• MEAT •

MEAT

A LOVE STORY

SUSAN BOURETTE

G. P. PUTNAM'S SONS

New York

PUTNAM

G. P. PUTNAM'S SONS

Publishers Since 1838

Published by the Penguin Group

Penguin Group (USA) Inc., 375 Hudson Street, New York, New York 10014, USA •
Penguin Group (Canada), 90 Eglinton Avenue East, Suite 700, Toronto, Ontario
M4P 2Y3, Canada (a division of Pearson Canada Inc.) • Penguin Books Ltd,
80 Strand, London WC2R 0RL, England • Penguin Ireland, 25 St Stephen's Green,
Dublin 2, Ireland (a division of Penguin Books Ltd) • Penguin Group (Australia),
250 Camberwell Road, Camberwell, Victoria 3124, Australia (a division of Pearson
Australia Group Pty Ltd) • Penguin Books India Pvt Ltd, 11 Community Centre,
Panchsheel Park, New Delhi–110 017, India • Penguin Group (NZ), 67 Apollo Drive,
Rosedale, North Shore 0632, New Zealand (a division of Pearson New Zealand Ltd) •
Penguin Books (South Africa) (Pty) Ltd, 24 Sturdee Avenue, Rosebank,
Johannesburg 2196, South Africa

Penguin Books Ltd, Registered Offices:
80 Strand, London WC2R 0RL, England

Library of Congress Cataloging-in-Publication Data

Bourette, Susan.

Meat : a love story / Susan Bourette.

p.   cm.

ISBN 978-0-399-15486-7

1. Meat industry and trade.   I. Title.

TS1955.B68   2008   2007048661

641.3'6—dc22

Printed in the United States of America

1   3   5   7   9   10   8   6   4   2

Book design by Marysarah Quinn

While the author has made every effort to provide accurate telephone numbers and Internet
addresses at the time of publication, neither the publisher nor the author assumes any responsibility for errors, or for changes that occur after publication. Further, the publisher does
not have any control over and does not assume any responsibility for author or third-party
websites or their content.

For my mother.
Thank you for all of those wonderful Sunday dinners.

CONTENTS

· MEAT ·

• PROLOGUE •

Violent winter winds lash against the streetcar as it rattles down Toronto's Queen Street West. Past the Gap and Starbucks. It rumbles by a vegetarian café where diners can be seen sucking hemp through straws and chopsticking at their tempeh salads, their sallow faces obscured by white clouds of steam that rise halfway up the window. Once the domain of hippie bicycle couriers, the café tonight caters to people who have their BMWs parked outside. The students and artists long ago priced out, the counterculture has given way to the country club. The restaurant's clients tonight are soccer moms who shop at Roots a few storefronts away, and the executives and bean counters who toil in the nearby corridors of commerce.

The streetcar clatters to the next stop. The doors open and riders are assaulted not only by a chilly blast but by the overpowering and unmistakable whiff of hot dogs on the grill. Dressed in a toque and fingerless gloves, the cart vendor works frantically folding dog to bun, his workspace clearly segregated.

On the west side, the hot dog peddler has his Polish sausages and frankfurters cooking. On the east, that's where the veggie dogs go. Just as the bacon bits and HP Sauce are relegated to one side, condiments like corn relish and sauerkraut to the other.

The streetcar lurches again, crossing an invisible dividing line. A place that not so long ago looked like it was cut out of a vintage postcard, circa 1956. A neighborhood where Euro-style delis are filled with sausage links that hang like stalactites from the ceiling, buttressed up against old-world butcher shops and grubby bars. Slavic-looking men with noses shaped like the kielbasa that decorate their stores, their moustaches about as long and coarse as the brooms they push. Shops like the Prague Deli, where you can order from the same bill of fare served up here for decades: classics like Gypsy goulash, tripe soup, and pierogies slathered in sour cream and bacon.

But recently there's been an invasion. A different one from the one that had marked the arrival of immigrants here, starting in the '20s. The delis and butcher shops are still here, but the street is now being crowded by upscale shops like Art Metropole, the Downward Dog Yoga Centre, and Clafouti Patisserie et Café. A haute onslaught; pouty models sharing the sidewalks with guys in bloody aprons. These days, it's a haven of carnivore chic. A place now considered hallowed grounds by the hipster cognoscenti, most of whom would see the old street as kitsch rather than tradition. Those like the twenty- and thirtysomethings standing here beside me tonight for an introductory course in butchering.

We're shivering in a cold, cramped room at the Healthy Butcher, a place where the new and old commingle. The smell is as old as time—harking back to the days when the caveman clubbed his first woolly mammoth. The aesthetic is as new and shiny as the latest Marc Jacobs. We are culinary tourists here, the new face of Queen Street West.

I'm fighting to keep my balance on this slippery concrete floor and out of harm's way. A good distance from the four-hundred-pound slab of flesh dangling on a meat hook, or "on the rail," as they say in the vernacular of the trade. On one side of me is a thirty-year-old Johnny Depp look-alike, who looks like he wandered straight off the set of *Pirates of the Caribbean*. He's wearing a striped shirt, a dozen small silver hoops, a tuft of hair on his chin, and a self-satisfied smirk. There's a married couple at the back, who whisper conspiratorially, subscribers to magazines like *Gourmet* and *Bon Appétit*; an art director and Bobby Flay–wannabe; and a doctor-cum-gourmet with a special interest in nutrition. There's also Ryan Donovan, the clean-cut head butcher and onetime chef who grew weary of the terrible pay and even worse hours before trading in his chef's hat for a butcher's apron. And finally, observing from the sidelines is Mario Fiorucci, a former lawyer and vegetarian turned organic-meat mogul, and the brains behind the operation.

We've been granted a backstage pass to a show typically reserved these days for an industrial underclass employed on the meat-factory floors and a handful of butchers across North America intent on resurrecting a once-proud tradition. At the show here tonight, the central cast members are a $1,600 heap of beef and the store's head butcher. "There's no definitive way to get from A to B—to take apart Humpty-Dumpty," Donovan says, waving a knife in his hand as if to underscore the point. "There are lots and lots of ways you can take down an animal."

Take down an animal? Sounds like a pep talk at a hunting lodge. I had expected that this would be a purely clinical exercise—with diagrams, skeletal cutaways—like the kind of illustrations you might see on the walls at the doctor's office. Maybe they do have something like that in the advanced classes. But one quick look at our how-to guide, *Breaking Down the Beef,* and I can't help thinking that this is *Butchering for Dummies.* Our handout looks like it's been printed for third-graders.

There's a cartoon cow painted in hues of hospital green and Pepto-Bismol pink. She looks almost gleeful, if not a little frisky—like she's trying to get away. Who can blame her? To this artist, she's clearly not a member of the sacred Bovidae clan, but food with a face. Meat wrapped in a leather case and divided into primal cuts: the chuck, rib, loin, hip, sirloin, shank, flank, plate, and brisket. But this simple approach does make some sense. After all, I doubt there are many among us who have ever laid eyes on meat that hasn't already been cleaved into individual and family-size portions and shrink-wrapped. For some it may even come as a shock: Meat comes from animals!

Fiorucci begins to deconstruct the handout for us, piece by piece. "Let's digest this information carefully," he intones before launching into an explanation of the differences between tough and tender cuts of meat. How the "locomotive" muscles at the front of the cow propel her around the pasture. And how the rib, loin, and sirloin muscles are used to support her frame— muscles that typically will be less exercised and more tender between the molars.

Meanwhile, Donovan is hard at work with a knife called a scimitar—using a grip I've never seen illustrated in Miss Manners's guide to etiquette. He makes a few cuts before disposing of the knife, ripping into the flesh with his bare hands. The fat between muscles gives way with a pop, pop, pop—like bubble wrap in the hands of a kid. Soon the cow's kneecap is exposed, glistening under the lights like fine porcelain. Donovan hacks away until four hundred pounds of Toronto's finest organic beef is dangling by a single tendon. It's hard to think of suspense in butchering, but the buildup truly is something out of a Ruth Rendell novel.

"We could call it *Death in the Queen Street Crypt.* It was the butcher that did it," Johnny Depp cackles in my ear.

Meanwhile, the punk band The Viletones are playing at the Bovine Sex Shop club down the street and a Michael Toke installation is going up at the Fly Gallery nearby. But here, it's butchering as performance art. The butcher as star in the eyes of this audience, the reception no different here from a crowd putting their hands together for the band or patrons lingering appreciatively in front of the art installation. Those old Slavic butchers never realizing that what they were doing was anything other than a job. Never mind that it was art. And up until recently, no one else seemed to, either. Not so long ago, this same crowd would have been lined up for veggie cooking classes featuring dishes like Virginia Sham and Beetroot Carpaccio. Up until now, the idea of anyone other than Jeffrey Dahmer forking over $80 for an introductory course in butchering—unthinkable!

The carnivores are back. It's like a bitch-slap to all those reedy, high-minded herbivores who have demanded nothing short of a bloodless revolution, dictating the parameters of the discussion, decreeing the rules for years. Now it's the meat-eaters who have wrested control of the food debate.

What's changed?

It's hard to know with certainty how it all started, although the cultural signposts these days are everywhere. Maybe the tipping point came with the makeover of New York's meatpacking district into one of Manhattan's more fashionable addresses. Today, there are new meat temples cropping up everywhere—from high-end butcher shops like this to Madison Avenue's Nello, where a fourteen-ounce Wagyu sirloin sells at a heart-stopping $750 a steak.

And what are we to make of fashionistas like Sienna Miller posed provocatively on the cover of *Esquire* in little more than a T-shirt featuring a moose head? And the antlered taxidermy, the rustic realism of bars and restaurants cropping up in glossier neighborhoods around Los Angeles and Brooklyn? For me, though, nothing pointed to a shift in the cultural zeitgeist more clearly than the purse I coveted in the window of a Yonge Street store in Toronto. Stitched together from recycled materials, it was emblazoned with big gold letters that screamed: I LOVE BACON. A rallying cry not just to porcine lovers everywhere but also to all of us lapsed vegetarians, who—according to a very informal and unscientific survey—eventually were lured back to meat-eating by the overwhelming savory and glorious aroma of bacon.

Like so many others in my urban, middle-class circle, I've dabbled in vegetarianism throughout most of my adult life. In fact, it was my first act of self-determination when I moved away from home. My first cookbook? *Diet for a Small Planet,* of course. Still, I can't claim any real stick-to-it-ness. Not like my partner, Gare, who is a sportswriter, celebrating thirty years of meat-free living. And while I must confess I have never really been more than a vegetarian dilettante, I've been stunned to watch my longtime vegetarian friends and acquaintances fall like dominos. Tamsen eating a hamburger. Lisa chewing on chicken wings. Carolyn mowing through a steak. And Khalil, the nineteen-year-old soft-spoken and thoughtful artist, reared almost exclusively on peanut-butter-and-banana sandwiches, now living on raw meat.

Pound for pound, as North Americans, we're eating more meat than ever. On average, we consume 260 pounds of meat a year. But, up until recently, when many of us did consume meat, it was with a supersized side order of guilt. We know all too well the arguments against meat-eating: It clogs our arteries, destroys the ecosystem. It's a cruel massacre of innocent victims. A slaughterhouse horror show I witnessed firsthand, believing—at least for a time—my days as a carnivore were over forever. The sin, the immorality of meat-eating has been the overriding leitmotif of the past few decades, ever since those first pot-smoking, bead-loving longhairs hijacked the debate and determined what the nation *should* have for dinner. Still, it gnawed. Deep in our guts, we knew Homer Simpson was right when he told his meat-eschewing daughter on the way to a neighborhood barbecue, "Lisa, you don't win friends with salad."

So, we began to rally. To reclaim our rights as meat-eaters. After all, where would the world be without the contributions of carnivores like Beethoven, Faulkner, Lincoln, and Trudeau? It's true that the vegetarians once held the countercultural high ground. Now, it's the carnivores who rule cool. Meat is the new black.

Maybe it's our last hurrah. One last shot at getting our fill before what some are gloomily predicting will be an all-out meat apocalypse. A world, according to those like Harvard anthropologist James L. Watson, in which meat-eating will be a historical footnote, something future generations will only read about in books of antiquity. Why? Mad cow disease, Professor Watson postulates, is just the first in a host of new and deadly diseases that eventually will infect our animals, wiping out whole species, one sacrificial lamb, cow, pig, and chicken felled after another. The upshot of factory farming, he argues, which has all but wiped out biodiversity.

Meanwhile, the evening is drawing to a close here at the Healthy Butcher. Our cow carved and sizzling on the grill, we gather at the front of the shop to swap notes, to chew the fat. Students are clamoring for a few last morsels of wisdom from Fiorucci. Growing up, I didn't know anyone who wanted to become a butcher. The butcher's life seemed to hold little in the way of adventure, of romance. But watching Fiorucci hold court, his students laughing, hanging on his every word, I can't help wondering: Is the butcher the new celebrity chef? And more important, why are we so obsessed with meat in North America? These are the questions I will grapple with on a protein pilgrimage of sorts—my year in meat. But not before I wrestle my classmates out of the way, wielding my toothpick like a dagger, to get at the New York sirloin now being sliced into shards and served on a platter in front of us.

1
· BUTCHERED ·

WE'RE DEEP IN THE SHADOWS, in the bowels of a building with walls that sweat gristle and blood. A modern-day chop house that serves up pork bellies and picnic roasts, loins and shoulders, and the odd human finger. A sprawling leviathan of steel and pipe, hidden in a wheat field, in the heart of the Canadian prairies.

We're standing in a semicircle on the kill floor at Maple Leaf Pork in Brandon, Manitoba. Two dozen fresh recruits, our mouths agape. Mike, a short, squat factory-floor veteran, stuffed into a bloody lab coat, is leading our tour. Hundreds of hogs swing by on a conveyor line; flayed and shackled up by their hind legs, their heads dangling by a flap of skin, they smack together like bowling pins.

Shivering against the cold, dressed in flimsy cotton jackets, we take in the floor show through a haze of steam that rises from the cement like vapor off a swamp. We stare at the blank faces of men dressed in the uniform of the meat trade: steel toes, mesh gloves, safety glasses to shield against the blood spray, and ear protection to ward off the shrieking white noise. They plunge in and out of the hogs' bellies with knives, yanking out glistening tubes of red and gray entrails, bowels, hearts, and livers that eventually will be chopped up, packaged, and shipped off for the dinner table.

No one strays too far from the pack. Undoubtedly worried they'll be swept onto a conveyor belt, hung on a hook, and eventually shrink-wrapped.

"We'd harvest the farts if we could," Mike offers with a certain morbid glee. "Yup. We use just about everything. Only three percent of the pig goes to waste around here."

I squeeze my eyes tight, trying for a moment to block it all out. Trying to envision my mother's roast pork fresh from the oven, studded with cloves and smothered in maple glaze. But I can't get past the reek of guts and scared animals. My head begins to swing like a seesaw. "Don't you dare puke," Mike snorts, grabbing at my helmet to take note of my name, displayed there in bold lettering. "Suck it up, Princess."

I'm praying for a miracle. That I won't toss my cookies. Or worse, be tossed out ass over teakettle my first day on the job. "It's the smell," I respond weakly. And then with all the bravado I can muster: "I'll get used to it."

With that, Mike cocks his head and inhales deeply before he begins a spiel he's surely mouthed dozens of times before. "You know what that smell is?" he growls rhetorically. "That," he says, leaning in for emphasis, "that's the smell of money."

It *was* all about the money. That's why I was here. I wasn't looking to do a story about meat but rather the meat business. I came to work undercover for a Canadian business magazine, to give the white-collar class a glimpse into a world inhabited by workers whose blue collars are splattered with blood. I came to try to explain the rationale behind a business that grinds up and spits out its workers with the same breakneck speed that it uses to turn pig into pork.

I had the suspicion that Maple Leaf wasn't so concerned about feeding a pork-hungry public but more about boosting the bottom line. A corporate strategy built on cheap labor and high volume to compete in a low-margin business. Maple Leaf's strategy here in Brandon essentially was the formula of Big Meat that had been perfected by companies like Tyson Foods and replicated cookie-cutter-style by every major pork, beef, and chicken processor in North America.

I had come here to tell the story of an industrial underclass, an army of more than 200,000 workers in North America's slaughterhouses. It was for good reason that a meatpacker had never made it on *Fortune*'s list of the "100 Best Companies to Work For." Yes, it was awful, filthy, and dangerous work. But was it necessarily so? You might imagine that these weren't the kinds of questions you'd broach with your boss on the first day at work. Not if you wanted to keep your job. Or your sanity. Besides, I knew that I'd never find all of the answers here even if I stayed until retirement. The truth was, I couldn't think any further ahead than punching the clock at the end of my shift.

I had no way of knowing that my time here in Brandon would be so utterly transforming. That I would leave the factory floor and swear off meat forever before being lured back— inexplicably—by a short-order cook waving a strip of bacon.

Brandon simply would be the starting point in a much longer journey that would take me whale-hunting with the Inupiat in Alaska and sausage-making in small-town Acadian Louisiana; to working on an organic farm in New York state and dining with a bunch of hippy-dippy New Agers at a raw-meat potluck in Colorado. My year in meat would be spent exploring the philosophical, social, and historical underpinnings of our obsession with meat in North America.

All that was to come, but in Brandon I was focused on my assignment, the one story that would set all the other stories in motion. After my orientation tour, I headed straight for Maple Leaf's HR department. That put me across the desk from a sober, stern-faced twentysomething. She scanned my résumé. One I'd admittedly doctored. Unlike all those crafty business types I'd read about getting creative with their résumés—adding degrees, pumping up job titles and work responsibilities—I had taken the opposite tack. Erasing any hint of the time I'd spent at university, my years toiling as a reporter at Canada's most prestigious media address. Just as I sat there in the chair in front of the HR person, completely unadorned; no makeup or jewelry, no lavishly overpriced shoes. No big-city attitude. Did I mind working overtime? she asked finally, glancing up from my résumé, a glint of pity discernible in her narrow-set eyes as I chirped merrily about working long hours in my previous jobs. Did I have transportation to work? Did I have any sexually transmitted diseases? And so on, until all the boxes had been checked off and my interviewer whisked me to the door and smiled weakly. "We'll call you," she said.

I waited and waited. So when the call finally came in two

weeks later, I found myself squealing into the phone. Truthfully, I didn't know whether to be overjoyed or mortified. Happy I could complete my assignment or petrified that I had just landed one of the most dangerous and gruesome jobs on the planet. For $9.45 an hour, I would join the ranks of some 1,300 other workers in Canada's largest meatpacking plant. A slaughterhouse team with titles I'd never seen in any employment directory: knockers and stunners, pig chasers, jawbreakers, and kidney poppers. I was assigned a job in the rookie part of the plant, working in "by-products," slicing the cheeks out of hogs' heads.

How bad could it possibly be?

Monday. My first day on the job. I had thought the orientation tour a couple of weeks earlier had steeled me for anything, but this morning I have the jitters. Other first days had been filled with expectation and hope, but now I'm filled with dread. It's just past 6:30 a.m., and the sun hovers low on the horizon, casting a faded wash over this pretty patch of prairie also known as Wheat City, about 115 miles west of Winnipeg. A steady stream of pickups and rusted-out station wagons is already on the road. Their headlights bounce along a dead-end stretch of highway, toward a low-slung building situated in a field of hay bales, a fifteen-minute drive from Brandon. The parking lot is already teeming, filled with dozens of young men in muscle shirts and women pinched into low-riding jeans. They walk two by two, the sound of gravel skidding beneath their feet. In the distance, a truck is busy unloading a shipment of today's hog kill. The constant drone of the engine muffles the sound of their collective squeal.

Inside, workers are lining up at the punch clock—looking for all the world like the pigs being herded in through another door on the opposite side of the building. We're not the first workers on the kill floor. The first stage of the assembly line has been in full swing for nearly an hour. Some workers are busy working in tag teams struggling to load these obese porkers onto the gam table. Others are already covered in blood. Hacking into the hogs' cavities to extract the bung—the pig's intestines and anus—a task these men will perform 21 times a minute, 2,500 times before the morning bathroom break, and 10,000 times before the day is out.

Meanwhile, upstairs, high above the kill floor, twenty-five of us are gathered in a large room. The floor beneath our feet is rumbling, set into motion by the thrum of the butchery below. The walls are festooned with posters trumpeting Maple Leaf products: chops, hams, ribs, and roasts. The artwork, the meat, primped by stylists like Hollywood stars in a *Vanity Fair* spread, bears no resemblance to the stuff we saw on the floor. I can't even imagine that the workers below would recognize it as the fruit of their labor.

I had expected that our job training would be two to three weeks, working alongside a factory-floor veteran. I thought that we would work our way up to a shift on the factory floor after spending days learning how to sharpen a knife and the rules of health and safety. But this process apparently has been sped up, just like the pace of disassembly. In its wisdom, gleaned over years of recruiting, Maple Leaf apparently has come to the conclusion that everyone is far better off if new employees aren't left to meditate too long on the job they've been hired to do.

That must explain why we are about to roll out onto the floor and into our workstations after lunch following a morning that is not so much practical training as it is a case of being sold and hectored, charmed and threatened by the man now standing at the front of the room. The face of management: Robert Panontin, a thirtysomething labor-relations specialist.

Panontin scans the room, sizing up this unlikely group of greenhorns warily. I'm sure that there are common threads that run through the two dozen among us, the most obvious one being economic necessity bordering on desperation. Yet our backgrounds are varied. It was almost like we had been plucked at random—or that we had all fallen on hard times, had taken different roads to reach this dead end, this last stop.

There's Tina, a velvety-eyed thirty-year-old mother of four, with hair sculpted like a porcupine. Her background is in retail. She stares at her hands, folded in her lap. At the next table, there's Jenn, a mid-twenties, golden-haired anthropology graduate in wide-leg pants, who smiles shyly. She looks least likely to fit in. But, in fact, she may be most suited to the job, having worked gutting bears at her grandparents' hunting lodge in Northern Ontario. At the back of the room, Joe, a transplanted Newfoundlander with big teeth and a know-it-all sneer, is fresh from working the oil rigs in Alberta. And there's Andrew, built like a boulder at six-feet-two and 270 pounds. Four years as a short-order cook have given him what the company values most: knife skills. The group also includes two Chads, Enoch, Phoebe, and Tim, who's back after quitting eight months ago. He's been assigned to the overnight sanitation shift, cleaning up guts and gore.

The indoctrination begins. Panontin sidesteps the reality of our poverty and pitches our employment here as an opportunity. "You have been chosen to be part of the Maple Leaf team," he explains, his baritone voice filling the room. "This is a big investment for us. To train you. To give you the kind of skills that you can take with you wherever you go. We are investing big in each and every one of you."

We listen quietly as Panontin expounds on Maple Leaf's commitment to the community and its employees. Just as I had listened to the company president elucidate corporate strategy for shareholders who nibbled on finger sandwiches at the company's annual meeting in Toronto. Maybe it was the cynical reporter in me—or the dearth of party food here—but I'm not buying it. It's only now that I realize that there's no chance I'll ever be coopted by management. If I'm going to sympathize with anybody, it's going to be my coworkers and the pigs.

And maybe that's why Panontin suddenly shifts gears. He senses he's losing us. Talk now turns to a language every low-wage worker can understand. How working at Maple Leaf can make us richer in ways we'd never expect. Perfect attendance over a month? An extra dollar an hour paid retroactively for the month and a shot at a company draw for $1,500. Extra time on the company clock will also translate into "pork bucks"—a kind of funny money printed here at the plant that allows us to buy our ribs and back bacon at factory-floor prices. Yes, even the perks are pork.

Panontin finishes his sales pitch, gathers his materials, and makes his leave before stopping short of the door: "I just want you to know we're watching you like a hawk," he snarls, looking around the room one last time to make certain his tone has elicited the intended effect. "You have signed an employee-employer contract with us. We've agreed to pay you a wage and you agree to come to work. I have a really good friend in security at the mall. If I'm doing an investigation on you, I'll go down there to watch his security videos. God help you if I catch you goofing off at the mall on video."

We sit in silence, beholding him with a collective wince. But Panontin knows the statistics aren't pretty. He knows most of us—yes, "the Maple Leaf team"—will flee long before we reach our three-month probation, like thousands of other workers since Maple Leaf opened the doors of its megaplant here in 1999.

Just like the worker who was waiting to board the bus I arrived on in Brandon before my first week of work. A young man with a world-weary look, whose hands were crippled by too many long hours spent working with a knife, whose blue eyes were ringed by dark circles. I imagined his nights were haunted by the same dark and surreal images that filled his days on the factory floor. Passing him in the terminal, I couldn't help staring, thinking about Jurgis Rudkus, the central character in Upton Sinclair's muckraking exposé of the meat industry, penned over a century ago. Did Sinclair's work still have relevance?

Although it was a work of fiction, *The Jungle* had the feel of journalism. And more than the feel—it reeked of the real-world stink of the Chicago stockyards in which Sinclair vividly depicted the horrifying living and working conditions of a family of Lithuanian immigrants toiling in turn-of-the-century meatpacking. An instant bestseller. Readers were horrified by

Sinclair's portrayal of a meat supply infected with vermin, animal feces, human blood, and body parts. How bribed inspectors looked the other way when diseased cows were slaughtered for beef; how filth and guts were swept off the floor and packaged as potted ham. The book elicited outrage, prompting Congress to pass the Pure Food and Drug Act and the Meat Inspection Act, both signed into law by Theodore Roosevelt in 1906. Sinclair, however, reportedly was disappointed. He had written his book with the hope of improving conditions for the working man. "I aimed at the public's heart," Sinclair lamented, "and by accident I hit it in the stomach."[1]

For a time, it may have seemed like Sinclair's appraisal was unnecessarily gloomy. As it turned out, successive cycles of industry-labor rancor over the next few decades would improve the working man's lot. By the 1950s, more than 80,000 workers in North America's slaughterhouses were covered by national agreements that standardized wages and working conditions. By the 1970s, wages in meatpacking were 18 percent higher than in the rest of the manufacturing sector.[2] Workers could participate in the luxuries of the middle class: buy homes and new cars and take vacations.[3] Conditions that would have been unimaginable to those who worked in the slaughterhouses of *The Jungle*.

Maybe it was inevitable, but the gains weren't permanent. Beginning that same decade, industry upstart Iowa Beef Packers began to rewrite the rules for killing, chilling, and shipping beef. Other meatpackers jumped on the bandwagon to compete in an increasingly competitive industry. One by one, they shuttered the doors of plants with entrenched unions. They pulled up stakes in big cities, reopened sprawling new plants in rural areas, and began to recruit immigrant and migrant workers from Mexico and Asia who were willing to do the job for half the wages.[4]

By the late '80s, the U.S. meatpacking industry had restructured. Big Meat had seized the same opportunities as other major corporations, riding a wave of anti-union sympathy in both the public and political arenas. That trend was best illustrated by Ronald Reagan's successful showdown against air-traffic controllers. His breaking of their union was portrayed as a profile in courage.

Competitive pressures in the marketplace finally began to push across the border. By the early '90s, weakened by the recession of the previous decade and feeling squeezed by more efficient producers in the United States, Canadian packers began to look to the American behemoths for lessons in how to reposition themselves in a newly competitive landscape. "What are we waiting for?" the executive in charge of Maple Leaf's meat division asked provocatively at a conference of industry colleagues. "Wal-Mart to come to town and put us out of business?" Maple Leaf began to gobble up competitors, close inefficient plants, and squeeze concessions from its workers much as the industry had done in the United States a decade earlier. It also began to recruit cheap labor from beyond its borders. With 35 percent of its workforce comprised of workers drawn from countries like Mexico and El Salvador in 2006—up from 8 percent in 2003— the Brandon plant is quickly moving to a U.S. model. A prototype in which its workforce is made up of recent immigrants and—in the United States at least—undocumented workers.

In recent years, meatpackers have come under increasing

scrutiny. Smithfield Foods, for example, was found to have created "an atmosphere of intimidation and coercion" by spying on workers, harassing them, and even firing them for backing the union trying to organize them. Large U.S. plants have also been the target of recent crackdowns on illegal immigrants. Some critics question what they see as the moral myopia of the industry. While meatpackers publicly denounce illegal aliens, critics charge that in reality they privately turn a blind eye to having them on the company payroll because undocumented workers are unlikely to complain about working conditions or push for union representation. In 2005, a scathing 175-page report issued by Human Rights Watch, titled *Blood, Sweat, and Fear: Workers' Rights in U.S. Meat and Poultry Plants,* denounced the U.S. meatpacking industry for "systematic human rights violations." "What's happening here," said the report's author, Cornell University professor Lance Compa, "is a modern-day version of *The Jungle.*"

Maybe that's why so many of the workers here look so glum, so desperate. As they stream into the company cafeteria, they pass by a sign that reads HAMLET'S. There's not even a flicker of recognition for what might pass as abattoir humor. Inside, the din of coffee cups is muted by the singsong of chain-link belly belts that chime as workers file in line for today's grub. Today's special? Pork chops, mashed potatoes, and gravy.

Jenn sits across the table from me. Her face full of dread. Like me, she's not hungry. She leans forward, head bowed, one hand on the table, another holding a cigarette. She doesn't usually smoke, but the anxiety has been building all morning. In a few minutes, she'll be on the factory floor, hacking away at a pig's head. She thought she was ready. "I had a nightmare last night," she sighs softly and pauses. "I was being chased by hogs' heads. It's still freaking me out." She draws long on her cigarette, then snuffs it out abruptly like she's exorcising a demon.

Soon, our posse is herded back to the training room, where we'll be fitted in the costume of the factory floor. Rubber boots with steel toes; whites still stained with the memory of yesterday's slaughter; a belly belt to protect the organs; earplugs, a hair net, and helmet; and a mesh glove that extends to the elbow. I'm now dressed to kill, or at least butcher.

Jesus Zavala stands ramrod-straight, hands clasped in front of him, looking like a no-guff factory-floor statesman. Jessie, as he is affectionately called, a Mexican-trained butcher, has worked his way up to trainer in less than two years on the job at Maple Leaf. He is to be our mentor.

Zavala leads us deep into the basement of the building. A crypt, really, where there are no windows, no vestiges of the outside world.

It's now 1:30 and workers are busy on the dressing floor, pulling on hearts and livers they'll place on the spikes behind them. Further down the line, men and women are carving into slabs of pork to make picnic roasts and loin chops. Their arms move in a mad flurry of butchery, making it difficult to distinguish one human body from another. One or two slipups and there's a bottleneck. The quotas must be met or it will mean overtime— part of our collective agreement with the company. One hour. Two hours. Whatever it takes to get the job done.

Our first day on the line, and we learn we're in for an hour's overtime. No choice but to accept. There's a problem at the gam table, first stop for the freshly killed hogs as they topple from a tumbler to have their tendons slit and be skewered up by their hind legs. Several workers are off sick. Sherri, our floor supervisor, a pretty woman of grandmotherly vintage, arrives, clipboard in hand. Her heavily caked eyelashes flutter as she peers out from behind gold-rimmed glasses. "Four," she finally bellows in a husky voice. "I need four real strong guys on the gam table."

A half-dozen hands shoot up. Andrew, the guy who's built like an offensive tackle, is waving his arm anxiously. Sherri picks off the men individually: "You, you, you, and you." Andrew smirks, and falls into the parade of burly men who trail Sherri down the hallway. "I have no idea what the hell a gam table is. But it's gotta be better than the gore in there," he avers as he rumbles out.

It's showtime for the rest of us. Zavala clamps on his protective hearing gear, slips on a pair of goggles, and motions us through. We enter a room reverberating in a chorus of hum and hiss, clang and thud. I step over strings of slippery yellow gristle and pools of blood, past plumes of steam that rise from the floor to my workstation.

On the right, workers are hunched over a conveyor line of disembodied heads. Some are sawing off ears with pneumatic knives. Others are skewering heads onto spikes. The thrum of the line triggers the beasts' mouths in motion, as though they're in conversation. They round the corner, tumbling onto another conveyor belt. Piled three by three, they're headed straight at me.

Zavala is already in a dance of kinetic perfection. With all of the skill and artistry of a sculptor, he reaches forward, picking a head up by the esophagus, and begins chiseling. First slicing the cheeks from the outside of the head, then the inside. He plops the flesh onto a smaller conveyor belt below, and thrusts the hog's head down a chute, on its way to rendering. "Now you try," he says, handing me a razor-sharp knife and smiling with encouragement.

I grasp at a snout, and haul twenty pounds of head toward me. It's heavier than I imagined, and I stumble. The head rolls from my carving station, falling faceup on my boot. Mouth ajar, eyes still open, cheeks twitching, it stares up at me as if stuck in some sort of somnolent scream. I do better next time. Soon, dozens of hogs' heads later, I can feel the blood trickling down my cheek and seeping into my bra. But what makes me really woozy is the sensation of warm, sticky flesh on the other side of my plastic glove each time I lay hold of an esophagus.

By quitting time, my carving hand is starting to give out. My back aches. But it's my cheeks that hurt the most from sucking my lips in all day, hoping to keep the blood and guts from getting into my mouth.

We gather around the sink to clean the little pieces of fat and meat from our tools. Jenn's hosing down a scabbard when she lets out a yelp. The hose has slipped from her grasp, and she's shooting a spray of scalding water into the face of a fellow worker. The water has soaked into her glove. Her hand is starting to blister up in welts.

On the way to my locker, I look for Jenn as I pass by the nurse's station. A half-dozen workers are slumped in chairs, waiting for treatment. A typical day. The cost of putting those pork chops on the dinner table. Human bodies lined up against a nonstop tide of animals. Where what were once hundreds of heads processed per day are now thousands; what were thousands are now tens of thousands. Even in state-of-the-art plants, the companies have been unable to make major gains through automation. Because every animal is unique, the most important tool in the plant is still a sharp knife. Therefore, the internal logic of modern meatpacking is based on ever faster line speeds and low wages to extract bigger profits.[5]

It sets the conditions for a human bloodbath: workers being beheaded by dehiding machines, others chopped up while cleaning out blood cauldrons. Those are the stories that make the headlines. Not the armies of workers who eventually become crippled by the knife, making more than 10,000 incisions every day and under constant pressure to step it up. In Canada, meatpacking has five times the national rate of industrial injury. In the United States, it's nearly four times the overall rate, although critics believe the figures actually are much higher, because immigrant workers are less likely to complain about unsafe working conditions and injuries for fear of being fired.[6]

It turns out that what's unsafe for the worker is unsafe for the consumer. The product is compromised just as much by the pressure to produce. Eric Schlosser, the author of *Fast Food Nation,* and the man who inspired one of the movie industry's more unforgettable lines of late, "There's shit in the meat," puts it this way: "The same things that contribute to contamination of the meat make it more likely that people are going to get hurt. The only reason it's been allowed to continue is that people don't know. Even if you have no compassion for the poor and the illegal in this country, if you eat meat, or the people you love eat meat, you should care."[7]

Increasingly, our meat is a Pandora's box of pathogens. The list of outbreaks keeps growing: Hundreds poisoned with *E. coli* and one dead after eating at Jack in the Box restaurants. Thousands more sickened over the past decade while eating beef at church banquets, company picnics, school lunch programs, and so on. The Centers for Disease Control and Prevention estimates that there are about 73,000 cases of *E. coli* 0157:H7 poisoning every year, including sixty-one deaths. Some restaurants, worried about liability, are now posting warnings about undercooked meat in fine print at the bottom of their menus.

Not surprisingly, the number of deaths from food-borne illnesses has climbed since the USDA began relaxing meat inspection procedures and standards, beginning in the 1980s at the behest of the meat industry.[8] These days there are about 7,500 meat inspectors overseeing 88 billion pounds of meat and poultry a year in the United States. But those figures don't take into account chronic inspector shortages around the country. In 2006, for example, 25 percent of inspection jobs were vacant in the New York City area, while vacancy rates were between 9 and 11 percent in other parts of the country. The upshot? Other inspectors have been forced to assume responsibility for those plants not covered by vacancies, imperiling the safety of the food supply even further.[9]

Inspectors admit they are overwhelmed by the jumped-up pace of production. A newspaper series in the *Atlanta Journal-Constitution* chronicled the worries of eighty-four USDA inspectors at thirty-seven plants overwhelmed by the pace of modern production in the poultry industry. Every week, "Millions of chickens leaking yellow pus, stained by green feces, contaminated by harmful bacteria, or marred by lung and heart infections, cancerous tumors, or skin conditions are shipped for sale to consumers," the newspaper paper reported, summarizing the poultry inspectors' frustrations.[10]

USDA inspectors were once required to condemn any bird with fecal contamination inside its body cavity. But lobbying efforts by the poultry industry eventually convinced the USDA to reclassify feces from a dangerous contaminant to a "cosmetic blemish" and allow workers simply to rinse it off.[11] Perhaps former USDA inspector David Carney summed it up best when he said, "We used to trim the shit off the meat. Then we washed the shit off the meat. Now the consumer eats the shit off the meat."[12]

Maybe there's good reason that I arrive back at my motel room after my first shift on the factory floor too sickened to eat. Little wonder that Jenn's having nightmares. I lay awake too after that first day, pondering the sorts of questions I would ask Maple Leaf executives given the chance. Not the sort of questions you would ask as a business reporter. Not the kinds of questions that would be informed by annual reports, past clippings, and press releases. The questions I had now came directly from what I saw on the factory floor; questions that arose from my own experience and from talking to other employees. They weren't the kinds of inquiries that could be answered adequately by one of the handpicked flacks the company pays to speak to reporters.

If I dreamed that night, I don't remember a thing. Once I got out of Brandon, I was going to make it a point to get in the face of the Maple Leaf execs—I'd live the dream that my coworkers only allowed themselves to fantasize about.

I arrive for work the next morning. We gather for roll call. There are three no-shows among the recruits. Jenn's been pulled from the line and assigned to kitchen duty while the wounds on her hand heal. Andrew's downing Tylenols. His body is throbbing from yesterday's work on the gam table. "It was crazy," he says, his face flaring red in exasperation. "I couldn't grab them fast enough. It's too fucking hard. I'd rather pull assholes any day."

Joe, the mouthy Newfoundlander, wanted a job on the kill floor, but he's been designated to work in rails, stacking boxes of meat. "First they tell me I'm doin' this, then I'm doin' that," he declares. "You don't take a piss unless it's on your scheduled break. This job sucks."

No one disagrees.

It's the last glimpse I'll have of most of my fellow trainees, many who have fanned out across the factory floor to fill in for both injured and absentee workers. For two more days, I hone my knife skills, carving into hogs' heads until I'm both numb with pain and desensitized to what I'm doing.

By my fourth day on the factory floor, something odd happens. I'm suddenly feeling squeamish, ready to puke again at the thought of touching flesh dead just forty-two minutes. For the next few hours, I slow my pace until I am miraculously granted a reprieve: I've been tapped to help out in packing for the rest of the afternoon. I spend the rest of the day picking diaphragms out of a giant tub and packing them, layer upon layer, into boxes destined for the Japanese market. I'm working as fast as a rookie can when I hear the lead hand behind me: "Come on," he roars. "You're holding us up. I need you to pack like a madwoman."

With that, I begin throwing the organs furiously into boxes until the tubs that were once overflowing are empty. I leave at day's end alongside hundreds of workers who spill into the parking lot, carrying their lunch buckets. Some wait for the bus. Others clamber into their pickups. In a little more than fourteen hours, they'll be back. I know I won't be returning. I can't stomach another day.

My gut queasy, my mind churning, I walk across the parking lot pondering the logistics of modern meat. So this is the cutting edge of meat processing? This is what they mean by hog futures? Hogs have no future. Bacon is not a career. Not for me, not for any human being in a rational and moral world.

I LEFT BRANDON the way I came. On the bus. I didn't tell anyone why I was here. I didn't tell anyone why I left. As the bus pulled out, I didn't even bother to look back, the real-life factory floor long in the rearview mirror. My magazine assignment still in front of me. I kept an eye out for stories about Brandon over the next few days. I pored through the archives of the business pages to try to track the history of Maple Leaf. There were stories about adding a second shift at the plant. Stories about the company angling to get federal funding for a water-treatment facility.

A few days later, I called Maple Leaf for an official interview. I came clean, disclosing that I was a reporter who had just worked undercover in the plant. After the initial shock, and moves by the company to try to kill the story, they put their best face forward and offered up human resources manager Steve LeBlanc for an interview. Only in hindsight could I possibly sympathize with LeBlanc. After all, his was an impossible PR exercise, defending the indefensible. I asked how Maple Leaf could possibly expect employees to do such difficult work and to get by on the same wages that high school students were pulling in at McDonald's down the street from the plant. A few hundred dollars a year above poverty level. "Our wages aren't the issue," LeBlanc explained. "They're actually very competitive as far as our local market goes." If it wasn't low wages, then how could he explain a turnover rate of 100 percent every year since the plant had opened? LeBlanc said the turnover rate was expected to improve the next year—dropping to 80 percent. I pushed him on workplace injuries. A rate of five times the national average—how could Maple Leaf consider that acceptable? "Compared with the rest of the meat industry, Maple Leaf is doing better than average," LeBlanc responded.

There was to be no gotcha moment in speaking with LeBlanc. Still, I was surprised when a letter arrived the very next day from his office. I hadn't bothered calling in to offer my resignation when I walked out of the plant—the whole undercover thing was just too complicated to explain to my supervisor. The letter was registered, and it advised me that Maple Leaf had decided to terminate my employment, effective immediately. "The company recognizes that this line of work may not be for everyone and that you may be suited to a different line of work," the letter read. "You are advised that should you choose to reapply for employment in the future, when your situation has stabilized, your application will be given due consideration."

Two months later, my story finally appeared in the *Globe and Mail*'s *Report on Business,* a national Canadian business magazine.[13] I was flooded with calls and e-mails from friends and colleagues, asking if I was still eating bacon. Admonishing me for not apprising them of the article's content before they sat down to read it over breakfast. Some wondered how I'd ever managed to pull it off. Truthfully, I wondered, too.

That same day, Maple Leaf shut down the production line and summoned workers to talk about my story. They said I'd gotten it all wrong. They reminded them of how lucky they were to have a job at the plant. I wish I had a pork buck for every time Panontin evoked "the Maple Leaf team." I could imagine the old hands on the floor—they had long grown deaf to the bullshit in the same way that they were inured to the smell on the kill floor. I heard some workers were silently pleased about the article. Happy that the Brandon community finally would understand what they were up against.

The local paper followed with a front-page story, headlined "Magazine Knifes City Plant."[14] The headline was of a size customarily reserved for declarations of war. LeBlanc told the reporter it was unfortunate I hadn't seen other areas of the plant—because if I had, my story "may have been much different." True enough, though not in the way he had intended. If I had been hired to kill the pigs, to rip out their guts, or clean their intestines of half-digested food, my story would have been even less flattering to Maple Leaf—or any meatpacking company in North America, for that matter. Truth be told, I was embedded in something less than the most gruesome position on the line.

The *Brandon Sun* article also quoted a provincial politician, who said he wasn't at all surprised by the content of the article. After all, working in meatpacking is hard work, Scott Smith said. "I'm sure she did suffer some culture shock," he told the newspaper. "The meat processing plant is worlds away from her environment of a quaint outdoor café sipping on cappuccino and nibbling on a ham sandwich in Toronto." I'm sure Smith would suffer some culture shock too if he ever came to Toronto and tried to order a ham sandwich at a chic sidewalk café.

I thought that this was the perfect comic postscript to my Maple Leaf experience. But a couple of weeks later, just before Christmas, my vacation pay from Maple Leaf finally arrived— barely enough to cover the cost of a cappuccino. Attached was a note informing me that the company was still keeping my file active in case I was considering returning to work.

Yes, I could even tell them when I planned to start: When pigs fly.

2
• MEAT, MYSELF, AND I •

Truly man is the king of beasts, for his brutality exceeds theirs.
We live by the death of others: we are burial places! I have from
an early age abjured the use of meat, and the time will come
when men such as I will look on the murder of animals as they
now look on the murder of men. —LEONARDO DA VINCI

AS A BUTCHER, I was an utter failure. I had only ever cleaved meat with a steak knife before landing my assignment to write about life on the line at the Maple Leaf plant. A week spent on the kill floor being tutored in the art of slicing the cheeks out of hogs' heads did nothing to improve my slaughterhouse skills. While my classmates graduated to jobs on the factory floor, I was hopelessly ham-handed, as much a threat to my coworkers and myself as I was to a hog brought in for slaughter. Worse, at least for a carnivore who typically ripped into a pork roast like a crazed hyena, I found I could no longer stomach the thought of meat.

I had an epiphany—or so I thought—one day over lunch at the Maple Leaf plant. Actually, it was at the very moment that I nearly lost my lunch. Above the thrum of the butchery machinery and the collective squeal of hundreds of pigs being herded to their death just outside the cafeteria doors, all I could hear was the voice of David Bowie being piped in over the sound system. He was instructing Major Tom to take his protein pills and put his helmet on. An omen, I thought. Meat was the past, and I was determined to live in the future. On the flight home from Brandon back to Toronto, I opted for the vegetarian meal. From here on in, I vowed, my protein would be limited to chickpeas and lentils.

For a time, I managed to shut out all those glorious holiday memories: the smell of rosemary-encrusted flesh wafting from the kitchen; the dressing scooped fresh from the turkey carcass, plumped up with onions and giblets. A few weeks out of the slaughterhouse, I spent that Thanksgiving under a mound of vegan cookbooks, my mother cursing at me from the kitchen as she poured grease drippings from the bird to flavor her celebrated gravy made from an old family recipe. The end of traditions, I decided, and a recipe that wouldn't be passed on to future generations.

Since I was of a certain age and certain political leanings, this wasn't my first brush with vegetarianism. It was my third. My first attempt lasted nearly a year after I left my hometown—yes, one set of traffic lights—for the big city. It was the mid-'80s. I was a student at the University of Toronto, a sprawling Ivy League kind of school then crawling with some 50,000 students—a place, predictably, where young conservatives in suits butted heads with disheveled pinkos. Back then I had a hunger for Big Ideas and the Great Thinkers. My passions were logic and the philosophers of ancient Greece. And against these things, the material world and its conventions looked awfully small. Along with giving up meat, I also took a vow of poverty. I must have lifted the idea straight from Pythagoras, the philosopher best known for his geometrical theorem but also founder of an ascetic group that swore off both animal flesh and private property. I really can't remember my precise reasoning. I can't even remember with any clarity making the decision. In those days I was devouring books, gobbling up as much learning as I possibly could. Given the option of eating or thinking, I'd push the plate away.

Near the end of my undergraduate study, a nasty hamburger put me off meat again. This time, I lasted eight months, right up until before exams. I was barely living proof that mere rejection of meat won't make you the picture of health. If a doctor had examined me, he would have rushed me to the hospital for tests. My raccoon eyes, my lethargy hinted that something was amiss. I was so tired I couldn't lift a pencil, let alone write an essay. But the tests would have defied diagnosis. All the physician had to do was probe into my diet. A muffin for breakfast. Green peas and rice for dinner. Oh, yes, and I was drinking about twelve cups of coffee a day. On the street I'd give a quarter every day to a homeless panhandler who was eating better than I was, down at the mission. This offshoot of vegetarianism—rejection not just of meat but also of any semblance of nutrition—is not as uncommon among college kids as you might think. Junkatarianism, some call it. For me, it was stress-induced self-abnegation.

Only when I started back on meat, started to savor it and other food, did I pull myself out of the downward spiral.

But this time, this time, I was convinced my vegetarianism would take, and it wasn't just because I was older and wiser. No, I thought of it as applied vegetarianism. Not an impulse in the throes of intellectual asceticism, not a reaction to a bad meal. No, I wanted to make it a well-considered life choice. To rework Socrates, I truly believed that an unexamined diet wasn't worth eating. I would *work* on my vegetarianism. I didn't just buy vegetarian cookbooks. I read the gastro-philosophical treatises of the moment, everything from *Fast Food Nation* to the *Sexual Politics of Meat: A Feminist-Vegetarian Critical Theory*. I pondered the arguments of animal-rights philosophy. I began to ask myself, "Does a halibut think? Do cabbages have feelings? Meat is murder, sure, but are eggs theft? Is cheese exploitation? Is yogurt cultural appropriation?"

Not that I was alone in this. Hardly. The fact is, I had plenty of company—and not just Pythagoras but the like-minded Plutarch, who once raged, "What frenzy drives you to the pollution of shedding blood . . . to slaughter harmless, tame creatures without stings or teeth to harm us, creatures that I swear, Nature appears to have produced for the sake of their beauty and grace. . . . Do we hold a life cheap?"[1] Even the original Epicurean, Epicurus himself, found pleasure in forgoing animal flesh. It's not certain whether Socrates and his student Plato partook of meat, but when they imagined their ideal state as set out in *The Republic,* it was a vegetopia. Vegetarian times took a turn for the worse, though, in 1208 when Pope Innocent III declared war against those who eschewed meat during the Albigensian Crusade. Tens of thousands were slaughtered in defense of carnivorous Christianity. And then again in 1231, during the Inquistion, Pope Gregory IX established courts in France to conduct inquests into the piety of vegetarian infidels.[2]

Vegetarians may have gone underground for a while, but by the late seventeenth and early eighteenth centuries, questions about whether man should banish meat from his diet began to swirl in the salons and cafés where freethinkers and revolutionaries gathered to debate the issues of the day. The notion that the ethical sphere of man's responsibility extended beyond humans to animals were not just high-minded concepts, but a philosophy they'd seen played out in real life in their recent travels to India. These questions fulminated in radical circles before being seized by the great thinkers of the time. Philosophers like Descartes and Pierre Gassendi—consumed with the relationship between God, man, and nature—also began to advocate a vegetarian diet.[3] It was a formative period, Tristram Stuart writes in *The Bloodless Revolution*—an attack on the "bloodthirsty luxury of mainstream culture," a nod to ancient ethics of abstinence and early medical science that helped reshape the values of Western culture.[4]

Maybe I could be swayed by Descartes's arguments. But really, all I had to do was take one look at my friend Dawn for my conversion to vegetarianism to be complete. A beautiful colleague at the newspaper where I worked, she was in her thirties and had glossy, dark locks, perfect skin, and perfect teeth; she was full of peppy optimism and good, clean fun. An overachiever, Dawn went to law school while holding down a full-time newspaper job. She was a mountain biker and a snowboarding fanatic.

She shopped low-end but always somehow looked like she'd just walked out of a *Vogue* photo shoot. She transcended cool. If ever there were a poster woman for vegetarianism, Dawn was it. It worked for her; surely it could work for me too.

And I did want to prove to my mother that a vegetarian diet was a healthy alternative—she being self-appointed spokeswoman for the Meat and Potatoes Party. I was growing weary of her withering looks, her snipes when I visited and bypassed the prime rib for squash, cauliflower, salad, and apple pie. It was as if I were rejecting not only her cooking, but also her values. As if I were rejecting her. I wanted to reassure her that I loved her cooking (I did) and that I loved her too. But she remained steadfast in her opinion of my dietary choices, convinced I was headed for ruin. "It's no way to live!" she seethed, evoking the tragic example of a neighbor. "Jean's daughter is a vegetarian and she looks like death warmed over. You're going to get sick."

Still, I tried. Maybe others were able to stick it out long enough to answer those questions about the cognitive functions of tuna and all the rest. I never got around to it. Before I could come up with answers, I was in the throes of a protein deficiency, a debilitating one. I was as pale as sticky rice, as weak as Scotch broth, and my head was spinning like a Mixmaster. This wasn't a craving so much as a junkie's withdrawal. I staggered into my favorite diner, the Detroit Eatery, a Toronto institution, and slammed my fists down hard on the counter, shrieking at the rattled cook sweating over the grill, "Give me meat! Make that bacon!"

Five weeks and thirty-seven hours. That's how long it took before I fell off the vegetarian wagon and boarded the gravy train. The fact is, I didn't even hold out for a first-class ticket on the train. I was seated at the diner's counter, a greasy spoon frequented by hungover university students, struggling musicians, and slumming brokers. I finished the lumberjack breakfast and then shouted at the cook again, "Keep the carnage coming, I'll have a burger!" I then upgraded to steak. Why bother leaving room for dessert when I could go for seconds? I was determined to work my way through the entire side of the menu. I felt guilty. But damn it, meat tasted so good! Hearing Bowie going on about Major Tom's protein pills, that wasn't an omen, just proof that Maple Leaf's music programmer had a twisted sense of humor. I somehow doubted that I'd really had an epiphany—probably more like a bout of posttraumatic stress.

It wasn't just the taste, mind you. No, I felt good. Strong, zippy, and cheery—the best I had felt in weeks. Proselytizing vegetarians—the PETA crowd and fellow vegan travelers—will claim that I must have messed up, missed out on some essential nutrients. But it wasn't true. I did vegetarian like a scientist—I stopped short of setting up a test group with a placebo diet. This time, I made sure to color my plate in a rainbow of vegetables *and* eat my fair share of tofu, beans, and lentils. I went into the vegetarian mode expecting it to take. I had anecdotal evidence (my friend Dawn) and statistical evidence (the life expectancy of the Seventh-day Adventists).[5] I truly believed I was on the side of the angels (the philosophers' chorus backing me up).

And yet I failed—or the diet failed—miserably.

With my B_{12} boost giving me new clarity, I set about investigating the modern history of vegetarianism—and those who would debunk it. Although vegetarianism had made cultural inroads back at the turn of the twentieth century, those who did not eat meat resided in the lunatic fringe—at least in the view of the majority of right-minded people. The popular media reinforced that attitude—perhaps sometimes with hard science, but also with a derisive touch. I took it all in, including a story published in *The New York Times* back in November 1907, headlined "Beefsteak Eaters Beat Vegetarians," about a grudge match between two college football teams: "The Rutgers College second football team today defeated the Macfadden Physical Culture City team of Spotswood by a score of 30 to 11. The game was of peculiar interest because a vegetarian diet is compulsory at Physical Culture City and Coach Gorton at Rutgers develops his men on thick beefsteaks. The Physical Culturists came to town in a hay wagon, accompanied by a crowd of pretty girls in bloomer costume." Yeah, that would have been me on the sidelines with the other vegetarian cheerleaders, fainting dead away.

It took years, but eventually the cultural dietary winds began to shift. It began in earnest, sometime in the '60s, when those commune-bound, organic-touting, soy-loving hippies began to rage against corporate control of the food supply. Two decades later, the science was in. All the journalism and academic study on the meat industry had the tone of scolding those who eat meat.

Still, I was resolved: I was going to have my meat. But I couldn't help but wonder if there wasn't a better way to get meat on the dinner table than the horror show I had witnessed at the Maple Leaf plant. And isn't there some way that the meat industry could rebut the arguments for giving up meat? Something more than simple PR and spin?

While I hoped to soon forget the stench of the slaughter-house—the sight of still-warm entrails stuck to my work boots, the feeling of pig's blood seeping into my bra—I had come out the other end of the disassembly line not as a vegetarian but rather a kinder, gentler, more thoughtful carnivore.

It was the beginning of my journey—the quest for the perfect meat. In many ways, it's been our constant quest through the ages. Some scholars have argued that the quest for meat can be traced back to the origin of the species, throughout world history, and right up to the settlement of the New World. If they are right that this is such an elemental part of our collective history, then perhaps the search for the perfect meat is one that everyone can identify with. We worry about the meat we eat. We obsess about it. Whether it has too much fat, or not enough of the right kind of fat. Whether it's destroying our environment. We also worry about whether meat is a breeding ground for lethal microbes like *E. coli* and mad cow disease.

Yet for most of us, meat is a mystery. We know less about how it arrives on our plates than ever before in our history. In part, this can be traced to urbanization, a population disconnected from agriculture and major corporations investing in the industrialization of meat production. But something more is at play: our knowledge of foodstuffs is gleaned from a reading list of ingredients on the back of the package and not from hands-on experience. This veil of invisibility helps us avoid the often violent necessities of food production, creating a psychological distance between the flesh we eat and its source. There is a world of difference between pig and pork.

Meat is the ultimate symbol of North American affluence.

To consume a hamburger is, in a sense, to fulfill the promise of democracy and prosperity in middle-class America. But long before the first immigrants landed on the shores of the Americas, meat had been considered a mark of power and privilege. The origins of *pecuniary* (in *pecus*, Latin for "herd") and *capital* (in *capita*, Latin for "head of cattle") are a reminder that meat was long a measure of wealth.[6] Human history, the controversial anthropologist Marvin Harris has argued, has been driven largely by the need to secure a steady supply of high-quality protein—a cross-continent, cross-cultural pursuit of the mythological horn of plenty. "That people honor and crave animal foods more than plant foods and are willing to lavish a disproportionate share of their energy and wealth on producing them" is what Harris calls "meat hunger."[7] Peace in Western democracies, then, can be attributed largely to society's supplying its citizens with enough animal protein. European emigrants fled to the Americas and Australia for better lives—and better lives meant having meat on the table. Three square meals a day, seven days a week.

It's no exaggeration to say that America was settled as a result of the quest for meat. Though it doesn't show up in the Constitution or the Bill of Rights, meat is a significant if unspoken subtext of the founding of the nation. The very push for the New World issued from battles over animal flesh. One of the most bitter and largely ignored social struggles in European history was over the right to hunt game. When warlords took possession of great tracts of land and became landlords, they took control of wildlife too. European legend is full of stories of poacher heroes, just as the records of European law courts are full of draconian sentences for poaching.[8] What these records memorialize is generation after generation of class warfare over access to meat. Ultimately, life in the New World spelled the end of the stratification of societies into two classes: those who hogged the supply of meat and those who were forced to stuff their stomachs with grains. As J. M. Coetzee writes, it is a victory that still plays out every day at the dinner table. "America typifies the triumph of the common people in their historical drive for animal protein, and Texas is, in this respect, the capital of America. The Texan family sitting down to a meal of chicken and fried steak with French fries on the side is making up, atavistically, for European forebears who had to make do with milk and bread, or polenta. Day after day, meal after meal, their diet celebrates the New World."[9]

Men of power have understood our lust for animal flesh, invoking the promise of more meat on the plate to secure their positions in history. France's Henry IV, for example, told his subjects in the sixteenth century, "I want there to be no peasant in my realm so poor that he will not have a chicken in his pot every Sunday." It was the same pledge—"A chicken in every pot, a car in every garage," that helped Herbert Hoover and the Republican Party march to victory in 1928.[10]

The history of meat also has less material roots. Stretching as far back as the Roman Empire, meat has been at the center of celebration and community. When, for example, Emperor Vitellius gave a feast in honor of Minerva, the brains of a thousand peacocks and the tongues of a thousand flamingos were served—a hecatomb of birds for just one dish.[11] And when ancient Greek cities participated in animal sacrifice, they were not only honoring the gods, they were participating in a ritual that expressed calm, order, clarity, hierarchy, and consent. "The Greeks believed, however, that conventional meat-eating was entirely proper; cooking and sharing meat was even what made people human. Modern anthropologists agree that the cooking of food, and the agreements human beings make in order to share it out, are major differences between our behavior and that of animals."[12]

Meat has always had mystical, even magical elements, circumscribed by the laws of both man and the divine. How else, then, to explain the close association between priests and butchers—the need for a priestly presence in the slaughterhouse? Some anthropologists have even suggested that the custom of praying before eating is an effort to placate the angry spirit of the sacrificed beast.

Whatever the rituals, the truth was I'd already made my peace with the fact that I devoured animals and planned to eat many more in the future. Apologies to both Plutarch and my friend Dawn, but eating meat was no longer a question of ethics for me. No, when I set out on this journey—a quest to find the perfect meat—my concerns were of a different nature entirely. I wanted to know: Why are we suddenly so fascinated by foodstuffs like offal and sausage? Why have carnivores regained respectability, and why are they suddenly viewed through the cultural prism as leaders of a new meat chic? More important, I wanted to understand what Marvin Harris meant by "meat hunger." I wanted to comprehend what we, as North Americans, are really consuming when we eat meat. What are the social symbols underlying sacred rituals like the pig roast and the whale hunt? What are we really eating at the steakhouse and buying at the butcher shop?

What I couldn't countenance, I had learned from my experience working in the slaughterhouse at Maple Leaf in Brandon, was man's inhumanity to both man and the pig. All in the name of supplying North Americans with cheap meat. In the end, like any self-respecting carnivore, I wanted to find meat that I could feel good about eating. I hoped my journey would lead me to meat with superior flavor but also meat I could eat with a clear—or at least clearer—conscience. But even if there were to be any inner conflict, I wasn't going to let it spoil my appetite.

3
· THE NEW ·
· CELEBRITY CHEF ·

"WHAT'S THE MATTER WITH YOU?" Benny Pizzuco bellows from in front of his butcher's block, situated next to mine, where he's roughing up a piece of meat like a grade-school bully. I'm jittery. Trying to prove I can make the cut and soon graduate from chicken breasts to pork chops. But so far, my chicken tenders look more like chopped liver, destined for the resident cat's lunch bowl rather than a white-cloth dinner table. And this afternoon, Pizzuco is growing impatient, watching me cleave into his profit margins for the second day running.

"Get mad if you have to," he commands, clamping his massive fists around each end of a veal roast, hoisting it in the air before slamming it back down on top of his workstation. Clearly this prized piece of nursling—who bought the farm before he could progress from milk to Lunchables—isn't going to make it out the front door with PETA's "cruelty-free" stamp of approval.

Meanwhile, I'm hoping to tap into some of Pizzuco's mad-dog

energy by conjuring up a mental picture of my neckless nemesis. Having already cut into the bone, I throw my weight behind me, trying to snap the chicken's breast in two with my bare hands. But my tiny corpse—a domesticated descendant of the red junglefowl—won't budge. Dead for nearly a week, it seems to be fighting for dear life.

Pizzuco suddenly drops his knife, his blue eyeballs bulging, gaping at me with his mouth open like a sea bass.

"You sure ain't no Joe Weider," he finally avers in the direction of a handful of patrons who are lined up in his store, clearly enjoying the floor show. "Like I told ya already," Pizzuco continues, "it doesn't take a lot of strength. Just follow the dotted lines and you'll be okay."

Evidently, the paper-doll cutouts of my youth have done little to help prepare me for the grinding days here on the job at this legendary New York City shop. In the figurative sense, I have butchered many things in my life: a Beatles song, for example, a wedding toast. But it's a wrong-minded metaphor— if someone "butchers" something, it should be quick, clinical, precise. Clearly I've got a lot to learn about wielding a boning knife, despite a one-week crash course at the slaughterhouse.

At the Maple Leaf plant, my efforts were literally a dog's breakfast: the cheeks I gouged out of hundreds of hogs' heads were ground up, canned, and peddled as pet food. But the meat here at Florence Prime Meat Market is of a higher order—flesh culled from beasts who once occupied the pinnacle of the animal kingdom. A veritable Noah's Ark of the finest quality protein— from baby goats and lambs to specialty turkeys and the finest rumps of beef on the planet. And of course they're destined for the toniest high-society gullets at the center of the universe. Those who would not only forbid their beloved pugs and dachshunds from eating the pet food from Maple Leaf, but the people food that comes from there too.

Indeed, the well-heeled crowd gathered here this afternoon appears humbled just to share the room with these distinguished guests in their afterlife. They stare, transfixed, seemingly channeling Francis Bacon, who, peering into the window of his local butcher shop, once declared: "All that death, I find it very beautiful. And it's all for sale—how unbelievably surrealistic."[1] Leave it to a guy named Bacon to cut to the meat of the matter.

Undoubtedly, these shoppers come for the spectacle, to witness a living museum. Pizzuco plays curator—a throwback to another age. His shop offers a window into how we shopped before the supermarket, to an era when meat was more than just a commodity. Pizzuco seems to have one foot in another time. He's like Michelangelo who sculpts his masterpieces in meat. Here, meat isn't just a foodstuff, a lifeless chain of cells spiked with amino acids and B vitamins. Meat is what *he* makes it. And while his is one among a handful of shops across North America spearheading a Renaissance in old-fashioned butchering, at the Florence Prime Meat Market it's a tradition that's never gone out of style—one that stretches back to the days when the store first opened, in the 1930s.

It seems an ideal setting to begin my search for the perfect meat. You might wonder: Why not start at the chef's top table—with a plated meal? But so much of cooking is the art of deception. Of making the best of less than the ideal. Ultimately, there's no better place to start than a place without the filters and window dressing. And no one, arguably, is more equipped to discern the difference between lesser mammalian forms and the kind of flawless flesh that would have found a place on Henry VIII's banquet table. The butcher is without bias. Not like the hog farmer rearing pigs for slaughter at the local megafarm. Ask him about the perfect meat and he surely would describe the perfect swine—one judged solely on properties like how quickly he is able to plump up his little piggy for market. His breadth of experience in identifying perfect flesh may be even more limited than that of the Inuit living in the far north, whose choices include polar bear, reindeer, caribou, and beluga. But the butcher is limited only by his imagination. He's able to size up a hindquarter the way Hugh Hefner scouts his next Playboy bunny.

Pizzuco has promised to help me learn to separate the wheat from the chaff. To be able to identify the difference between a foresaddle and deckle, a porkette and a lamb chop.

It's with this in mind that I set out for lessons in Pizzuco's legendary shop earlier in the week. A retail landmark that has outlived many of Greenwich Village's celebrated roster of famous residents: Cole Porter, Lillian Hellman, Andy Warhol, Bob Dylan. The list is endless. Although, truthfully, few among them seem like meat-and-potatoes types.

It's two weeks before Christmas and a warm front has settled over the city. The streets are filled with shoppers and students dressed in bulky sweaters, brimming with preholiday cheer and postexam merriment. They wander up and down the narrow streets filled with idiosyncratic shops and celebrated restaurants like Babbo and its earlier incarnation, Po—the eatery that helped launch Molto Mario, aka Mario Batali, the potty-mouthed chef with the Falstaffian girth, into a household brand name. And, predictably, one of Florence Prime Meat Market's customers.

One street north, flagged by the Slaughtered Lamb pub on the corner, a green awning hangs over a lonely street. Inside, the decor is decidedly early meat market. Sawdust on the floors. Meat hooks jut out along a back wall. The sound of Spanish and the buzz of a hacksaw rise above an aria emanating from a radio somewhere in the background. A kinetic parade of men flit back and forth between workstations, their knives glinting in the glare of the fluorescent lights overhead. Strangely, there's not a drop of blood in sight. Not a hint of the smell of flesh. In fact, these butchers look more like estheticians—not just not stained, but never stained. If someone told you that food was coming out of here, you'd swear they were churning out tofu.

Along one shop wall there's a tribute to one-time celebrity regulars: funnyman Pat Cooper and former mayor Ed Koch, and a client's before-and-after pics of a crown roast. There's a bookshelf filled with works written by fans like chef Tyler Florence and writer Bill Buford. Untouched. Pizzuco hasn't yet had time to read them. He's too busy trying to keep up with orders to worry about his own nascent celebrity.

He emerges from a dry-aging locker at the back of the store with two Flintstone-sized racks of lamb, one on each shoulder— the kind of shoulders it takes to maneuver in a city of eight million.

"You want me to French it?" Pizzuco queries in the direction of a fiftysomething woman lolling beside his workstation.

"Oh, yes, please give it the French look," she says, smiling appreciatively.

Standing six-feet-two, Pizzuco sports the same thick, black moustache he's worn since his days as a beefcake bartender. However, his pimped-up, bell-bottomed, polyester ensemble has been given an update, replaced by a cotton golf shirt, khakis, and the requisite butcher's apron. At fifty-two, his hairline has matured too, rising high above a face as broad and rosy as a roast. He keeps undertaker's hours, arriving at 3:30 sharp to begin his work at the meat morgue. His body language—his threatening posture, the way he grips the knife—remind me more of an enforcer on the cast of *The Sopranos* than the beloved urban-village butcher.

Moments later, Pizzuco picks up his cleaver and begins to swing wildly at a half-dozen rib tips splayed on the table like a fistful of fingers.

"Why are you doing that?" I ask, shielding my eyes from the bone spray with one hand, a pen at the ready in the other, hoping to glean some of the butcher's age-old secrets.

Dead silence. "Because this is the right way to do it," Pizzuco replies finally, clearly irked by having to answer such a bone-headed question. "Besides, it's ugly and I want to make it look nice."

Apparently, you can dress up a piece of meat the way you can titivate a cleavage. After all, didn't a savvy, young, and then unknown actress named Jennifer Aniston allegedly use chicken cutlets to fill out her B-cup?

All of this has got me reflecting on the butcher shop of my youth. The only one I ever knew: Sam's squeaky-clean shop on that squeaky-clean family show *The Brady Bunch*. Alice, the Bradys' housekeeper—who presumably dated Sam so she could keep a lock on the best meat to feed the family—kept her body parts under cover of a blue double-breasted uniform and thick sweater, just as the pork chops and pot roasts were out of reach, displayed behind the pristine glass of the meat counter.

Although the official history is undoubtedly different than this reporter's hazy recollection—my post-Brady years spent toiling in a sausage factory of a different sort, cranking out disposable news nuggets—it seems the butcher had all but vanished in popular culture. Much as the real butcher was shuttering his doors, disappearing from the retail landscape all across North America. Surely, one telltale marker was the transmogrification of the word itself. In the lexicon of my generation, the word *butcher* is more commonly used to describe a monster like Jeffrey Dahmer, whose idea of interior design included tchotchkes like a pail full of hacked-off hands and a jar with a pickled penis. And what about the Butcher of Broadway, Frank Rich, the man responsible for killing productions with one swipe in *The New York Times*? Or, last, in the verbiage of my own profession, typically an invective muttered under one's breath while cursing out an overzealous editor?

And just when it seemed the butcher had all but disappeared in pop culture, he (and it is almost exclusively he) made a startling comeback. First in the 1991 black comedy *Delicatessen*, where he did double duty, working stints both as butcher and landlord. In this surrealistic world where food is rare, he serves his tenants cannibalistic dinners made from the carcass of a star-crossed renter. And who can forget Daniel Day-Lewis as Bill the Butcher, the demonically magnetic sociopath in *Gangs of New York* (modeled after real-life butcher William Poole), who warred for power, maimed a few enemies, and eventually was murdered, just down the street from where Pizzuco plies his trade.

Undoubtedly, the butcher's reputation has ebbed and flowed with the vagaries of history. Back in the early days, his job was not only to understand primal cuts, but to stalk and kill food too. The first butcher shops were the riverbanks where the Neanderthals dragged animals as large as elephants and rhinoceroses to feed their families and small nomadic tribes. Their know-how with a flint tool placed them at the top of the pecking order.

And later, in ancient Egypt, the butcher worked almost exclusively for the upper classes, who reportedly had a rich and varied diet but consumed beef like there was no tomorrow. And when there was no tomorrow, they packed their protein provisions for their journey into the next world. For example, the food found in the tomb of a minor noble's wife at Saqqara from the Second Dynasty—sometime between 2890 and 2686 B.C.—included cooked quail, two cooked kidneys, a pigeon stew, boiled fish, and beef ribs. Meanwhile, commoners ate little meat except at feast times, and then it was usually a sheep or goat slaughtered for a meal among friends.[2]

But by the Middle Ages, the butcher's status in the community had become somewhat tarnished. His workplace in many European cities was the cobblestone walkways, where it wasn't unusual to hear the bleating of goats and cries of cattle any day of the week; a place where blood and entrails flowed out in the open and rushed down the streets. Because the public spectacle of the slaughter was so violent, it "led to the general opinion that the butcher's trade—since the butcher was also the knacker—was unworthy. The French eater demanded that, in processions, the butchers march behind the main part of the parade, and the English eater demanded that butchers not be members of juries when a decision had to be made about putting a murderer to death."[3]

However, over the next few centuries, with the formation of trade unions, the butcher regained some of his social status. In Hungary, for example, belonging to a butchers' guild was seen as a badge of honor, in part because it was difficult to gain admission. A new member could join under strict rules, and only if he was the son of a guild master or an assistant marrying the daughter or a widow of the master. Admittance also required six years of apprenticeship and passing a lengthy examination.

Meanwhile, by the early part of the nineteenth century, the profession was also getting a makeover in France. New laws decreeing a separation of slaughterhouse and butcher shop redeemed the butcher in the public's eyes. The sullied reputation of men with blood-soaked hands was transferred to the men of the slaughterhouse. This development also proved to be a critical juncture in between man and animal, creating not only a physical but psychological distance between the eater and the eaten. "Meat [was] no longer linked with the living animal. It became an anonymous substance, harmless and without history. Surreptitiously, slowly, the disembodied culture that characterizes the contemporary epoch fell into place. . . . Basically, slaughtering out of sight assured the eater a certain peace of mind and appeased the carnivore's conscience."[4]

By the time my grandmother was shopping for meat in small-town Ontario, the butcher was considered a confidant. Ethel

Mae not only relied on him to provide the best cuts of meat but also looked to him for cooking tips at her busy café in the Muskoka cottage country. Like most North American women who were responsible for supplying loved ones with their protein provisions, my grandmother patronized the same store for years, just around the corner from where she lived.[5]

But by 1930, industry experts began to predict a vastly different future. Converging in Chicago, the hub of the North American meat industry, corporate chieftains decried the current state of the butcher shop, in which consumers had to endure long lineups. Making it easier to shop, they believed, would bolster meat sales. Experts foresaw a future, reported *The New York Times*, in which the butcher would more closely resemble a "cafeteria chef, and clerks may serve out meats like a waiter."[6] Others emphasized that the "old-fashioned butcher shop with its old-fashioned methods of cutting and selling meat in unattractive surroundings" was "doomed for the discard." The butcher shop of the future as pictured by the packers' spokesmen would be "smart-looking shops designed to appeal to the fastidious woman shopper, with the cleaver and chopping block entirely disappeared." Fresh meats, cut into convenient sizes and grades, would be ready in "attractive, sanitary packages," they predicted, "this new method having already been tried successfully," according to the *Times* story.

By all accounts, they were right. Over the next three decades, the butcher gradually was being phased out. Retreating further and further behind glass panels that enclosed ever more sterile-looking cutting rooms. He still was visible in his white coat, but if you wanted to talk to him, you had to ring the bell. Somehow we lost touch. So you probably can forgive those like Jack Christie, the father of my best friend growing up. Like many among his generation, he might have been a crackerjack at his job as a biologist, but when it came to basics beyond the barbecue (forget about the Thanksgiving turkey), he was clueless. Even his wife, Susan, was stunned at his ineptitude when she put Brillo pad to pan the morning after she'd left him to cook on his own, wondering what had become so horribly burned to the roaster. Turns out that when Jack put his Shake 'N Bake pork chops in the oven, he didn't know he was supposed to remove them from the plastic bag before cooking and then eating them.

An extreme example? Maybe. But I would argue that few within my social group typically fare much better in the kitchen when it comes to meat. Case in point: The panic at the household where friends were planning their annual pre-Christmas party. On the day of the soirée, it suddenly dawned on the hosts that neither had ever cooked a prime rib—like the $120 roast from Cumbrae's sitting in the fridge. Finally, numerous panicked phone calls later, they located Kaspar, the only person on a guest list of twenty-five who had ever cooked a roast. Apparently, you have a better chance of finding a doctor—even a specialist—at a party than someone who can use a meat thermometer. Kaspar was dispatched to the gathering two hours early and gallantly saved the evening from ruin.

I would have liked to have thought that somehow I was different, having watched my mother all those afternoons prepare her prime rib for Sunday dinner. Still, a couple of years back—when my non-meat-eating boyfriend was off on assignment—I decided I was going to cook a roast. Admittedly, I was hankering for red meat, but I also figured Gare's eighty-seven-year-old father, Toby, could also use a protein boost to supplement his twice-daily servings of Campbell's Scotch Broth. I hit the supermarket, scouring the meat cases for a small prime rib that would feed two, with leftovers for sandwiches. I stood, rooted in the same spot for more than an hour, manhandling one roast after another, completely flummoxed. What did a good piece of meat look like? How much did I need? I finally settled on one of those prepackaged numbers because it also provided cooking directions—along with its own gravy—on the side of the package. Back home, some forty-five minutes later, I extracted my muffin-size roast from the oven. Bursting with anticipation, I hacked into the side of it and hoisted a piece to my mouth. Seconds later, it lay steaming on top of the garbage. The gravy tasted like industrial cleaner, the meat was as tasteless as a shock jock's joke. Inedible.

Two years later and Toby's still waiting for his roast beef dinner. At the very least, I'm hoping my week spent here at Florence Prime Meat Market will teach me a thing or two about how to select a good piece of meat as well as how to cook it.

As soon as I met Pizzuco, I knew I had come to the right place. He and his store manager, Maria, were huddled over the meat case, staring at a photograph, oblivious of my arrival. "Beautiful," Maria cooed softly. "Yeah, I don't see why we can't send this out as our Christmas picture this year," Pizzuco confirmed, his eyes glazed over like those of a teenager in the blush of a first crush. Edging closer, I caught a glimpse of his beloved: a standing rib roast, shaped like a crown. "Think you can do that?" Pizzuco smirked while handing me a butcher's apron, the formal introductions now out of the way.

Truthfully, I'm not sure I'm ready for prime time. But it's not long—in the flurry of the morning's work—before I realize I've lost my performance anxiety. Pizzuco first puts me on lackey standby, poised and ready with the "veal cutlet pounder"—a weighty instrument that would have ably done the job on Colonel Mustard in the conservatory. First up for Pizzuco? A six-rib roast. Followed by a ten-rib roast. Eight pork chops. Six chicken cutlets. A veal roast. A rack of lamb. The order list is piled high this morning, just like any other weekday morning.

Pizzuco glides across the sawdust like an ice dancer on skates, disappearing into the locker before emerging with the back end of a steer. "This is where the good stuff is," he tells me, pointing to the meat muscle on the inside of the ribs, right in front of the loin.

He should know. He's been handing out these pearls of wisdom from behind the butcher's block for nearly thirty years. Showing a little too much attitude for his teachers, he dropped out of school at seventeen. He landed a job at his best friend's father's butcher shop in Queens—a meat-market holdout in the burgeoning days of the superstore. Pizzuco stayed four years, learning the basics of the butterfly cut and how to prepare a Delmonico steak before being sucked into bartending in the last days of disco. At twenty-seven, completely burned out, he returned to butchering to learn the trade in earnest. "It's a clean job," Pizzuco says, explaining the lure of the work. "You know, you're not digging holes or dealing with the elements."

He bought his first shop in Baldwin, Long Island, before eventually setting his sights on acquiring a more prestigious address: a place where people wouldn't haggle over costs, a place where he could sell only premier goods—dry-aged prime beef, as well as the best veal, lamb, and chicken on the planet. So, when a FOR SALE sign went up on one of New York's most celebrated butcher shops, Pizzuco pulled out all the stops. At the time, Florence Prime Meat Market's owner, Tony Pellegrino, said he wanted the new owner to continue in the store's longstanding tradition to uphold the art of butchering. "There are not too many left like us," he said back in 1996. "We go to the market every day and pick a piece of meat that is nice for the customer. Veal Parisienne, veal Pellegrino, the Newport steak, we invented here. We wrap nice. We present nice." Pizzuco lined up beside five other butchers, auditioning for the job for six months before Pellegrino finally agreed to sell him the store. Maybe he had an extra edge: although Pizzuco was from the Bronx, his parents, like Pellegrino, were Sicilian. Whatever the case, Pellegrino was impressed with Pizzuco's butchering skills. "I'm going to miss it, I'm going to cry," Pellegrino told *The New Yorker*'s Nick Taylor as he set to hand over the store keys and settle into retirement. "I'll come back on weekends and give a hand to Benny for a while, because it's like family, this place, and he doesn't know everybody yet. But then he'll be better than me."[7]

As Pizzuco gouges deeper into the roast with a boning knife, it's clear that he takes his role as torchbearer of the tradition seriously. "See? This is how a prime meat market works," he says, before expounding on the differences between a butcher shop and a prime meat market. Most notably, that old-fashioned types like him start with primal cuts—the two-hundred-pound slabs of meat—before cutting them into secondary pieces and then to the customer's specifications.

Pizzuco's all New York hustle. His mouth moves as fast as his knife. He's a one-man power grid of high-octane, fist-pumping opinion. Just don't get him started on the supermarket butchers. "Those schmucks," he cries in exasperation. "They wouldn't last here five minutes. They just take stuff from the box and cut it and put it on a platter in a showcase. They bring out a pork roast and it looks ridiculous. It looks like something a four-year-old kid did. It's nasty. Horrible. That's not butchering," he declares, waving his hand dismissively.

But there's plenty of scorn, plenty of vitriol to go around. Pizzuco doesn't reserve it just for other butchers. It's only now that I realize I have breached the inner sanctum, the who's who of New York's Grub Street, when Pizzuco launches into a butcher shop confidential, tearing into one of the critics' darlings, a chef who shall remain nameless. The only one he's ever turfed out of his store, so far. "He didn't know what he was talking about," Pizzuco seethes. "What can I tell ya? I just don't deal with morons."

"This is me," he sighs, and shrugs, suddenly eyeing my tape recorder. "I can't hide who I am. Someone gets mad? What do I care?"

I pause, pondering whether it would be appropriate to pry into his dealings with the legendary tyrannical perfectionist who shops at his store, mostly via assistant. The one I've watched fuss over a trussed-up piece of poultry under the TV lights on more than one occasion. Would I be taking advantage of a man mid-rant? I can't help myself. A journalist, a gossip at heart, I find myself finally blurting out my question: "What's Martha like?" Pizzuco's eyebrows shoot up before he stretches his mouth into a wide, sly grin. "Ahhh," he pauses. "She's great! And you know why? Because she *listens* to ME."

So much for shop talk. Pizzuco turns his attention back to the roast, one that's now been butchered to about half its original heft. "I've got to straighten this out," he explains, lifting it in the air and throwing it on the butcher's block. "You should write this down," he instructs over the sound of big hands slapping wet flesh. "Meat is malleable." As if to prove the point, he tugs on one corner of the roast before rolling it up like a cinnamon bun. But the job's not finished yet. Next, he fetches several blocks of dense white fat, shaves them into dozens of thin slices, and arranges them on the roast like a puzzle before placing a sheet of waxed paper on top. "This is to keep people from themselves," he explains, patting the paper in place. "To keep them from overcooking it."

Finally, I'm called to duty. Pizzuco assigns me my first job: flattening out the fat with the veal cutlet pounder. I must admit the first pummel feels a little awkward, but I quickly find a rhythm and I'm soon lost in my thoughts, envisioning all those beef-loving Englishmen who used to bolster their spirits by singing "The Old Roast Beef of England," imagining a postwar world when they could once again dine on the national dish:

> When mighty Roast Beef
> Was the Englishman's food,
> It ennobled our brains
> And enriched our blood.
> Our soldiers were brave
> And our courtiers were good,

Oh, the Roast Beef of old England
And old English Roast Beef.[8]

Even Shakespeare acknowledged beef's almighty impor-
tance in nourishing the troops in *Henry V*: "Give them great
meals of beef and iron and steel, they will eat like wolves and
fight like devils."[9]

Pounding away, I realize I'm happy to contribute to the
sustenance of the modern-day warriors—those who work in
the glass towers and nearby corridors of American commerce.
Twenty minutes into my pummeling and I peel back the wax
paper to reveal a thin layer of fat that looks like vanilla cake
frosting. "Alex is one lucky guy," Pizzuco says of a regular, wrapping the fat around the roast and securing it in several places
with butcher's string. "In here, you work hard, you make somebody a nice roast and they go home and say, that's beautiful. If
it's $40 or $80—it don't matter. Out in the suburbs, you make
something like this and they'd try to start a fight with you. They
go for that Costco crap. Here, we get sensible people."

Sensible. And happy. By day's end, my body feels like a
transducer, vibrating from a day spent wielding the pounder
to fashion security blankets for these upscale roasts. It somehow seems well worth it as I watch customers leave the store
with their roasts and chicken cutlets under their arms, wrapped
neatly in old-style butcher's brown paper. A smile on their lips,
a bounce in their steps, visions of perfect rump roasts fresh from
the oven dancing in their heads.

By eight the next morning, I find myself straggling, struggling
to keep pace with Pizzuco, who marches along the sidewalk of

one of Manhattan's most fashionable streets like he owns it. The place where perfect steaks and perfect chops and perfect racks of lamb are holed up, hidden far from the public eye, deep inside nondescript warehouses. A neighborhood where the trendiest thing worn up until recently was a blood-stained apron—a uniform slowly being replaced by designer labels peddled in neighborhood stores, like Stella McCartney and Diane von Furstenberg. Walking along West Fourteenth Street, the meatpacking district's main artery, I'm struck by how much it looks like Rodeo Drive until we pass a truck unloading a shipment of bodies. A lone truck in the street where fleets once teemed, servicing the neighborhood's 250 meat plants and slaughterhouses.

"That's where I used to buy my pigs," Pizzuco says, aiming a beefy forefinger at a building with a sign that reads KUSY'S PROVISIONS, formerly Adolf Kusy Co. Fine Pork and Provisions, a shop that turned out the lights in 2001 after seventy-five years in business.[10] Like so many other meatpackers squeezed out by an onslaught of tony retailers, hip nightclubs, and ultra-chic furniture stores. For fifteen years, it was one of the first stops on Pizzuco's rounds throughout the district, although these days he's more likely to dispatch his minions to pick up his precious cargo. Now, his suppliers understand his needs. They know he'll ship it back if he's not happy. He *should* get what he wants. After all, he's been known to grease a few palms.

"I take care of them," Pizzuco explains matter-of-factly as we scale the stairs of Walmir Meat Market, supplier not only to his meat market but steakhouse luminaries like Peter Luger and the Old Homestead.

"Like a tip?" I ask.

"If you want to call it that," he says. "Sometimes, during the holiday season, things get short. I just tell them, 'I don't care. Tell someone else, don't tell me. It's not my problem.' I'm a good customer. I pay on time. They make sure it's somebody else's problem."

We step into a cold, damp grave, arguably North America's most elite meat locker. It might as well be a bank vault, overflowing with the riches of the best Angus beef, Herefords, and Brahmans in all God's green acres. No doubt, the inventory more valuable than the entire showroom at Alexander McQueen's a few streets away. Row upon row, thousands of seemingly identical hindquarters and frontquarters hang side by side, like freshly pressed garments at the dry cleaners. Rigor mortis never looked so good. Nothing but beef as far as the eye can see. Otherwise, the decor is austere. There's a small plastic pig on a shelf, and a girlie calendar on the wall, which features Miss December, who's wearing little more than the teddy bear clutched in her arms, presumably to keep warm.

"Benny!" a guy wearing a white lab coat, yellow hardhat, and genial grin hollers. "It's been too long," he continues, sidling up beside us and slapping Pizzuco on the back. "To what do we owe this honor?" Pizzuco explains he's brought me, his cousin from Toronto, here on vacation for a look-see. A sneak peek into the backrooms of packers and their brethren. Sure to be a keepsake moment in my vacation, a little boho travel, off the traditional sightseeing grid, he explains. "Ahright," the guy in the lab coat finally pronounces. "But NO pictures."

Pizzuco and I begin the tour. Our purpose? To observe the differences among prime, choice, and select cuts—the three grades used by the USDA to identify the quality of beef. In other words, a search for the perfect beef. Walking down the first row, I feel like I've just entered a cartoon panel of Where's Waldo. Every aisle identical, I worry I'll get lost, left behind in cold storage before being loaded onto the back of a truck. I scramble to keep pace with Pizzuco, who's marching nonchalantly, seemingly giving little more than a passing glance to each carcass when he suddenly stops dead in his tracks. "See this?" he asks excitedly, running his finger along a maroon-colored piece of flesh, heavily laced with speckles of white fat. "That's the strap. When you get the fat broken up like that. That's prime. Ah, now that's just beautiful. A beautiful piece of prime."

"I'm a traditionalist," he sighs. "There's nothing better than American grain-fed cattle. There's nothing better than dry-aged beef. There's no such thing as dry-aged organic. It all comes in a plastic bag. That stuff's nasty. It's got no flavor. You don't buy into that organic crap, do you?" I sputter. I stammer. Truthfully, I don't know how to answer his question. No matter. Pizzuco turns on his heel to round the corner. He doesn't bother to wait for a response. He doesn't need to take any cues, any counsel from a green pea like me.

An hour later, Pizzuco's acquainting me with the wonders of his house specialty—culled from another upscale piece of prime meat direct from the same supplier. We're sitting at the lunch table that does double duty as the sausage-making station. It's the same place Pizzuco eats lunch every day. If not here, then at one of the city restaurants he supplies with meat. "I don't like to take chances," he explains. "You don't know what you're getting. I only know what I'm getting if it comes from here." He's grilled us a couple of Newport steaks—invented by the shop's original owner to feed his hungry student clientele from nearby New York University. A cheaper cut, a one-inch triangle of beef cut out of the bottom butt. A steak apparently so coveted by onetime mayor and former member of the House of Representatives Ed Koch that he ordered ten of them every week to take with him to Washington.[11] The Newport is to be fortification for my first afternoon spent on the floor learning knife skills. "You eat one of those Newport steaks with a salad. Where you gonna eat better?" Pizzuco asks before answering his own question. "I'll tell ya, you're never gonna eat better than right here." He's right. I slice into the Newport and marvel at how wonderfully its crust is charred. One bite in I know the steak gods are shining down on me. Nutty and buttery. Maybe not perfect. But delicious.

Too bad it's the last time I'll even come close to touching a Newport for the rest of the week. Pizzuco doesn't tell me at the time, but I'll later learn that he doesn't want to risk his high-end inventory in the hands of a novice like me. Besides, it's a long-standing tradition in the butchering trade to train on chicken breasts—the cheapest of butcher shop proteins.

There's no time to linger. No time to relish the feast we've just finished. It's time for my first lesson. In truth, Pizzuco couldn't be a more patient teacher. But twenty minutes in, I'm tempted to call it quits. Butchering is much harder than it looks.

So here it is, the verbatim account of how my first half-hour unfolded, with instructions and color commentary straight from the mouth of the maestro. Just press replay for a full account of the rest of the day.

"You take the breast bone like this. See, it snaps right open. Take this out. Right here, this wishbone's gotta come out. Yes, like that."

"Cut away from you."

"Hit it so it will pop open. Turn it around. Grab that piece in the middle right out. Bring your finger right along here like you're doing surgery."

"No. No. No."

"Hold the knife away from you. Don't get tangled up with it. If the knife gets greasy, it could turn on you. If the board gets slippery, it's dangerous too."

"You cut it crooked like that, you're going to ruin it."

"See? You ruined it."

"No. No. No."

"Listen, there's no diagram. You're just going to have to do more of them."

"Don't hurt yourself. Keep your hand steady."

"That's it. That's it."

"No. No. No."

"Okay. Bring out the next hundred fifty. She's gonna need some practice. Lots and lots of practice."

At day's end, my fingers look like they've been soaking in a pickle jar, they're so puckered and soggy. I'm dead tired. The chicken breasts have more life left in them than I do. But it's not just my body that's broken. It's my spirit too. I hang up my apron and leave feeling completely disgraced.

The next morning, just before eight, I arrive to greet my fellow workers. No one will meet my gaze. The reviews are in from yesterday, and apparently I stink. Pizzuco starts from the beginning, patiently explaining it all over again. I spend the day carving, cleaving, and cursing—I just can't seem to get it right.

By my last day, I'm assigned to "help" Maria, the store manager, with the customers. I learn to wrap meat in brown paper and tie it with string. I had begun my week here in an entry-level position—the most junior job in the place. Now I've carved out a niche for myself that's even lower in the pecking order of butchery. I was dispatched to pick up the company Christmas photos, to get coffee. My legacy? Enough mangled chicken breasts to feed the staff and the resident cat, Veronica, for a week.

I decide to cut my last day short. I bid my good-byes. I tell Pizzuco how much I'd enjoyed the experience—at least hanging out with him and his staff. I tell him that I'd love to find a way to live and work here, somewhere in the neighborhood. Maybe I could even get a full-time job here, I say. A look of panic suddenly flashes across Pizzuco's face—dissipating only when I assure him—"I'm only kidding."

"Well," Pizzuco sputters with relief, "if this were a supermarket, I could teach you to be a meat cutter in about two weeks. But here, in a prime meat market like this, it takes two years to learn. You? Maybe five.

"All I can say is that chicken really beat the shit out of you."

He probably meant to laugh with me rather than at me. But his words cut like a knife. Actually, his words cut more like me wielding a butcher's cleaver. But there's no dressing up the facts, which are as cold as a meat locker and as hard as T-bone: there are many things that I have little talent for, but apparently none less than butchering.

In the end, I decide it's best to leave the heavy lifting to the greats, the giants of the industry, like Pizzuco. For him, it's simple. He's just a guy who gets his jollies by sending people home with a prime rib roast—one he's "made" with his own hands. "I just like making people happy." He shrugs and sighs. "When you make people happy, your whole life is easy."

4
· OFF THE ·
· EATEN TRACK ·

I'VE COME TO THE TOP of the world for this haute cuisine, readying myself to unleash a reactionary head butt on the ranks of the politically correct, as well as to trump my fellow carnivores in terms of sheer carnivoraciousness. I've come for a meat that you can't find anywhere else on the menu in North America, a culinary staple that has been consumed here for millennia. Never varying in recipe and seasoned only by God, it's typically served freshly chilled straight from the world's largest naturally occurring meat locker. If launched as a product for mass consumption, it surely would defeat all but the most ironic advertising copywriter: "Best served before the eighteenth century" and "Hundreds served since 1 A.D."—probably carved into soapstone somewhere.

This afternoon, I'm sitting in a dark and cavernous room, a dining room in northern Alaska that has the ambience of a members-only club. I feel like I'm an interloper in a secret society, like I've just stepped into a meat-eaters' speakeasy. As I am staring down at the slab of pallid flesh on the plate in front of me, my stomach suddenly has the heebie-jeebies. I can't help thinking that gate-crashers in this culinary underbelly might do better taking their first bite in private. In the seclusion of the living room of my imaginary igloo, for example, right next to the latrine. Anywhere but here, under the watchful stare of this exceedingly polite and expectant audience, because it might not be pretty.

I'm spooked not just by the idea of eating an utterly alien being, but by the significance of my gustatory exploits. The very act of consuming this creature has sparked violent global clashes as well as vitriolic debate on everything from cultural imperialism to the nature of consciousness and intelligence. Depending upon which side of the moral divide you sit on—north or south of the 58th parallel—I'm either about to participate in a sacred custom or a profane and unholy act.

I feign excitement, forcing a smile and nodding to the group as I ready my fork, finally hoisting a piece of muktuk, or whale blubber, to my mouth. I pray that one bite will suffice, that one mouthful will give me a peek into a society that pins its entire identity on an endangered animal. A place where a whale must die so that a culture can live.

IT'S EARLY SUNDAY, late April, in Barrow. From the sky, the town must look like a defiant human footprint in the snow, set amid the polar bear tracks, 330 miles north of the Arctic Circle. The last gas station before the North Pole on the most northern shore of continental North America. The sun glitters in an endless sky. Its rays seep into tar-paper roofs, through oilskin curtains, and through the icy panes of the Northern Lights restaurant, where locals are gathered this morning, swapping fish tales. Stories about the capricious whims of the winds and currents and ice. And stories about the one that got away. "It won't be long now," one of the town's elders declares loudly between bites of toast and reindeer sausage. "I can feel it in my bones," he continues. A dozen heads swivel in his direction. "You get to know these things," he pronounces. "Someone is going to catch a whale—maybe even today."

Down the street, inside a small church, the congregation is gathered in prayer. Heads bowed in unison, they ask God to provide a plentiful bounty and to bring the community's hunters back to safety. Outside, children race on bicycles up and down streets like North Star and Okpik. Pedaling as fast as they can, they pass a whimsical signpost with arrows pointing in all directions: Paris, 4,086 miles, Los Angeles, 2,945 miles, and so on. They pass dozens of brightly painted green, yellow, and blue houses perched on stilts, high above the tundra. Dressed in shorts and T-shirts, oblivious of −20 degree Fahrenheit weather, they pass by Arnold Brower Sr.'s house.

Brower's already busy at work, loading a wooden box with today's sustenance. Provisions: two frozen Arctic graylings, several chunks of bearded seal, a baggie full of salmon, and a tin of Spam. Notably absent: cutlery, dishes, and napkins. All of which has got me thinking about matters of etiquette on the ice floe: Will we be served from left to right? Who will get the prime cuts of meat? And will my Inupiat hosts introduce me to any curious customs—like the Egyptians who dined wearing cones of scented fat on their heads? Or hosts in Melanesian New Ireland, who threw pig bones at the table to signal to their guests that they could begin eating?[1]

As in all ancient cultures, what passes here for good manners is so ritualized it's almost instinctive. Like this morning's preparation for the hunt, one Brower has performed as far back as he can remember—long before the town was patched into the electrical grid and the advent of Gore-Tex. Still, today's food box is much lighter than it once was. Brower no longer has to pack rations for his dog sled team. He upgraded from his squad of hardworking huskies to the snowmobile along with the rest of the town back in the 1960s.

"This food will keep us warm," he tells me, peering out from behind a wolverine ruff of fur with brown eyes framed by thick black eyebrows that lend him a gentle and quizzical expression. He twists a piece of twine around the box and places it on the ground before pulling a rifle out of a canvas bag attached to his machine. Reaching with hands as thick and brown and lined as old catcher's mitts, he grabs a half-dozen bullets and loads the gun, the sound of metal against metal piercing the brittle air. Stuffed into a white hunting parka and blue snow pants—and standing a squat five-feet-five, the eighty-four-year-old Inupiat looks more like a vintage and politically incorrect child's Eskimo doll than the most revered whaling warrior this side of the twenty-first century. His is the face of a man who has lived large and close to nature—as a reindeer herder, World War II parachutist, businessman, father of seventeen, cancer survivor, and widower—as well as the most legendary whaler to ever step a Sorel on this side of the tundra. "No agvik today," Brower pronounces, staring west into a cloudless sky. "You want to catch a whale? Then you've got to think like a whale. Like me. For I am hunter, I am wildlife," he says, curling his lips into a playful smile.

I figure he's playing it up for the crowd—admittedly a crowd of one—me. I laugh, dismissing his utterance as a bit of good-natured bonhomie on the local whaling circuit. It's only much later, as I come to know and understand Brower and his culture, that I am able to grasp the true meaning behind this seemingly offhand and playful comment. In the manner of an elder handing down the wisdom of hunters learned and shared over generations, Brower is, in fact, instructing me to harness my inner beast.

"An animal knows much more than you do," Brower intones in a hushed voice, brimming with reverence. "If you watch them, you can learn from them as I have done." Perhaps the evolution of man into whale is off the Darwinian trajectory, but to Brower it is his own natural selection. However, I'm a little bewildered when he assigns me to an avian analogue, suggesting that my inner beast is better adapted to flying over the ice than migrating beneath it. "I like your voice," he tells me. "You sound like a goose." I can see from the look on his face that it's meant to be a compliment, although I can't help thinking it might well explain my thwarted career in radio—a good thing, perhaps, that I opted out of broadcasting to find my voice in print.

Undoubtedly, I am feeling somewhat feral, without the trappings of urbanity and wrapped in several layers beneath a down jacket and Kodiak boots purchased years ago for a camping trip I never took. My mink hat—belonging to my partner, Gare, and pilfered from the hall closet without his knowledge—is my only concession to fashion. I'm here on a crash course for the kind of tutoring you can't get at any Ivy League school or from instructional tapes shilled on late-night TV. In just two weeks, I hope to glean the secrets of what it's taken this Inupiat Eskimo, my mentor and ultimately my friend, a lifetime to learn.

I'm sitting in a sled roped to the back of Brower's snow-mobile, and fretting as I ponder the perils that await me. Will I make it back with life and limb? And more important, with Gare's $500 hat? Had I understood what was really at stake—that my role here would be pivotal in determining the outcome of the hunt—I would, in all likelihood, have bolted.

"Are you ready?" Brower asks. Before I've had a chance to answer, he's yanking on the rope to ignite the engine. "You'll be on polar bear watch today," he avers, laughing over the basso roar of the machine, and we steer into the Chukchi Sea. We're headed ten miles northwest, out onto a frozen plate of ice to spring whaling headquarters—the first of two trips I will make to the camp. It's a scouting mission to check out the site while we wait for the polar ice to crack into an open lead, as the Inupiat call the open water, allowing the whales to pass and the hunt to begin.

My head jogs up and down like a cheap bobble-head doll, banging against the back of the sled as we climb up and down a chaotic jumble of pressure ridges formed along a vast expanse of ice. I'm singing at the top of my lungs, hoping my off-tune ditty will ward off any hungry polar bears. Believe me, if any-thing will scare off a bear, it would be my rendition of the Bee Gees' "Stayin' Alive." Either that tuneless karaoke or my new

Goth look—cheeks streaked in black mascara, eyelashes lined with tiny icicles, and a prefrostbite pallor reminiscent of *The Addams Family*'s Wednesday Addams. For a moment I'm able to forget my fear, as I take in this utterly astonishing vista: miles and miles of tangled ice shards, jutting up in every direction. A bleached-out blanket—whiter than white—embellished with icy blocks of aquamarine that look like precious jewels in the snowscape.

ONE CAN IMAGINE but no one knows for certain what the hungry nomads saw thousands of years ago as they crossed a now-lost land bridge from Siberia, in pursuit of caribou and other game that thrived along the Arctic coastlines and inhabited its ice floes. Anthropologists believe that the Inupiat are the descendants of a second wave of migrants to cross the Bering Sea about 4000 B.C. and that they were whaling as early as A.D. 800[2]—about the time that the pyramids were being built in Yucatán's Chichén Itzá. Within two hundred years, a subsistence whaling tradition had spread across the entire circumpolar region—stretching from Alaska through Canada's far north to Greenland and Siberia.

Much like the buffalo for the North American Plains Indians, the ability of the Inupiat to harvest a whale often meant the difference between life and death; the struggle for survival not just between man and mammal, but for individual hunters and entire villages. When American Robert J. Flaherty filmed *Nanook of the North* around Canada's Hudson Bay in the early 1920s, he was paying homage to the Inuits' perseverance in an inhospitable world in a way that he probably never fully understood at the time. It is, perhaps, a sadly appropriate footnote that the subjects in this landmark documentary perished shortly after the film was released—the victims of starvation.

In many of these small villages, in places like Kotzebue to the west and Nuiqsut to the east, one bowhead whale could feed an entire community for a year. Whale was their food, but also their heat and light. Nothing was wasted. The baleen from the "feathers" of the whale's mouth, and the bones, were used to help build sod shelters and to make household implements and weapons. Whaling also provided a social structure for the Inupiat, led by the whaling captains, in which the community pooled its resources.

When the first Yankee whalers from New Bedford, Massachusetts, appeared on Alaska's northern shores in the 1880s, the Inupiat showed that they were a tradition-respecting culture but not a hidebound one. They were eager to adopt the best of the Yankee technology while maintaining their sacred traditions. They traded up from spears to powdered bombs, for example, but held fast to the umiaks, or sealskin boats, they had used for centuries. They weren't hostile to those who came from away—they were more like welcoming hosts, providing food and clothing and crewing on the white men's ships.

An estimated two thousand voyages set out from New Bedford alone,[3] hoping to cash in on the boom in bowhead whale products. Its blubber produced a high-grade oil that was used to light the streets of the new industrial age. Its baleen was used to make everything from buggy whips to carriage springs, corsets, and parasols. But two decades later, the fickle whims of fashion and technological change would herald an end to this era in whaling—and by default, save the bowhead from extinction.

All around town, the influence of those Yankee whalers is everywhere. New England names like Leavitt, Adams, and Pederson crowd the thin pages of the Barrow phone book, many of them still among prominent whaling families this century. However, no white man left a bigger footprint on the Arctic's North Slope than a buccaneer from New Bedford, Massachusetts, named Charles DeWitt Brower. Brower arrived in Barrow in the mid-1880s at age nineteen, aboard the ship *Beda*. Though commerce brought him north, it was the people that kept him rooted there for more than half a century. The Inupiat taught him how to live in their igloos, hunt seals and caribou, and whale as they had for centuries. In less than ten years after his arrival, Brower owned his own commercial whaling operation and had established the region's first trading post, as well as a fifty-seat café that still bears his name, located on a lonely strip of tundra on the outskirts of town.

He married his beloved Toctoo, a local Inupiat woman, who died in 1902 in a measles epidemic. He then hired Asianggataq to take care of his children, and later married her, raising fourteen children in the tradition of the culture. He included some of the Arctic's greatest explorers among his friends—those like Vilhjalmur Stefansson, Knud Rasmussen, and George Wilkins. Humorist Will Rogers was on his way with Wiley Post to visit Brower when his plane crashed into a lagoon twelve miles from Barrow in 1935.

Writing in his memoir *Fifty Years Below Zero: A Lifetime of Adventure in the Far North* in his twilight years, Brower noted the impact of modernity on the place he called home for most of his lifetime. "Electric lights! Radio! Shortwave sending station. 'Daily' papers six times a year." Yet how strangely unchanged it was from the days of his first arrival. "Ghostly sounds…which typify the Arctic to me. I hear them plainly as I work—the rhythmic beat of the devil-driver's drum, wind-swept shouts of a triumphant crew, or, mingling with the boom of ice, the dying swis-s-sh of a bowhead whale."[4] His autobiography was an instant bestseller. An ode to the Arctic's early explorers and adventurers and a souvenir for his children—including his only surviving offspring, my mentor, Arnold Brower Sr.

Brower sits at the kitchen table, buried under a stack of old maps, but there's no dust on him. He rises before five every morning during whaling season, puts on a pot of coffee, and tunes in to the CB radio for the latest weather conditions. He listens for news about the day's winds and currents—clues as to when the glacier ice will crack into an open lead, allowing the annual spring bowhead hunt to begin. "Happy fiftieth, George!" a thin voice crackles on the squawk box. "Heard anything about how the girls' basketball tournament is going in Anchorage?" another disembodied voice queries. No word of an open lead yet.

Dozens of photographs line his bookshelves, from sepia tone to digital. There are pictures of his beloved and now deceased wife, Emily, smiling shyly from behind bright red lipstick and holding a vanilla ice cream cone while visiting relatives in San Francisco. There are photographs of his children and great-grandchildren. "There's so many of them, I don't even recognize them all," he sighs and shrugs by way of explanation. There's a crucifix on one wall, a painting of the Last Supper on another.

Hidden in one corner is a box overflowing with tokens of conquests—the eardrums of nearly a hundred whales harvested over a lifetime. The walls are festooned with hunting snapshots: a fifty-ton whale lying on the beach, ready for butchering; a picture of Brower beaming from the front of his umiak, as well as a number of close-ups of stone and ivory harpoon points that look like they belong in a museum case. "Look," he commands. "You've never seen anything like these before," he announces matter-of-factly. He's right. And until a little more than a decade ago, neither had any of the world's top scientists. The harpoon points had been cut out of recently harvested whales, but hadn't been used by whalers for more than 120 years.[5] It meant these same bowheads harvested by Barrow hunters had been swimming the oceans during the Civil War, as far back as when Abraham Lincoln was president, before Canada was even a country. Their discovery sent tremors across the scientific community, and corroborated what scientists had long suspected—that the bowhead may well be the earth's oldest living creature, and certainly its oldest mammal. For the Inupiat, it simply validated what they already knew: The mighty bowhead was an oracle that should be worshipped, killed, eaten, and worshipped all over again in an elaborate festival.

In a town of 4,500, gushing in billions of dollars of oil revenues over the years—in a place where you can dine on sushi, pizza, and burritos any night of the week—in a community where many have desk jobs, carry cell phones, and watch satellite TV, it's difficult to fathom hunting on such an epic scale or to understand the Inupiat's cultural need to slay its own dinner. But to understand the significance of whaling to the Inupiat, one needs to look to the past, to an ethnological tradition in which man and animal shadow one another.

In Inupiat cosmology, men and animals coexist in a world of reciprocity and respect. In *The Whale and the Supercomputer: On the Northern Front of Climate Change,* writer Charles Wohlforth describes the Inupiat view of human-animal relationships in this way: "What others saw as a playground or a church, they saw as home. Inupiat hunters still felt kinship and real admiration for polar bears, foxes, wolves, eagles and other predators with capabilities they lacked, like colleagues admiring a co-worker facing the same challenges. . . . Traditional Inupiat did not distinguish between spiritual and practical life. They performed rites and observed rules every day to negotiate a world in which the animals they subsisted on had spirits similar to their own—complicated rules that limited the kill of certain animals, helped hunters demonstrate respect for their prey and often required a lot of effort and sacrifice."[6]

It's not known whether the then governor of Texas, who blew into town for a whirlwind tour, clearly understood those elaborate rites and rituals. But George W. Bush's wife, Laura, and the entourage of political wives who crowded around Brower's table that afternoon, clearly appreciated the fruits of the hunters' sacrifice. Dabbing politely at their mouths, having just finished a dish of raw whale meat fermented in its own blood, the ladies who lunched then took out their pens, politely inquiring after the recipe. "They kept licking their lips, saying, 'This is so good,' Brower recalls, sitting at the same table where his visitors dined on mikigaq more than a decade ago now. "One of them said it tasted like a bitter wine. She wanted to make it for her husband," he says, his eyebrows shooting up before he sputters with laughter, keenly aware that fermented whale meat isn't likely to ever make it onto the White House menu, alongside eggs Benedict and barbecue.

Today's menu isn't quite so elaborate: coffee, biscuits, salmon jerky, and leftover caribou stew. Brower speaks slowly, in the singsong cadence characteristic of his native tongue, as he tries to explain the Inupiat ways—much as he had done that day in the company of the woman who would later become First Lady. How a hunter must follow strict ritual for a successful hunt. Those rituals included blessings offered by a shaman. Crew members also carried amulets and tied talismans to their sealskin boats, believing they not only brought luck but showed respect to the bowhead. The sweep of Christianity that arrived with the missionaries in the tiny villages and inlets all along the Alaskan coast wrought subtle changes in the ceremony of the hunt. Christian prayers replaced the shaman's drumming ceremony. And these days, Brower doesn't have any good luck charms—just me. All of which seems shocking to his own family members, one of whom announced grudgingly to a collective gasp: "Anything for Susan. She's even allowed in the boat!" It's only at this moment that I am able to grasp how much my mentor has been willing to give up for me. That I am able to understand how much he has broken with an age-old tradition that forbids women from participating directly in the whale hunt. As one whaling captain's wife informs me, women are taboo, banned from the whaling boats because "women's moon cycles can weaken the strength of the hunters' oars."

Brower is too discreet, too generous, to even mention this

to me. It's a sacrifice he seems willing to make just this once to share his cherished culture—to offer a window into the Inupiat's sacrosanct relationship with the whale. "The whale gives itself to a respectful hunter and crew that work in harmony," Brower explains to me. "It will allow itself to be killed and only its body dies. Its spirit returns to the ocean, to the other whales, and it tells them, 'My hosts were good to me.' The other whales listen to that whale and they return to that camp the next spring.

"That is what I believe. That is what the elders taught me."

Brower's apprenticeship began when he was twelve, under the watchful eye of the community's best whalers. It was the same year his father spelled out his life choices: he could either go to school in California and study to become a surgeon like his sister, or stay in Barrow. "I was an Eskimo. I couldn't imagine living a life without hunting," he tells me. He wants to be perfectly clear. His life wasn't one thrust upon him. There never were any lingering doubts about what he wanted to be.

He spent his boyhood performing menial tasks for whalers, breaking trail and cleaning the hunt camp. All the while, listening and watching, soaking in his elder's wisdom. Learning how to camouflage yourself in the snow and how to mask your scent from passing bowheads. How to paddle with stealth and in silence. But the most important lesson of all? An intimate understanding of the winds and currents and ice. One whaling captain's knowledge was the product of thousands of minds over centuries. Lessons that had to be learned, rules that could not be broken, not just as a matter of cultural respect but as one of life and death.

Lessons passed from elder to youngster, father to son, uncle to nephew. Like family recipes, precious heirlooms, handed down generation to generation. Recipes, however, that don't include the *Ursus maritimus*. "The girls are starving!" a voice booms from around the corner, before Brower's youngest son, Louis, bursts into the room. He looks like an Inupiat version of Brad Pitt, with a thick black mane and a wide, boyish smile. "There's polar bear in the yard," his father tells him. "A whole leg if you want," he says. "They're fussy," Louis explains between bites of salmon jerky. "They don't want polar bear, they want caribou."

Brower and I finish our lunch and follow Louis outside for a tour of nature's ice cellar. Sliding along a well-worn path in the ice, we pass by two snowmobiles, a pickup truck, a new minivan, and a polar bear skull lying in the snow on the way to a wooden shed. "Look in here," Brower implores, garnishing his command with a proud smile while peeling back a fur flap to reveal a smorgasbord of meats. A caribou head piled here, a hindquarter of polar bear there, and dozens of unidentified legs poking up haphazardly, like a game of Twister gone horribly wrong. "Wow," I say finally, at a loss for words. "I had a busy fall," Brower offers by way of explanation, and waves me in the direction of another storehouse, bolted tight with a heavy padlock. I figure the best cuts of meat must be kept in here. Brower opens the door and I peer in. I crane my head into a tiny room where a ladder leads about six feet down, deep into the permafrost. It's empty, save for a four-by-four-foot square of whale blubber and what looks to be a small fur purse but I'm told is actually a piece of walrus. The cellar is pristine, recently scrubbed and covered in a fresh coat of snow. "I paid my grandson ten dollars to clean it," Brower tells me. "It must be done at the beginning of every spring because a whale will not give itself to you unless it has a clean place to rest."

Meanwhile, Louis is busy working a frozen hindquarter at the Butcher Boy in the nearby garage, shaving a haunch into slices like meatsicles. "It's good just like this," Louis shouts above the hum of a saw cutting through frozen muscle. "But even better if you dip it into seal oil. It makes good munchies, you know?" I expect him to smile, but he says this with a face as straight as the blade of his saw. *Munchies?* Hard to imagine leaving out a tray of toothpick-lanced caribou at a dinner party, but that's exactly what Louis is getting at. What's more, caribou has nothing on the bearded seal, which is sort of the Inupiat equivalent of the cocktail wiener. "Muktuk, some caribou, and the ultimate—the bearded seal. Serve that with a cup of tea—now that's really living!" Louis laughs and winks.

If only the heavyweight food critics in the lower latitudes could get a load of this. At the very outside, they'd award Chez Louis a single star. They wouldn't offer their readers a review so much as a warning. "Slabs presented in seal oil reduction. Heaping portions, less for the gourmet than the gourmand. Decor less simple than spartan. No wine or liquor available at the restaurant—or in fact anywhere in Barrow (a dry town). Meat cellar open upon request. Children's menu, takeout, and private parties."

This high-protein nutritional regime has fueled Brower for hundreds of hunting trips, long past the time when many other octogenarians would have retired to the bridge table. I also can't help noticing how wrinkle-resistant my elders look. Women ten years my senior appear at least a decade younger. Could it be the rich stores of vitamins C and A in the whale blubber? The essential fatty acids in the bearded seal? I consider ditching my $200 jar of Crème de la Mer for takeout muktuk. Over my two-week stay, I will hear my hosts extol the health benefits of the traditional Inupiat diet over and over again. "You'll never get sick from this. It will keep you warm and cozy," Louis tells me one day, offering up a piece of frozen walrus. "Sick people want to take it," Brower agrees, nodding with encouragement. "They get healed from it." But I decline. One whiff suggests to me that it's about eight months past its best-before date.

Vilhjalmur Stefansson, apparently, also felt squeamish when he was introduced to Inupiat food back in 1906. After abandoning his position as a junior member of the Anglo-American Polar Expedition, the Canadian explorer from Gimli, Manitoba, took up with the Inuit, living among them on the banks of the Mackenzie River. From the beginning, he was determined to subsist on a native diet because it was easier. At first, his hosts roasted his fish for him, the way they knew "whites" preferred it. Eventually, though, Stefansson began to eat it boiled, as the Inuit did. And within three months he began to prefer it that way. He also came to agree with his hosts that the head was the best part of the fish, that fermented whale made a tasty condiment, and that partially rotten fish was something to be savored. More important, the experience taught him that he could stay fit and healthy living exclusively on fish. Over the course of three expeditions, spanning ten years, he added caribou, seal, whale blubber, and other meat to his diet. "By necessity at first, later by choice, I followed the rule of doing in Rome as the Romans do, which included living on Eskimo foods prepared in the Eskimo way," he wrote in his book *Not by Bread Alone*. "In that process my tastes underwent a gradual change, and I came to realize that many of my former beliefs about the wholesomeness of food and about 'normal' likes and dislikes were due to the locale of my birth and upbringing; they were matters of social and biological inheritance."[7]

A decade later, returning from his northern explorations, Stefansson vigorously advocated the medicinal benefits of an all-meat diet in the medical journals of the day. But his claims were ridiculed. He eventually devised a plan he was certain would waylay his critics and prove the veracity of his assertions once and for all: he and fellow explorer Karsten Andersen would check themselves into New York's Bellevue Hospital and live on meat alone—a research project fittingly bankrolled by the American Meat Institute. For a year, first in the hospital and then at home, the two gorged on a high-fat, high-protein diet that included calves' brains fried in bacon grease, while researchers kept a close eye on their basal metabolism and overall health. The world was stunned when in 1929 a New York gastroenterologist revealed his findings in the *Journal of the American Medical Association*. Not only had both men remained in good health—their blood pressure, kidney function, and calcium levels remained normal—but there were a few unexpected benefits. Both lost about five pounds, Andersen's hair stopped falling out, and Stefansson's constipation was cured. Stefansson also noted that the men's feces had become "practically odorless" and that he felt more energetic and optimistic on this high-protein diet than he normally did.[8]

Maybe that explains my reluctance now. Not enough fatty flesh in my diet, no monies from the Meat Institute to fund my next project. The fact is, no money could possibly get me stoked for my next job. I'm filled with trepidation, shaking in my snow boots as Brower and I move to the side of the house where a polar bear skin is airing out on the tundra. Brower has enlisted me to help him scrape the fat from the skin of this freshly culled beast, lying peacefully in the snow—now a mere shadow of its former invincibility. A full 1,200 pounds of predatory impulse, reduced to a pancake of fur with claws. "I couldn't shoo him away," Brower tells me, climbing into a pair of orange plastic coveralls before beginning to scrape away a thick layer of fat. It's the nearest thing to liposuction in Barrow. "Too much stink in the boat," he explains, and I immediately understand his meaning, having stood within spitting distance of the traditional seal-skin boat the Inupiat use to stalk their prey during the spring hunt. What smells like dinner to the polar bear makes me want to retch. "My second polar bear this month," Brower continues. "They won't be happy at fisheries and game." It's only now that I learn that this hide belongs to a bear Brower spied on our first night at the hunting camp. Why, he confesses now, he suddenly wanted to get me out of there before returning on his own. His personal safety was one thing; mine, something entirely different. Truthfully, I've had to deal with my share of hostile subjects in the name of journalism, but none that was ever a threat to eat me.

We work quietly for the better part of an hour, the only audible sound the scraping of metal on hide and the call of an eider duck somewhere in the distance. It's a make-work project, while we bide our time, waiting for the winds and currents to shift, causing the ice to crack into an open lead.

Meanwhile, a few streets over at the public school, the boys are getting ready for subsistence leave. The classrooms soon will be half-empty, transported to the ice. The boys are poring over their textbooks, boning up on the fundamentals of whaling. Chapter one: Understanding clouds and weather terms. Chapter two: How to butcher a whale and distribute it to the community. Chapter three: Understanding the role of the gunner, harpooner, floatman, and paddler, and so on.

Turns out, I'm struggling to keep up with my own lessons in skinning and tanning this afternoon. Brower seems a little put out when I slip on the polar bear skin and nick its hide with my scraper. It's not really my fault. With the mercury rising to a balmy −10 degrees Fahrenheit, the animal fat has melted into a yellowy glop. Brower waves me away, dispatching me to help his daughter Jenny prepare food for the hunt camp while he sees to his hunting equipment.

Jenny's a petite woman in her mid-fifties, dressed in a pink sweatshirt, with a mild-mannered smile and pretty, almond-shaped eyes framed by large gold-rimmed glasses. She's the eldest of Arnold Brower's brood and the Betty Crocker of the family. She spreads her arms as wide as her smile. "I just want to hug you," she chirps, and grabs my hand, leading me inside the warmth of the kitchen where biscuits are baking. Like many other women in whaling families across town this afternoon, Jenny's taken the afternoon off from her job as a cultural administrator to cook for the hunt camp. Sharing a pot of herbal tea and our family histories, we plan the hunt camp menu: salmonberry pie, fish spread, and caribou stew. We linger for a few hours sipping tea, while I drink in Jenny's story as well as the history of women in whaling. "The women's role is sacred too," Jenny tells me, peering with intensity from over the top of her glasses. "Without woman, a hunter can't achieve all that he does for the community."

It's only now that I clue in to what's really playing out behind this opaque cultural curtain. The carefully orchestrated dance between man and whale requires the participation of a woman, too, to be fully successful. I wrestle with this new knowledge, realizing that I am—at least symbolically—Arnold Brower Sr.'s wife. Now, don't get me wrong: Brower's a wonderful man— his charms, his prowess are legendary in these parts. ("Let me tell you about Arnold Brower Sr.," a young man told me one afternoon at the local outfitter's store. "Why, there's more man behind that name than you'll ever know.") No, what's got me in a funk is the sudden comprehension of the enormity of my responsibility here. After all, my job, as stand-in wife, is to lure the bowhead to Brower and his crew.

Anthropologist Barbara Bodenhorn describes the woman's role this way: "Among Inupiat, as among Northern hunters in general, hunting is a sacred act. Animals give themselves up to men whose wives are generous and skilful; it is also the man's responsibility to treat the animal properly, but it is the woman to whom the animal comes. . . . When a woman sews for her husband, her needle is creating a second skin that will attract the animals. . . . The generosity of the wife in sharing meat and the skill of the needle 'makes the hunter.' . . . She is acting ritually as wife the hunter. It is her job to maintain amicable animal/ human relations."[9]

Women are called upon not only to cook for the whalers and

to sew the men's white hunting jackets, but to braid the caribou sinew that will be used as thread in the traditional boat. And then, in the most elaborate ritual of spring, they will gather in prayer before beginning their most important task of the hunt: sewing the umiak's sealskin cover together. "You must forget your troubles," Jenny explains, "you cannot talk about anything upsetting, or you will risk the safety of the crew."

Jenny and I set out to perform another important ritual, although in the Inupiat timeline, a distinctly modern one. Grocery list in hand, we head to the nearby AC, a well-stocked supermarket lined with rows of radicchio, kale, and fresh cilantro—where eight dollars will also buy you a pint of blueberries. Beneath the glow of the pink fluorescent lights, locals are loading up their grocery carts with lamb and hamburger, worried they'll be caught short, having cleaned out their cellars of the vestiges of last year's catch. A group of elders are huddled in the foyer, minding the grandchildren, speaking animatedly in Inupiaq. "Something must be wrong," one of the old women finally whispers in English. "There is disagreement," she continues. "The whales are not coming!" Last year at this time, the whaling crews had already brought home three bowheads. "If something doesn't happen soon," the elder adds glumly, "we can't trigger the festivals. There will be no Nalukataq [one of the year's biggest Inupiat festivals], no Thanksgiving, no Christmas."

Indeed, the whole town is on tenterhooks. But not Jenny. Loading our grocery bags into the back of the car, she tells me she's not worried because she has had a divination. "I saw a small bird flying low on the horizon two days ago," she intones in a voice barely above a murmur. "It's a signal—the whales are coming. They are coming soon!"

The wind is blustering out of the east and the air is adrift with frost crystals, casting an icy sheen over the whole town. A perfect day for a few tourist snapshots. We drive to the edge of the tundra, to the site of Jenny's grandfather's historic café, where I mug for the camera beneath a bowhead jaw that looks like a giant wishbone. A few clicks of the shutter later, our cheeks frozen, our fingers numb, we scramble into the restaurant to warm up with a hot cup of coffee.

Scurrying to the back of the restaurant, we pass a couple waiting at the counter for ice cream cones, as well as two of Jenny's sisters lunching with their spouses at separate tables. "Hello!" Jenny trills without stopping. "It's hard to be a Brower without running into a family member anywhere you go," she tells me as we climb into a cozy booth.

Her small hands cupped around her coffee mug, Jenny tells me about growing up in Barrow in the 1960s, painting a portrait of a community that glints like sunshine on surf. How she and her siblings practiced for weeks to enter the annual goose-calling contests; and the joy of sliding up and down the backs of freshly harvested whales. Did I know her mother was the first Avon lady on the North Slope? Oh, the trouble she and her sisters caught after sneaking into the customer kits and using up all the red lipstick! Jenny sighs as the conversation turns to more painful memories. She pulls at a strand of her dark hair distractedly as she begins to unravel the story of her community's bitter fight for self-determination. About the lonely years she spent attending a residential school, far away in Anchorage. "Do you know that when I returned, I was to become like an elder? That I had to teach our parents how to live in the new world?" Jenny asks, her voice incredulous now.

She stares out the window, collecting her thoughts before suddenly bolting upright in her seat. "Look!" she cries, pointing to the sky. "A watercloud!" I peer out the window to witness a magical sight: a blue ribbon cutting a swath across the polar sky—a reflection of water between two frozen plates of ice. An open lead!

We clamor for the bill and get into our coats, speeding up and down the gravel roads on our way to Arnold Brower's house. The town is already abuzz with the news. We pass a stream of snowmobiles snaking their way out of town, as far as the eye can see. Rounding the corner onto Brower's street, we drive by a family gathered around an umiak, heads bowed in prayer—a final blessing, a prayer for fortune and goodwill while hunting.

Stepping into Brower's kitchen, I can hear him commanding his platoon over the radio in the next room. "Check the bomb box," he instructs, his thumb releasing the button of his CB radio. "Don't forget the dental floss," a voice crackles back from somewhere far along the ice edge.

It's finally showtime, and Brower clamps his lips into a thin, tight line, his mind rummaging through a laundry list of tasks and supplies. He motions me to a corner of the kitchen where he has assembled my outerwear: a pair of snow pants, an insulated pair of his boots, and a white hunting shirt that I am to wear over my puffy blue coat—camo gear designed to help disguise me in the snow. Moments later, we're on the Ski-Doo, climbing up and down crumbled mountains of ice toward the camp. This time, I'm too busy listening to the pounding of my heart to notice either the cold or the treachery of the terrain.

Rising over a peak of a jagged shard about thirty minutes

later, I am finally able to pick out a half-dozen white snow shirts against the white of the canvas tent. "Agvik," Brower's son Gordon shouts in our direction from atop a perch of snow. "Big one. Fifteen minutes ago. I threw the harpoon, but it was too far away."

Brower and I join the rest of the crew on the ice edge at a bench hidden behind several large blocks of snow. "Welcome to our humble hunt camp," Louis proclaims, rubbing his eyes as he emerges from an afternoon siesta in a nearby tent warmed by a kerosene stove. "Have some cowboy coffee," Gordon says, thrusting a cup of rich and gritty coffee in my hands, a handful of coffee grounds dumped into a pot of melted ice.

Truth be told, I'm not anxious to eat or drink anything, given that there's a snowball's chance in hell I'm ever going to use the outhouse here. A makeshift powder room that is really just a yellow rut in the snow, situated on the east side of the canvas sheet. Here, on this remote expanse of ice, where paw prints outnumber footprints, you'd think this comfort station would be as private as the presidential suite at the Ritz-Carlton, right? Not if you take into account the forty other crews camped out nearby, up and down the glacier, binoculars at the ready. I'll gladly go hungry, happily stay parched. Besides, I'm terrified to stray too far from the pack for fear of becoming polar bear nosh.

The sun is blazing high overhead, surrounded by sun dogs. Over the next few hours, a thin sheet of ice as delicate as eggshells forms over most of the open water, obstructing the hunt—at least temporarily. The second of three groups of whales in the annual spring migration between mid-April and June is passing here today, Brower tells me. It's May 5, and for decades, if not centuries, on this day a pod of bowheads has begun to pass by. "The ducks are affected by the weather," Brower explains. "But the bowhead comes on the same date every year. These are the good ones," he continues. "They're small but chubby, and their meat is soft and easy to chew. And the easiest to pull up onto the ice."

We spend the afternoon waiting, telling stories. I opt out of snack time while my companions gnaw on slices of bearded seal and walrus. Talk eventually turns to hunts past. In the old days, Brower would slip into a sealskin wet suit to keep warm, riding on the back of his prey before plunging a lance straight into its heart. Then he'd butcher his whale right there in the water.

One by one, everyone takes a turn, relaying stories of being surprised by whales, of accidents with mishandled guns, of close calls—and death. Men forever lost in the sea after being flipped out of a boat by an angry whale. But mostly they talk about death wrought by the whimsical and unpredictable ice. Everyone has a story of hearing the ice shelf creaking, followed by a booming "Clap, clap, clap!" of ice shattering beneath their feet, of jumping splintering cracks in the glacier to safety, of floating helplessly out to sea. My ears suddenly are filled with the eerie cries of lost whalers. Their ghosts creep up on me, whispering in my ears, telling me their secrets, their tragedies. Brower admits, he is haunted by them too. "I can still see him, even now. Like yesterday," he now recalls solemnly, perfectly etched snowflakes dancing, catching in the dark ruff of fur that surrounds his face. The whaling captain who suddenly became wedged between the shorefast ice and a fast-moving, shape-shifting floe. He died twenty minutes later. "His corncob pipe still between his lips. Isn't that strange?" Brower asks. I don't know how to respond. What I don't say is that, sitting here now, I am utterly petrified.

Brower himself has had many close calls. A few years ago, he was among the more than 150 whalers who drifted out to sea after a large pack of ice splintered. No one noticed for hours as they floated toward Siberia. They eventually were rescued with the help of their GPSs and their cell phones. Airlifted, one by one—along with their snowmobiles and their whaling boats— to safety.

The conversation turns to global warming. How the Arctic ice is thinning; the glaciers are receding. But no one raises the inevitable question: Will there be a day when climate change will forever bring an end to their most important cultural and gastronomical tradition?

We sit in silence for the better part of an hour, waiting and watching. Listening to the creaking of the ice in the distance, maybe a bowhead butting its head against the ice, reaching for air. I eventually follow Louis back to the tent. We take off our boots and jackets and huddle by the kerosene stove. I wrap myself in a caribou blanket. Louis tells me his dreams often fore- tell the future. Two years ago, he dreamed that his crew would be the last one to catch a whale that spring. And guess what? He was right. "Someone will get a whale this season. I saw in a dream two months ago. It was my very good friend. And it was his very first whale," Louis says, now staring at his hands rest- ing in his lap before tears suddenly begin to spill with urgency down his cheeks. "I'm sorry," he says finally, unable to make eye contact. "It's just that it's such a joyous thing. An expression of life. I don't think I can explain that to you."

Meanwhile, the ice has frozen solid again. I already have extended my stay for another week, desperately hoping to participate in the harvest of the community's first spring whale. But the weather is refusing to cooperate, and Brower has sent me back to town. It's time for me to go. Later, I will hear that local whalers killed three bowhead. Each time, a prayer of thanksgiving came over the CB radio, and the whaling captain thanked God for a safe and successful hunt. "In Jesus' name," the successful harpooner intoned through the speaker to his community, followed by the traditional whaling cheer, "Hey-hey-hey."

Over the next twenty-four hours, townsfolk came out in shifts to help haul the dead whale onto the beach with a rope and pulley. Soon, the beachfront was an extraordinary blood-splattered sight. Dozens of men climbed atop the carcass, hacking away at strips of skin and blubber. Children bounced on and slid up and down its body. Finally, the meat and tongue and internal organs were taken out. The baleen was scrimshawed, and given to local artists and later sold to tourists. A few weeks later, Inupiat from all across the North Slope descended on Barrow to celebrate the bowhead harvest. The most important festival of the year.

The women had been working for weeks for this day. Officially, it's known as Nalukataq, but it could also be called National Meat Day, or Women's Day, for this is when women divvy out shares of whale meat and blubber to the community. Barrow becomes a catwalk, as the women finally unveil their summer finery, the glittering and colorful summer parkas they've spent the winter months sewing. By noon, the whole town is at the outdoor gathering, spooning duck and goose soup. By mid-afternoon, it is time for muktuk, followed by oranges and tea. At dinner, the whale meat that has been fermenting in blood for the past four to six weeks is finally served.

Sated, the elders gather around for the highlight of the evening, the traditional blanket toss. Hundreds of people gather, grabbing hold of a sealskin blanket fashioned from the successful whaling captains' boat, and toss audacious youngsters and teenagers as high in the air as they can. The Arctic's equivalent of Scary Ride at Coney Island.

Arnold Brower will tell me later that he enjoyed this year's festival like any other. We talk for a stretch about my time in Barrow. He makes no mention of the fact that his crew didn't harvest a whale this spring. He doesn't utter a word about my failure, as his symbolic wife, to lure the mighty bowhead to his camp. He's too charitable to mention how I let him down. Almost anyone else would be second-guessing his decision to have me along on the hunt, but not Brower. I can't imagine that he second-guesses anything.

Even as I got ready to leave Barrow in early May, I couldn't help pondering Brower's generosity. I couldn't help thinking that it wasn't only the whales that gave themselves to the community, but so did he. Over more than eight decades, he's risked everything to preserve his culture. To provide not only physical nourishment but spiritual sustenance to his community. Before I left, I made one last trip to say good-bye. He was baking buns when I arrived, but he left the kitchen for a moment and returned with a gift in hand. I tore off the wrapping to find a piece of baleen art. A beautifully etched drawing of a whaling crew paddling out to sea in their umiak. We hugged before I headed for the door. "Keep yourself right," Brower shouted after me. I hesitated, looking back over my shoulder, but Brower was staring out the window. He didn't turn around. I made my way to the car, thinking of how lucky I'd been to be granted this interlude with one of the world's great whalers.

But before my plane took off later that day, I vowed to accomplish what I'd come so far to do. To eat a piece of muktuk. I could hardly claim to have gone native if I didn't at least try it. It wouldn't be cultural immersion so much as tourism if I didn't make this culinary leap.

I headed to the cultural center, where seniors had come out in force to relive old times and to feast on traditional foods at a noonday potluck. After spending so much time out in the killing cold, I was overpowered by the bouquet of exotic aromas. The buffet table was lined with cauldrons of goose soup, caribou stew, and biscuits, as well as a large silver bowl filled with last fall's catch—a bowl of blubber slices. I found a seat at a table lined by dozens of older women in traditional garb, flowery dresses and mukluks; the men donning jeans, fur-lined vests, and fleece. They toasted one another with their teacups, and spoke softly in Inupiaq, and bowed their heads in prayer. Finally, it was time to eat. *"Bon appétit,"* one of the elderly ladies said, giggling and nodding in my direction. I glanced hesitantly at my plate. A couple of slices of crusty bread on one side. A lone shard of muktuk—maybe three inches or so—as sandwich filler. The epidermis was still shiny black, the blubber a white-gray hue, the color of a well-worn undershirt. This piece was a fraction of a kid's helping—the size a mother here would give a teething infant.

I poked at it, finally spearing it on the end of my fork. A silence settled over our table as my hosts smiled anxiously. I lifted my fork, placing the muktuk on my tongue. My mouth was soon swimming in oil. It wasn't horrible. No, it wasn't the taste I found so disagreeable. I chewed. And chewed. I found myself wishing for a mouthful of the same diamond-tooth blades outfitted on Louis's Butcher Boy saw. My jaw muscles started to spasm. I couldn't even make an impression on this piece of flesh. To say that it had the texture of the sole of a shoe doesn't quite suffice—imagine gnawing on a Doc Marten or a construction boot. It seemed to have been reinforced with a steel shank. My guests exchanged a look of shock when I suddenly began to make gagging sounds and spat the muktuk out into the center of the table. No one looked up. No one said anything. Words weren't needed. My humiliation was complete.

It brings to mind an old adage: One man's meat is another man's poison. Conjure up thoughts of the most appalling food you can think of, and there's a good chance somebody somewhere is savoring it. Flamingo tongues. Elk droppings. Rodent fetuses. Or haggis, the national dish of Scotland, for that matter: you might well consider that a dog's breakfast. And what about a dinner of dog? A barbecued delicacy in the Philippines, a smoked meat treat in the European Alps. Clearly, there are no hard and fast rules as to what constitutes a delicious or utterly horrific meat meal. It is culturally determined.

At that potluck in Barrow, I realized that in order to enjoy muktuk, I had to belong rather than just play along. Taking in the quiet joy around me, I found myself hungering for something in the room. It certainly wasn't muktuk. No, it wasn't anything on the menu. I found myself longing for the generosity and community spirit with which this food was given and received. Deep in my belly, I longed for something I could not name.

5
• THE NEW PONDEROSA •

ON THE OTHER SIDE of the continent, in a place as seemingly remote as Arnold Brower's whale hunting camp, another way of life is also threatened. Here, in South Texas, where people look to the Lone Star rather than the North Star for guidance in how to conduct their lives, ranchers are fighting to preserve their culture. It is the culture of America's other first families. A way of life built on the kind of gritty work that puts calluses on your hands, dust in your eyes, and beef on the table. A place that fills the dreams of every American boy—boys like Cuatro Brown.

It's eight a.m. and Cuatro's horse Levi is kicking up a cloud of dust. While most other second-graders are just climbing out of their pajamas, Cuatro's been at work since sunup, riding alongside his dad and grandpa. Three generations of cowboys, a posse bunched together as tightly as the cattle they drive this morning.

While other seven-year-olds play with plastic toy cowboys, Cuatro rides with the real ones. His long, lanky legs—too big for his body—hint at the man he'll soon become. His white-blond hair, his sun-freckled face, the boy he still is.

It's the middle of spring roundup. A blue sky pushes low on the South Texas mesquite brush. It's a scorcher. Hot, dusty, dirty work. What the Brown Ranch cowboys have been doing for more than seventy years: separating the six-month-olds from their mothers. Traumatic? Not compared with the upset these calves will face before the day is out.

I'm trailing behind in a dirty white four-by-four, driven by Daniel, a ranch hand who speaks little English, a fixture on the Brown ranch for nearly twenty years. Daniel doesn't meet many from the outside. He breaks in few new workers. So, the idea of me showing up here as casual labor is about as unlikely as showing up at the Ponderosa—you'd have to be well off the beaten track, thoroughly lost to come looking for work here. A place where a family heritage is held tight and yet seems destined to fade into the twilight.

It's a white-knuckle drive, lurching along a parched landscape garnished with tumbleweed and varmints—jackrabbit and quail, skunks and rattlers. The ranchers ride tall. Their cowboy hats rise and fall in the big sky as they push the herd toward a holding pen. The sound of eight hundred hooves in our ears. A lone calf breaks ranks, bawling as it darts into the brush. Austin Brown III, or A3 as he's known here on the ranch, whistles and pulls hard on his horse's reigns. He two-steps to the left of the calf, and motions Cuatro beside him for a lesson in how to "gentle-down" a Holstein. After all, tender on the ranch means tender on the plate.

"Hey, hey, hey! Yo, yo, yep," A3 hollers, slapping his chaps and giving the calf a wide berth, respecting its flight zone, so as not to spook this five-hundred-pound baby. One of the secrets of "cow whispering," the language of man and bovine, passed on here from man to boy, father to son, generation over generation.

"Yep, yep, yep. Hey. Hey-a-ay," Cuatro echoes, and we watch the calf fall into line, disappearing into a whirlwind of dust and a mass of moving animal.

Time has stood still here in this austere sweep of prairie brush. The same lariat tricks. The same smell of burning cowhide. The same hickory-smoked wisdom dispensed over a ribeye, stretching back to the days when Austin Edwin Brown bought his first parcel of land in 1924—here in the southern plains of Bee County, an hour's drive either way of San Antonio and Corpus Christi.

The Browns are a stoic clan, clinging to a way of life that existed long before the boom-bust cycle in the oil and gas industry and the rise of the prison industry. They may carry cell phones and walkie-talkies and sell their bulls in cyberspace, but these ranchers are firmly steeped in tradition. They still work their cattle on horseback with dogs and break in their own stallions. Ranching traditions you'd be hard-pressed to find anywhere else—even here—in the cradle of the North American cattle industry. Today, peering out over the wide-open prairies with narrow, hooded eyes, the sixty-three-year-old family patriarch, Austin Brown II, recalls the legacy of the men who came before him. The cowboys who not only tamed the frontier and forged a nation, but sustained a land that would provide America with its most coveted food.

"In those days, the land was only as good as the cattle on

it, only as good as the rancher," A2 explains in a drawl as slow as the Pecos River. We're sitting in a low-slung bunker, across from ranch headquarters. The morning roundup complete, the Brown women have prepared lunch for their husbands and their ranch hands. Nana, A2's wife and sweetheart since she first danced with him at a Christmas party at age fourteen, is busy pouring iced tea. She smiles a pretty smile, her pink lips matching her brightly colored blouse. "There's nothing like the pride that goes with selling a good set of steer," A2 continues. "Nothing like the pride that comes with producing good, quality beef. Those ranchers, they took pride in being able to feed the nation."

I can't help thinking that in the old days, we'd probably be having this conversation around the chuckwagon. The only real address a cowboy ever had. A place where he got a haircut, got his broken bones mended, and swapped the day's stories while feeding on "chuck"—cowboyspeak for grub. A traveling kitchen dreamed up and designed in 1866 by Charles Goodnight as a way to fortify his workers, to keep them happy during the great cattle drives out of Texas. A place where buckaroos like me would be served up more than their fair share of beef, in addition to prairie strawberries (beans) with Texas butter (gravy), swamp seed (rice), and sinkers (heavy biscuits), and, of course, "son-of-a-bitch stew," made from the first freshly killed calf of the spring.[1]

Today's lunch is one of traditional cowboy fixin's: brisket, beans, pork sausage, biscuits, and grits. Just like the lunch you might have expected at the Cartwrights' lunch table. In fact, the Browns look like they've been plucked straight from Central

Casting—ready for their guest spot alongside Pa, Adam, Hoss, and Little Joe on *Bonanza*. Dressed identically in perfectly pressed Wranglers, red handkerchiefs around their necks, and spurs that jingle as they hit the floorboards. Even the pint-sized Cuatro walks with a gentlemanly swagger. A quirk of the Texan genome—a genetic lineage that dates back to the arrival of the Longhorn.

"We just love the freedom," A2 explains between bites of brisket. "The independence. Make it or break it yourself." His son, A3, nods in agreement. "It's not really that different from what other people do," A3 adds. "It's just that my backyard is bigger than most people's, and we make meat instead of widgets."

On the one hand, this is a wilderness preserve, a place where history and environmental integrity seem to go hand in hand. And yet it's a meat factory. A prep yard for the slaughterhouse, much like the one in Brandon. There's nothing organic about the meat here. This beef is raised using antibiotics and hormones. These cattle are cogs in the great industrial meat machine, overseen by a handful of corporate monoliths that have contracted with small ranchers like the Browns across the country. And while these animals eventually will be cut down to size, wrapped in plastic, and served on styrofoam trays, the purpose of this operation is to beef them up. And that's why A3 is poking and prodding at this young calf this afternoon. It's why we've moved from the lunch table to the calf table. To get these boys' minds on feeding rather than fighting and procreating—so that they'll fatten up and fetch a higher price at the meat market.

But this ginger-haired Holstein seems to have other plans. He kicks and cries as he's squeezed into a metal contraption before being flipped on his side on the calf table, one leg roped behind him. It's a compromising position—one in which he'll soon be transformed from stud to breeding dud all in one carefully orchestrated surgical move south of the belly.

A3 stands tall at six-feet-five, outsized like everything in the Lone Star State. He has long, ropy arms and broad hands. A single stripe of gray rises through a head of dark brown hair, above a handsome face coppered over thirty-six years spent chasing steers in the hot sun. Clenching the calf's scrotum in one hand and a tool aptly named the emasculator in the other, he crimps the bull's sperm cord and extracts a glistening orb so white it's almost blue and plops it in the mud a few inches from my feet. A few seconds later, it's followed by another. "Cool!" Cuatro shrieks, his blue eyes as big and round as wagon wheels.

It's an unfolding drama that appears part Western, part *Fear Factor.* If they ever filmed Hoss Cartwright doing this, it was left on the cutting room floor. I try to imagine the gastronome first intrigued by the possibilities of this delicacy. The French have their pâté. The Italians, their pasta. Here, in ranch-country, it's what's variously known as cowboy caviar, cowboy hors d'oeuvres, or prairie oysters. A rite of cowboy machismo, typically deep-fried in cornmeal, or served between buttermilk biscuits and topped with gravy. Wincing at the wails of this young bull, I have to admit, I'm relieved this work is too dangerous, too complicated for a cowpoke-in-the-making like me.

But it's what cowboys like the Browns do every spring season. Doing what destiny has decreed of them. Taming the wild, bringing order to chaos in a world in which we're all God's creatures. Man and beast. Carnivore and herbivore. Beef-eater and vegan.

In many ways, it's a remarkable story, one mythologized over and over again in literature and through the whir of the film projector, nearly as long as Hollywood has been making movies. It's a story used to define the American heritage, the meta-theme of a nation. It has not only inspired scriptwriters and novelists but successive presidents, including Teddy Roosevelt, John F. Kennedy, and Ronald Reagan. "A settler pushes west and sings his song," read the lines of Reagan's second inaugural address. "It is the American sound. It is hopeful, big-hearted, idealistic, daring, decent, and fair. That's our heritage, that's our song. We sing it still, for all our problems, our differences, we are together as of old."[2]

Some have argued that no story is more fundamental to understanding the mythology of the cowboy, to Texas, or America, than the birth of the cattle industry. The story of meat. Much as the controversial anthropologist Marvin Harris postulated that all of human history has been driven by a quest to secure protein, Jeremy Rifkin and others have argued that the story of the cowboy isn't really one of gunslingers and heroes in white Stetsons. It's the story of how cattlemen forged an alliance with Eastern bankers, railroads, and the U.S. Army to reshape nature. A place that eventually would be utterly transformed from the land the settlers saw was desolate when they arrived in the Americas. When celebrated orator and politician Daniel Webster scanned the horizon in the early 1800s, he couldn't imagine that the West would ever be anything but a drain on the public treasury: "What do we want with this vast worthless area? This region of savages and wild beasts, of deserts, shifting sands, and whirlwinds of dust, of cactus and prairie dogs?...I will never vote one cent from the public treasury [for postal service] to place the Pacific Coast one inch nearer to Boston than it now is."[3] Less than one hundred years later, the landscape had been completely reimagined, transformed into a golden kingdom of prairie grasses and the world's largest cattle pasture.

The change was swift and brutal. Over a scant few years, beginning in 1871, gunshots rang out from every corner of the Great Plains. The buffalo, which had roamed the land for more than 15,000 years, were obliterated by the millions. It was just one element in a bigger scheme to make way for the new "cattle complex." Part of a strategic plan to usurp control of the land by exterminating the Native American's food supply. "While history books often explain away the mass slaughter of the bison as an act of wasteful exuberance, the facts point to a clear and systematic policy designed to replace the buffalo with the steer and the Indian with the cowboy,"[4] Rifkin writes in *Beyond Beef: The Rise and Fall of the Cattle Culture.*

Meanwhile, financiers from the land of "corpulent cows and opulent Englishmen," in Rifkin's words, helped secure the future of cattle culture in America. By the time the cattle industry had begun its massive expansion across America, Britain was scrambling to sate a rising appetite for beef among its elite and new middle class. A taste for the fat of obese cows had gripped the landed gentry for decades, keeping artists busy idealizing the bovine in the paintings that adorned their drawing rooms, and breeders fine-tuning a formula that would produce prize-winning cattle so large they buckled under their own weight and had to be wheeled into agricultural gatherings. Massive beasts, Rifkin writes, that "served as a physical metaphor for the wealth and prestige of the British ruling class.... The taste for fat was synonymous with the taste for opulence, for power and privilege, for the values that made these island people the feared and envied rulers of the world.[5]

British monies began to flow into the U.S. cattle country, bankrolling the expansion of the railway. And, by the early 1880s, the Brits launched a financial invasion into the western range of America, setting up cattle companies and securing some of the best grasslands for the British market. As Rifkin explains: "While the west was made safe for commerce by American frontiersmen and the U.S. military, the region was bankrolled by English lords and lawyers, financiers, and businessmen who effectively extended the reach of the British beef empire deep into the short grass of the western plains." Swept up in cattle fever, "the drawing rooms buzzed with the stories of this last of bonanzas; staid old gentlemen who scarcely knew the difference betwixt a steer and a heifer discussed it over their port and nuts."[6]

By the mid-1880s, British financial interests dominated many of the cattle associations. An anti-British mood began to fulminate. Homegrown beef barons, ordinary citizens, and politicians began to decry what they saw as an attempt to turn their country into a quasi-colonial outpost of the British empire. In 1884, James C. Blaine galvanized the anti-British mood of the country in his bid for the presidency with the slogan "America for Americans."[7]

In many ways, it's the same kind of circling of the wagons that exists here in Texas today. Although the threats of old—Indians, the Brits and Union soldiers, wild animals and pestilence—have been given a makeover for the twenty-first century. Ranchers like the Browns have been fighting the erosion of family values, faltering faith, Japanese trade barriers, militant vegetarians, and even Oprah.

Today, as every morning, Austin Brown II rises at four-thirty, drinks a pot of coffee, answers his e-mail, and thanks the Lord for all that's been given to him. An opportunity to live and work here, on the bare outposts of habitation, far away from the corrupting influences of the outside world.

"You have acres and acres between you and the rest of the population. Nobody bothering you. Nobody hassling you," A2 tells me, his pickup bouncing down the narrow ruts that pass for a road on his pastures. "If we stay in our environment, there's no crime. No drugs. No problems. You just don't have to deal with the same things the rest of the population has to deal with. When I drive around my ranch, I don't wait for anybody."

We're headed to nearby Beeville—population 13,200—for an afternoon at the cattle auction. Driving out of ranch head-quarters, we pass A3's house—one among a handful of houses on the property and the house where his grandmother had lived for years. The days before A3 moved in with his wife, Jody, after graduating with a degree in agricultural economics from Texas A&M, the same school his daddy and granddaddy attended before him. If all goes well, it's the same university Cuatro will attend too, once he's finished with home-schooling.

Driving toward town, we pass one motel after another, crouched so low to the ground they look like matchboxes strewn on the scorched gray earth. Low-rent destinations that service family members visiting loved ones in Beeville's three prisons. These days, the ratio of townspeople to inmates is less than two to one. "It's changed so much here—and not always for the better," A2 offers, his voice tinged with regret. Meanwhile, I suddenly notice the shotgun resting between our seats. "Oh, that there's for coyotes and varmint," A2 offers by way of explanation. "I've got a nine-millimeter in the glove compartment too. It's our right to own guns. That's part of the Constitution. We've got to protect ourselves."

Just like in the old days of the Wild West, the days of cowboys and Indians. A place that, according to one early Bee County settler, was "pleasing and only man was vile."[8] The place A2's grandfather's grandfather had settled from Georgia following the Civil War. An ideal location for his mercantile business, which thrived for three generations, until A2's grandfather decided he wanted to be a cowboy. He then began piecing together the land where the 11,000-acre ranch stands today.

"They'd get up before sunup in the mornings and they worked late into the day," A2 continues, recalling the old times. "They didn't go home for days, sleeping in cow camps on top of a bedroll under nothing but the sky. It was a real hard time back in those days."

Times still are tough. Consolidation and globalization in the meat-producing industry have wrought chronic distress to ranchers. Most are permanently cash-poor, forced to mortgage or sell off pieces of land just to survive. Others are being forced out. The Browns have scratched out a living—like most ranchers in these parts—by taking on other work. A2 moonlights as a mortgage appraiser and by managing other ranches. "The last three and a half years, we've seen good cattle prices and then just when we thought we were doing well, we get in a drought situation. Gas prices are really hurting the hell out of us too," A2 says as we turn into a parking lot teaming with trailers and pickups.

That could explain the laconic greetings. "How you?" met each time with a world-weary stare as we pass one rancher after another crowded into the auction room this afternoon. The men who bank on Mother Nature year after year, knowing full well it's a crapshoot. I tag behind A2 to find a seat in the bleachers, overlooking a score of Stetsons that float like fishing bobbers above the crowd. Some men are sipping coffee out of paper cups. Others scan catalogues, pencils pushed behind their ears.

This afternoon, the only sound in the room is the amplified echo of an auctioneer's machine-gun patter. "Okay, let's sell some cattle," he booms into the microphone and the Bovine United Nations parade begins. Blondes, brunettes, redheads, and tiger stripes. Each cow barreling back and forth across a dirt-floor stage, their hooves flying wildly—just like I remember in the Looney Tunes cartoons. The auctioneer barks out a steady waltz of breed names. "Okay, do I hear eight hundred. Eight hundred. Eight hundred. Do I hear eight hundred?" But bidding is reserved today, just like it was last week and the week before that.

I opt out of a snack at the auction house and head for a quiet dinner on my own at the steakhouse. Shorty's Place isn't exactly a high-end restaurant, but it's among the best in Beeville. The ambience is what you might call primitive. There's a stuffed kangaroo at the entrance and stuffed tigers and polar bears staged in predatory poses around the dining room. A reminder: It's a dog-eat-dog world out there. Eat or be eaten. It's a decor that's wholly unlike that of other steakhouses where I've dined recently. Like the Chicago Chop House and Barberian's in Toronto. Places where a nice steak can set you back more than a round of golf at Pine Valley. Here, a twelve-ounce T-bone goes for $8.99. But I figure this is a prerequisite of any wannabe cowpoke—anyone trying to understand what beef means to a Texas rancher. Leaving here without eating a steak would be like visiting Italy without sampling its olive oil, France without trying its cheese, Russia without tasting its caviar.

My T-bone arrived lickety-split, with a side salad of iceberg lettuce and a stack of fries. It was far more than I could eat. Far more than I wanted to eat. Two bites in and I pushed my plate away. I had to wonder if they'd mistakenly thrown kangaroo on the grill, although I knew it wasn't polar bear. It tasted nothing like the boiled white, bland flesh with the fishy smell that I'd eaten at Arnold Brower's house in Alaska a few weeks earlier. I swear on the Lone Star flag, this was the worst steak in all creation. It looked like a slab of dull-gray nothingness and was as flavorful as a cup of tepid water. It felt like sandpaper on my tongue. Full of gristle and maybe even tougher than muktuk. Clearly, not all cows are created equal. Staring down at my plate, I couldn't help but notice there was little in the way of fatty marbling typically associated with high-end grain-fed meat. The kind of fat that boosts flavor, acting as a lubricant between meat fibers, making it easier to tear apart with your incisors. The truth was, I got exactly what I paid for. Yes, this steak was enough to put me off beef—at least until tomorrow.

These days, it seems the beef barons and ranchers are a jittery lot. And who can blame them? They've long taken a beating in the media, as well as in laboratories and government offices from Washington to Ottawa. Beef's tough times arguably started with the publication of a dreary-sounding report titled "Dietary Goals for the United States" put out by the U.S. Senate Select Committee on Nutrition and Human Needs in 1977. It advocated eating less meat as one step to living a healthier lifestyle. However dull the paper's title, reaction to it was anything but—the beef industry threw a conniption and proceeded to put the report through its own spin cycle. Not surprisingly, it ground out a much meatier conclusion: instead of eating less meat, the beef industry said, consumers should "choose meats, poultry, and fish which will reduce saturated fat intake."[9] But it wasn't enough to stem the tide of negativity.

Even those the industry had once embraced as their own were starting to turn their backs on beef-eating. Canadian country crooner k.d. lang kicked up a storm of controversy when she came out not only as a lesbian but a vegetarian. In a slick TV spot called "Meat Stinks," produced by PETA in 1990, she hugged a cow named Lulu while she stared into the camera, intoning: "If you knew how meat was made, you'd lose your lunch. I know, I'm from cattle country, and that's why I became a vegetarian." Country music stations across the country pulled her music, while vegetarian activists like Paul McCartney and Chrissie Hynde rallied to the cause. Events got out of hand, however, when lang's mother was threatened in her hometown of Consort, Alberta. Signs that once read HOMETOWN OF K.D. LANG were defaced with EAT BEEF, DYKE. In the end, the controversy proved a boon to k.d. lang's music sales. Her album sales skyrocketed—the beef flap had brought her music to a broader crowd.[10]

So by the time Oprah weighed in with a TV segment on mad cow disease in 1994, it had just been one kick in the chaps after another. The cattle ranchers decided they'd had enough. A group from Texas launched a $12 million libel and defamation suit against the daytime diva after she declared that the rise of bovine spongiform encephalopathy in the United Kingdom had "just stopped me from eating another hamburger." A guest on the show, a former Montana-cattle-rancher-cum-vegetarian, didn't help matters after he told the audience that BSE had the potential to affect thousands in the United States—that BSE could be as infectious as the AIDS virus. Oprah didn't win regular Texans' hearts either. During the brouhaha the most popular bumper sticker in the state proclaimed, THE ONLY MAD COW IN AMERICA IS OPRAH. Two years later, however, Oprah emerged unscathed when a court ruled the ranchers had failed to prove their case.[11]

And just when it seemed like it couldn't get any worse, bestselling child-care guru Dr. Benjamin Spock stoked the fires again in 1998 with a final recommendation. In the seventh edition of his blockbuster book *Baby and Child Care* (published shortly after his death and second only to the Bible in sales), the legendary pediatrician had come to this stunning conclusion: children over the age of two should be raised as vegans.[12] The cattlemen went on the defensive. Their websites were overflowing with vegan vitriol, meat boosterism. Beefed up with bites of wisdom like "If animals weren't made to be eaten, then why are they made of meat?" and "Vegetarians don't live longer, they just look older," and "Beef makes men stronger, women more beautiful, and kids smarter."

These days, it seems the cattle ranchers' biggest challenges are coming from tweens and teens—the offspring of perfectly respectable carnivores—for whom beef is a four-letter word. Weaned on movies like *Babe* and a steady diet of news nuggets exposing the environmental woes of the meat industry, a growing number of youth are turning their backs on the most North American of traditions—and signing on to vegetarianism at twice the rate of adults. It's what *Time* magazine once dubbed "The Looming Vegetarian Crisis."[13] The industry has responded, not by denouncing these young herbivores but with carefully crafted messages and stealth campaigns to lure back young salad-eaters. For example, the National Cattlemen's Association launched an advertorial extolling the hipness and healthfulness of beef-eating in the form of a website, cool-2b-real.com. Its aim? To turn the sugar-and-spice set into red-meat-chomping teens. As the Internet magazine *Salon* noted, "At cool-2b-real.com, you can learn about how 'real girls' have 'strong bodies and strong minds' and 'friends who understand, friends who care, and friends who keep you real.' Friends like these nice cattlemen who'd like to get you on their ground-chuck gravy train from ages 8 to 80!"[14]

Some savvy cynic toiling in the blogosphere exposed that the Cattlemen's Association was behind the website, and it has since been dismantled. But the effort underscored just how panicky the industry is about its future. Vegetarianism is no longer a loony fringe movement but part of mainstream culture, promoted by both health and environmental organizations. A fact that casts a shadow over the meat industry, given that it's kids who keep the economy rolling.

On some level, I know just how the cattleman feels. Even

though my vegetarian partner doesn't seem to care if I eat pork or chicken—well, beef, that's another story entirely. On the one occasion that I happened to mention I was so famished I wolfed down a burger at the first fast-food joint in sight, Gare suddenly lost his composure. "You didn't!" he cried. "How could you?" I was flabbergasted. Since then, I've wised up to the ways in which he tries to keep me away from the beef I love. He doesn't flinch at picking up a "real burger" for his father at Licks, one of our favorite takeout joints in the neighborhood. Me? I ask for a burger and Gare always returns with a "nature" rendition of a hamburger, that is, a dried-out piece of cardboard slapped between a bun. So, I've learned to keep my beef-eating a secret. Cheating on him when he's out of town. Subversive acts that reportedly have landed other couples on the carnivore/herbivore divide in divorce court. Mediators brought in just to rule on tofu or chicken—what will nourish the children post marital collapse.

So, sitting here across from Austin Brown II this afternoon in his home, I understand why he gets so defensive. I understand why he gets worked up when ordinary folks ask why we should eat beef at all. "I love beef. We eat it every day," he tells me, his long legs stretched out in front of him as he lounges in his La-Z-Boy, the TV channel flipped to a live cattle auction. "Nutritionally, it's got what a person needs. It's full of iron and it's got enough fat to make it taste good. You take a T-bone, you strip away the flavor, and you've got chicken."

He stares at the TV, where a black bull is strutting across the screen, via satellite feed, when something suddenly triggers, something sets him off. "What those vegetarian whackos don't understand," his voice now at full volume, his chin cocked at an indignant angle, "is how hard ranching is…" His voice trails off just as Nana rounds the corner with a plate in her hand, filled with corn chips and a ham sandwich. She sets it on A2's TV table and tucks her feet up under her on a chair on the other side of the room.

"I sure wouldn't trade places with my husband," Nana says, staring at her hands in her lap. "He makes decisions every day that—well, if he didn't make the right one—we'd have to shut it all down."

I can't help but wonder about the future. What about their grandson, Cuatro? I ask. Will he find a way to stay here on the ranch as four generations have before him?

Nana brushes a strand of gray away from her soft brown eyes. "Well," she sighs heavily, "I think the biggest compliment a man can pay his daddy is to walk in his boots. To respect the same values. Cuatro will choose to do it like his family taught him. He'll get a good education and find the right woman to support him in what he does." Nana pauses, staring out the window at nothing but acres of desolate brush in front of her. "Sometimes, sometimes I see glimmers—that maybe he can find a way to stay on the ranch. Other times, I know that's it—that we're the last generation here. I do think he'll have to find another way to make a living."

"Maybe he'll go into politics," A2 interposes, a smile pushing at the corners of his mouth. "I think he might make a fine politician one day." It's not much of a stretch when you consider the state's biggest exports have been cattle, sweet light crude, and men bound for the country's top political office—including two of the last three presidents and three of the last eight. Watching

Cuatro ride alongside his father and grandfather, it's clear he's got Texas in his heart and more charm than a posse of wranglers put together.

It's not hard to picture Cuatro in the country's top office. His birthright has given him a fundamental understanding of the founding American mythology. An ideology built upon notions of conquest and subordinating nature in the name of civilization. For the early cowboys, it meant clearing out a desolate land where buffalo roamed to make way for cattle—to provide sustenance for a beef-mad nation.

This century, you might argue, those same notions are being applied in the laboratory. Diners got their first taste of a cloned porterhouse at a Los Angeles restaurant early in 2007. Grilled medium-rare with sprinkling of salt and cracked pepper, it apparently was indistinguishable from any other porterhouse. But not everyone was thrilled by the notion of this futuristic food. In fact, some partygoers politely snubbed an invite to the event. No-shows included self-described omnivore and author of *Fast Food Nation,* Eric Schlosser, who declined the invite, saying: "I'd rather eat my running shoes than meat from a cloned animal." Worse, perhaps, Lee Hefter, executive chef of the famed Spago (the flagship of Wolfgang Puck's group of restaurants), backed away from hosting the event at the company's new Beverly Hills steakhouse. "I don't want people to think that I would ever use it," he explained. "I don't want to condone cloned beef. I don't want to eat it. I don't want it in my kitchen." And while the Food and Drug Administration has approved cloned meat's safety (although it is commonly referred to as cloned meat, the meat is actually from the offspring of a cloned animal), consumers have besieged the agency, hoping to block moves to see it stocked in stores by year end.[15]

Will they feel any different about meat grown in a petri dish? That's right: lab-grown ground chuck that smells and tastes just like the real thing coming (possibly) to a supermarket near you. As far back as 1936, Winston Churchill looked into his crystal ball and foresaw a future much like this. "Fifty years hence," he wrote, "we shall escape the absurdity of growing a whole chicken in order to eat the breast or wing, by growing these parts separately under a suitable medium."[16] Indeed, scientists are now tinkering with formulas to mass-produce animal protein for a meat-mad world. Slabs of animal flesh that would be cultured from a single cell in a lab rather than carved from livestock reared on the farm and culled at the slaughterhouse. The implications are revolutionary. In vitro meat would be better not only for the environment but for human health too, protecting us from the scourges of *E. coli* and BSE. An added bonus: there's no animal cruelty.

Meanwhile, there's a growing chorus of critics questioning whether the idea that we *should* control nature has outlived its usefulness. They believe that a system of growing food in a massive monoculture, in which we feed animals food that makes both them and us sick, is at odds with what nature intended. Sustainable agriculture. Slow food. These are the buzzwords of a burgeoning global agricultural and culinary movement. It's a crusade that has been described as belonging to both the eco-gastronomy faction of the ecology movement and the culinary wing of the antiglobalization movement. It advocates a return to regional traditions and home cooking that is focused on local foods and following the rhythms of the seasons. Its proponents denounce factory farming and the hidden risks of agribusiness—the perils of relying on too few genomes. Alice Waters of the storied Chez Panisse restaurant in Berkeley, California, has been among its most influential advocates. She was a pioneer in organics and sustainable agriculture back in the 1960s, long before it became fashionable. "Most of us have become so inured to the dogmas and self-justifications of agribusiness that we forget that…most [food] was, for all intents and purposes, organic…and was also by necessity fresh, seasonal and local," she once wrote. "The fate of farmers—and with them the fate of the earth itself—is not somebody else's problem: it is our fate, too.…It's a return to traditional values of the most fundamental kind."[17]

Meanwhile, here on the Brown ranch, in a room filled with precious heirlooms that once belonged to Austin Brown II's grandfather, it's clear that traditional values are what the family holds most dear. The preservation of a way of life and a way of ranching that stretches back nearly a century. A2 finishes his sandwich and we meander one last time through the halls and corridors of his ranch-style brick home, filled with cowboy hats and boots and silver-tinged photographs of young men saddled up at the railhead, gathering for the cattle drives. Maybe the bioethicists and scientists growing meat in the lab would feel comfortable here, but I suspect Alice Waters and her disciples would be uneasy. I can't help but wonder if the future of ranching for Cuatro's generation might, in fact, be something more along the lines of what Waters et al. advocate—raising meat without antibiotics, growth hormones, and grain. I finally put the question to A2. "It's difficult enough for ranchers like us to make a living without imposing all kinds of restrictions on us," A2 offers after a moment. "What the environmentalists don't understand is that we are the real stewards of the land. There's nothing more natural than what we do. Man is meant to dominate nature. He has dominion over the land and the animals. That is what God intended."

He turns away from me to stare at a photograph of himself as a young man. Taken more than forty years ago, it's a picture of him roping a steer, not far from where we're standing, just on the other side of the pasture.

Nana comes to bid me good-bye. She's got a care package prepared for me, including recipes for grits and creamed spinach. I shake hands with A2, thinking what a privilege it has been to watch him work the ranch as cowboys have worked for more than a century, knowing I'll never meet another real cowboy. I take my leave, and drive toward the highway, just like all the drifters that have come and gone before me. Turning toward Houston, I watch the ranch fade behind me until it's a speck on the horizon.

6
· ANTLER ENVY ·

AND WHILE THE RANCHING TRADITION seems destined to fade into history, there is a growing number of carnivores for whom haute cuisine starts in nature's backyard. It's a walk on the wild side—no place for sissies. A mist-shrouded place like this on the northern tip of Newfoundland.

I flip through the Michelin Guide, but there's no rating for Tuckamore Lodge. Maybe it's because the omnipotent handbook to gastronomy and lodging is too uppity to rate a place more feted for killing flesh than cooking it. Or maybe it's because hunting guides have yet to achieve the same stature as the celebrity chefs who are as likely to be seen fleeing the paparazzi as the stars who glitter at their most coveted tables. But taking in the beauty of this sprawling chalet set on the edge of Southwest Pond, should the "Red Bible" ever deign to rate Tuckamore Lodge, it most certainly would be given three pelts.

It's mid-September, early in the hunting season. The air is fat with the scent of pine and the sea. Buttressed against the jagged Precambrian rock, Tuckamore Lodge sits like a beacon in the wilderness. It's a place where the hunting cognoscenti happily fork over upward of $500 a day just to get big animals in their sights and a little blood on their hands. Inside, the lodge is a warm expanse of blond wood, deep-seated couches, and scented candles. On the luxe side of rustic. My room—about the size of a schoolyard playground—is prettified in Egyptian linens and lush pillows that sit atop two poster beds where I will sleep on alternating nights—if I ever find my way out of the Jacuzzi. Downstairs, two women are bustling, clanking pots and silverware as they prepare a traditional Newfie dinner: toutons and molasses and partridge berry pie. In the next room, from the sparkling expanse of the bay window, I watch a snowshoe hare dart across the field into the nearby brush. It's picture-perfect. A snapshot worthy of the company brochure. The only thing missing? Other guests.

Oh, they are here, the staff informs me, pointing me in the direction of a dirt path leading to a shed at the bottom of a small hill. I follow the well-trodden path and sneak into the shed through a side door. A gray cloud, a mist? No, I am assaulted by the smell of wood smoke and testosterone. In a far corner, empty beer cases are piled high. The frying pan is sizzling with a heap of gnarled moose flesh. Directly in front of me, a half-dozen body parts are suspended on giant meat hooks. It's humble, bare bones in at least a couple of senses, but the staff and clientele would slam the door on Martha Stewart if she were offering to redecorate. These men who are gathered here in a semicircle in front of me are not looking for luxury—they're looking for the authentic, even primitive. And there's no doubt that they have that here.

This is the meat house. A meeting place and a meating place.

"That buck must die!" Terry, a fiftysomething coal miner dressed in hiking boats, camo gear, and a hunting cap declares, slamming his beer can down on the table.

"He's mine," Mike, a short, compact man with a wild-eyed stare interjects, lunging into the center of a group of men, some of whom have toothpicks jutting out beneath a patch of overgrown moustaches, while others look on with wild bemusement.

"We've seen him a few times at the bog," adds Dennis, one of the hunting guides, gripping a ripped-up piece of a cardboard box that's doing double duty as a dinner plate.

"He was at least a sixteen-pointer," Terry swoons. "Ohhhhh. What a rack!"

Apparently, Newfoundland's most-wanted fugitive is still on the run. And in this eternal contest of male bravado, it's going to be a drag-'em-out slugfest to see who is going to bring down this wily moose. A classic contest sparked by a deep-seated affliction of the male species: antler envy.

It is my first venture into this secret haunt of men. The grown-up version of the boys' clubhouse, set high in a tree and emboldened with a sign that warns: NO GIRLS ALLOWED.

It's a sacrosanct time of year across North America. From the backwoods of Texas, Pennsylvania, and Maine, all the way up to Alaska, across Canada—into the Yukon, Ontario, Quebec, and Newfoundland—and all points in between. A vestige of rural life that is tied to the land and the seasons and one inexorably linked to early frontier life. As American as Davy Crockett, Daniel Boone, and Teddy Roosevelt. A tradition that has been extolled for generations in literature, most famously, perhaps, by Ernest Hemingway and William Faulkner. But it was much more than a story line for both men; it was an atavistic compulsion and a passion. When Faulkner, for example, was reached at a backwoods deer camp in Mississippi with the news that he had just been awarded the Nobel Prize for Literature in 1949, he reportedly shrugged off the news, saying, "Hell, that's just money. They haven't got any deer meat over there [in Sweden]."[1]

Faulkner saw hunting as a fundamental right of passage. In pulling the trigger, he wrote, one ceased to be a child forever and became not only a hunter, but a man. He also reportedly exalted the post-punch bonhomie. As critical, he mused, to the hunting experience as the actual slaughter.

That may explain the liquid revelry currently under way. Randy, my driver and the lodge's all-around master of touring and hunting, suddenly spies me out of the corner of his eye. "Hey boys, 'dis is Susan," he pronounces. The conversation grinds to a halt. An interloper. A female intruder! Two dozen eyeballs are on me. "B'Jesus boys," Randy says, nodding his head in my direction and stretching his mouth into a wide, sly grin. "Don't you think she'd look nice in a camo bikini?" For a moment I feel what the moose must feel when spotted by a guide and his party—not that I'm standing naked, just that I'm a target. Apparently, those haunches aren't the only meat on display. Thankfully, I think to myself, at least nobody compares the moose's rack to mine. The room erupts into a collective snort, and for some reason, I can't help laughing too.

But, make no mistake about it, the men who are gathered here are deadly serious about their sport. Indeed, they are no ordinary killers. They're a distinct breed who don't just gun down animals but hunt them with crossbows. They revel as much in stalking their prey as mounting heads on the wall. They've traveled hundreds if not thousands of miles to hunt their quarry: the largest member of the Cervidae, or deer, family, and one of Canada's national symbols—one that seems to utterly defy the laws of physics. Proportionally, it's like a fullback trying to rush the end zone on a runway model's matchstick legs and spiky high heels.

And while these hunters get excited talking about velvet and points and racks, I'm fascinated to catch my first glimpse of this creature in its natural habitat rather than in a photograph. From a distance, the moose looks positively regal, its lustrous dark brown fur glinting in the sunshine; its glorious antlers the envy of cloven-hoofed animals everywhere. But upon closer inspection, it's a different story. With its droopy nose, overhanging lip, and scrubby hump, the moose looks like the love child of kissing cousins—like something has gone slightly sour in the genetic broth. And if there's any truth in the stereotype, the moose doesn't have particularly sharp vision, just a higher vantage point. In other words, natural selection may have gifted him more physically than cognitively. His most famous depiction? Bullwinkle J. Moose, a good-natured naïf, more threatened than threatening. One that is beset by a never-ending string of outlandish misfortunes and bailed out by a lowly squirrel. If only there was a moose defamation league. But talk here is almost reverential. No one mentions that the moose may be two bricks short of a load even within their own genus, their own subfamily within the animal kingdom. After all, the contest here is not only man against man, but man against beast. The ultimate trophy is, of course, the biggest rack.

My bets are on the garrulous onetime army doctor named Mike, with freshly shorn locks, a boxer's grill, and narrow-set eyes that flit nervously when he speaks. When asked by his geriatric patients in his Ohio practice why he has a stuffed bear climbing out of the wall in his office, he tells them that he kills bears so that he doesn't have to kill people. He likes to recite statistics from nameless science journals that apparently show that there are far fewer murders in societies where men hunt regularly. Mike's here with his diffident hunting partner, Bob, a freshly pressed business owner with silver hair and perfectly manicured nails. He's so tightly wound he looks to be set at hairtrigger. This hunt is really just a warmup for these boys from Ohio. In a few months, they'll test their mettle hunting cougars with a crossbow over Christmas in British Columbia.

There's also a Mennonite doctor from Topeka, with the mien of a cherished and tattered teddy bear, with deep-set blue eyes and even more deeply held convictions. He recently purchased eighty acres of land near his house so he could hunt. He's a regular fixture at Tuckamore, having hunted moose over six seasons, but he dreams of hunting bigger prey: musk ox in the Arctic. Doc is here with his friend Willie, a forty-something entrepreneur from the largest Amish community in the United States. He's as thin as a stick of licorice and full of self-deprecating humor. Aside from the pack of smokes poking out of his breast pocket, he's dressed in the uniform of his culture: a shaggy beard and a shirt and trousers made by hand and fashioned from patterns handed down over generations.

They are joined by a twosome who hail from West Virginia: Jerry, a tall, dimpled, mild-mannered sales exec with a pale-blue stare, and Terry, a slightly paunchy coal miner with jet-black hair, the group's wisenheimer and self-described hillbilly. There are also two advertising guys from New York. One is Bob, a former marketing entrepreneur and now retiree. He currently tinkers in the grass-fed beef business, when he's not hunting or touring Tuscany on bicycle. He has a penchant for cognac and foodie authors like Ruth Reichl and Nina Planck. And liberal politics. And last there's Bill, a slim city-slicker who came to hunting late in life. He owns a billboard marketing company and has yet to develop a taste for Canadian beer or Canadian people. He snipes at the help, chomps on a stogie, and sips Merlot when he's not hunting.

The men who will guide them to their game this week are all intimately familiar with the terrain, hailing from Newfoundland's nearby coves and villages. They know moose hunting the way rabbinical scholars know the Torah. They know the landscape like an art restorer knows oil paints from antiquity. They know where the big boys are, where they like to bed down, where and what they like to eat. There's Junior, Keon, Dennis, Tom, Clarence, and Brendan. And, of course, Randy, whose accent is so thick with Newfoundland swagger, I will need an interpreter to keep up.

Brendan, the lead guide here at Tuckamore, has drawn the short straw this week. He will act as my guide, taking me through the bogs and ponds and the tuckamore, in search of my first moose. We make arrangements to meet the next morning at five.

I awake with a start, smashing a fist frantically at a quacking-duck clock on the side table, fully appreciating for the first time why they are called alarm clocks. Propelling myself out of bed, I climb into my borrowed camo gear—including a pair of hiking shoes one size too small on loan from the lodge's owner, Barb—and down to the dining room.

The staff is already busy shuffling plates from the table to the sink. Apparently, I'm the last one out of bed and holding up the mission. Brendan is pacing the floor boards, fueled by his second Pepsi of the morning. Standing all of five-feet-six, he's bedecked in a forest-green hat and matching jacket and pants that are tucked into similarly hued boots. "Jesus, you don't look so good dis mornin', Susan," Brendan avers, cocking his head to one side, his lips pulled into a tight smirk. "Well," he asks rhetorically, "what do you want to do?"

"Catch a moose," I respond as cheerily as I can.

Brendan suddenly coughs and grapples for the safety of a table, contorting his face into a manic expression. I'm pretty sure he's laughing, but no sound is coming out. "Susan," he finally sputters. "You don't *catch* a moose."

I feel the blood rise to my cheeks. Much like the time when my grade-four square-dancing partner tripped in front of the school assembly, taking my crepe-paper skirt with him on his way to the floor.

"Okay. Stalk a moose," I correct myself. "Mow 'em down," I add, squinting one eye and pulling my arm back in a mock bow-hunting gesture for dramatic effect. "I'm sure moose tastes good if you're really, really hungry." It's so early I forget where I am. I'm overcompensating, like any female determined to prove herself in a bastion of machismo.

There's no time for breakfast this morning, and I fill up a coffee cup for the road and step out of the lodge. It's not yet morning. A harvest moon lurks behind an eerie fog. The only audible sound is the clattering of my teeth as I shiver beneath two jackets on my way to the pickup. We're headed out to Area 40—not to be confused with Area 51. The guards there have orders to take out trespassers, while the hunters here are licensed to kill.

We climb in the truck and Brendan flicks the radio to a country station. He leans his full body into the wheel, his heavy-lidded pale-blue eyes clicking like a camera's shutterbug as he scans the darkness. He's no predatory rookie. He bagged his first moose at ten. He's been working at Tuckamore Lodge, guiding hunters—mostly Americans and Europeans—for more than twenty years. He's had to learn a few things along the way. Like that first year when he led a hunter to the biggest animal he could find on the island, who then proceeded to thank him by throwing a fit. It wasn't poundage these hunters were after, Brendan discovered, but their fifteen minutes in the spotlight. A shot—both literally and figuratively—at the record books.

It may be the most obvious delineation between these two solitudes. Two distinct hunting cultures that intersect here for several weeks every year. On one side of the fissure, the big-buckled Americans, the dukes and duchesses as well as kings and queens, reportedly from as far away as Sweden, who come seeking a trophy, to earn yodeling rights, to complete their collection. On the other side of the economic and social divide, not only the guides who live here and juggle jobs to make ends meet but the vast majority of these northern Newfoundlanders, who hunt simply because they need to eat.

Up and down, we rumble past roped-off parcels along the

roadside, some trampled by animals, some picked clean at harvest's end. Gardens where locals tend to rutabagas, cabbage, and potatoes, situated atop a forsaken and unforgiving piece of rock in the mid-Atlantic. For more than two hundred years, it'd been home to an insular stock of people who set their teeth to howling gales and the tempests of the vicious North Atlantic winters, eking out a living in cod fishing. Today, it's a lonelier place. The cod is gone, followed by a heartbreaking flight of people. But those who have stayed are proud of their heritage, their achievements. They are celebrated for their legendary sexual prowess—the most active lovers in the Canadian Confederation, according to an oft-quoted survey—but also for producing an overwhelming preponderance of Canada's best writers, comedians, and musicians. They are a stalwart lot who hold tight to the homeland, their songs and stories, as well as their idiosyncratic language and accents.

"If you're not from around here, you don't know where you're to," Brendan tells me.

"Huh?" I respond, hoisting my eyebrows in italicized befuddlement. "Just stick close to me. Don't get lost," Brendan commands, switching off the ignition. We've arrived at our destination: Browsey's Pond, a shrubby landscape, booby-trapped with a honeycomb of hidden sinkholes, untold bogs, and tuckamore. Home to several bucks and their harem.

"Finally. The killing fields," I offer with all the conviction I can muster. Truth be told, I'm more inclined to hailing a taxi than calling a moose, more used to hunting for bargains than animals.

Brendan pulls his cap down low, and motions me into a fragrant canopy of pine and spruce. I breathe deeply, trying to summon my inner killer. One, I've been told repeatedly, is always there, lurking right beneath the surface. "Nothing scares you. You don't back away from a showdown with anyone," my first boss at Canada's premier newspaper said, smiling beatifically before offering me my first reporting gig after a year of piecemeal contracts. "You're a tiger!" a senior columnist at my same alma mater cheered on more than one occasion. "Boy, I wouldn't want to get on your bad side," my fellow cubicle-dweller at the paper squealed all too regularly. And so on. These comments, quite frankly, always surprised me. I'd never had any inclination to be a war correspondent—where the hunter and hunted are one—something for which I lacked the sangfroid, the nerve, the requisite detachment. And I didn't feel particularly hard-bitten. Although I always figured that my small stature and easygoing demeanor were like stealth weapons for a reporter. No one ever expected me to put him in a body bag. I took these compliments as they were proffered: the highest of praise coming from the paper's resident ball-busters.

But advancing deeper into the woods, a crossbow slung across my back, I can't seem to connect with my inner assassin. The dirty-dealing politician? The bull's-eye was clearly marked on his back. But this hapless vegetarian? My designated fall guy? Yes, unwitting, defenseless Bullwinkle. I can't seem to rouse any feelings about him whatsoever. Except fear. Truth be told, the thought of killing a moose scares me. Hell, the thought of eating moose scares me even more.

I steady myself, stepping carefully, looking for signs of moose scat. Shit! I have no idea why they call them droppings. Heaped like a sandcastle, as thick as axle grease and one degree to the east, I've just missed crawling in a pile that is still steaming. Yes, Brendan whispers, we're hot on the trail. "See those black dots," he mumbles, and points through the fog to a hill, a quarter-mile in the distance. "There's a big bull on the far left, right there." I squint, straining for a peek, but I can't see anything. Brendan assures me they are there. He pivots his head, glancing furtively from side to side before flicking a stubby digit in front of his mouth. The universal command for silence.

We snake our way along, half-walking, half-crouching. We are being followed by a thousand eyes that we can't see. A creek burbles in the distance. Every cracking twig, every rustling leaf is amplified—seemingly arising from no fixed address. While I am at the mercy of my senses, the moose is sustained by them, used to surviving by its wits.

We move surreptitiously. Two steps. Pause. Five steps. Pause. Starting and stalling. I'm afraid to breathe, let alone move. We track our prey for the better part of an hour until what was a smudge on the landscape now looks to be a towering creature, fifty yards away. He lifts his head, staring with glassy black beads in our direction, his ears oscillating slowly in the wind. A fourteen-pointer! I exhale reflexively—and reach for my cross-bow. Peering through the viewfinder, I search frantically for his vitals—the heart, the lungs, but the only thing in my sightline is his backside. And from what I've been told, you don't want to risk shooting him in the butt and ruin a couple of really good steaks. No matter. My moment of glory, my shot at the record books vanishes in an instant as I watch my buck suddenly take flight and disappear into a thicket of trees.

I came here wanting to fully participate in the hunt, but the reality is that there are some formidable obstacles to my success. It's not just that I'm not the outdoorsy type. What gives me pause is the thought of it being *my* arrow that would take the life of another sentient creature. We kill the animals we eat, so why should this be any different? If I am to consent to taking an animal's life to nourish mine, shouldn't I be willing to kill it too? If my life depended on felling this creature, I am certain I could pull it off. I'm just not sure I really want to.

Clearly, this hunt is about more than food. This is sport. The macho conceit of taking down a big animal—a concept that is utterly foreign to me. At the very least, I can soothe my conscience with the argument that this is an educational pursuit. However, no matter what intellectual arguments I come up with to prop up my justification for being here, the truth is practicality rather than philosophy is going to scuttle my participation. I've never fired a weapon more potent than a water pistol. When it comes to working a crossbow, I'm a babe in the woods—more of a threat to myself and my fellow hunters than to the moose. But it doesn't mean that I can't have fun playing along. Hunting a moose through my viewfinder.

It's to be the last moose we will see this morning, before the dawn splits the dark and daylight, illuminating the wonder of the woods. When the birds and animals come alive, like an orchestra. The moose have gone to bed down, to digest their morning's meal. They won't return until twilight. I return to the comfort of the lodge and linger in the Jacuzzi—no camo bikini in sight—before catching up on some shut-eye. I spend the rest of the day reading and picking partridge berries.

By eight p.m., having stalked their prey again for another two hours, my fellow hunters have hung up their bows for the night. We gather around a long pine table and tuck into a dinner of cod in shrimp sauce served with peas and carrots and mashed potatoes.

Bob, the former ad exec, organic beef farmer, and only straggler, announces his arrival from around the corner. "Oh, the mistakes I made today," he booms, limping on a sore knee before deflating in a chair. He pours a glass of cognac, swirls it methodically, and breathes deeply before he begins a ten-minute reconstruct of the day's hunt. His audience is listening with such spellbound intensity you'd think he was giving a play-by-play of the successful capture of Osama bin Laden in the caves of Tora Bora.

"I couldn't get a clear shot," Bob sighs, punctuating the end of his story with a swig of cognac.

The room explodes in a cacophony of voices. It's clear that these guys aren't just comparing rack sizes. Storytelling is, apparently, also a competitive sport. Tales from afar. Hunting brown bear in Siberia. Himalayan tahr in New Zealand. How one guy's son, a high school quarterback, a monster really, panicked at the last minute. Couldn't pull the trigger. Meanwhile, the wine and beer and cognac are flowing and talk gets more and more animated.

Bill, the snooty ad guy from New York, is expounding on his philosophy of the hunt. "Anybody can load a grocery bag," Bill says. "Anybody can go out and get a job and earn money and buy meat that's been slaughtered and mass-produced. We've been programmed to provide for our families, and hunting provides that fulfillment. It's about being able to stalk an animal, dress it and butcher it, cook it and consume it. It's an anchor to our humanity."

"Bullshit," someone shouts from the end of the table.

"That's overintellectualizing it."

"It's about being one with nature," another voice interjects.

"It's a passion."

"It's like taking a needle of adrenaline and jabbing it straight into your heart."

Ted Nugent knows all about the adrenaline rush. These days, the self-described Motor City Madman and badass '70s rocker is the most recognizable face of hunting in America. Nugent likes to elucidate the pleasures of hunting with his characteristic shoot-from-the-hip style—"There's no bag limit on happiness," he explains. A card-carrying member of the National Rifle Association, Nugent is also editor of his own hunting magazine, hosts a show on the Outdoor Channel, and is the author of titles that include *Bloodtrails: The Truth About Bowhunting* and the cookbook *Kill It & Grill It*. Nugent makes no bones about it. Hunting is not only a primal act but a sexual one: "The heated excitement of the shot...the shaft was in and out...complete penetration...I was hot...I was on fire...the kill is climactic...it satiated a built-up frustration."[2]

I can't help but wonder if it was Nugent who coined the term "buck naked." Nugent likes to wax philosophical while riffing on the bliss of sweet 'n' sour antelope and deer stroganoff. For him, the high notes of hunting are inextricably tied to the protein culled at day's end. His encores are proselytizing about his pastime. He is not so much a musician-hunter as a hunter once known as a musician.

Maybe it's my effete, middle-class, urban sensibility, an obsession with pumping my body full of the right nutrients, but the Nuge—to my mind—makes some pretty compelling arguments for bypassing the factory farm in favor of gunning something down in the backyard. "If you want your body to be healthier," he instructs, "get off the salmonella, *E. coli*, mad cow, assembly-line, toxic hell train!" In other words, if you want to eat meat, killing it yourself is better not only for the environment but also for your body.

The colonial settlers had no choice. When the first Europeans arrived on the shores of the eastern seaboard, they were besotted by the notion of a newfound land of bounty. As Daniel Justin Herman writes in *Hunting and the American Imagination,* "When John Smith—explorer, historian, and founder of Jamestown—reported early in the seventeenth century that two of his fellow colonists had killed 148 wildfowl with three shots, he inaugurated the idea of America as a 'hunters' paradise.'"[3]

In colonial America, everyone had the same God-given, democratic right to hunt and eat meat. Hunting was, Herman argues, an expression of what it was to be an American expressed in its purest form. The New World was not only a land of bountiful game and good hunting, it was a place "intended by providence to lure those of hardy and adventuresome spirit. . . . If Americans had not been a self-sufficient, liberty-loving, hunting people, what would have compelled them to stand up to King George III? And if Americans had not been skilled with rifle and musket, how could they have defeated the mightiest army in the world?"[4]

However, it wasn't until the nineteenth century—and the

rise of the popular press—that hunting began to dominate the canvas of American culture. For a new country, an instant tradition. The presses poured out thousands of hunting tales to slake a seemingly unquenchable thirst. Their heroes were Meriwether Lewis, Daniel Boone, Davy Crockett, and Buffalo Bill—men modeled after their colonial forebears. Hunting, thus, became a passion and a pastime, a way to not only mimic the heroes of the frontier. "By the late nineteenth century," Herman writes, "The hunter (as sportsman and backwoodsman) had become, in the phraseology of Antonio Gramsci, a 'hegemonic' figure, a cultural hero propagated by powerful members of American society to serve their ideological ends. The hunter became the human banner for imperialism, laissez-faire individualism, and patriarchy. As that banner, the hunter triumphed in the American imagination. But hegemonic cultural heroes play ambiguous roles as they wander across the prairies of history. If the hunter epitomized laissez-faire freedom and imperial conquest, he also became in the Gilded Age a symbol of the American common man (and in some instances, woman) and the nation's democratic ethos."[5]

It's hard to say how the hunter's once vaunted reputation began to be chipped away in North American culture. Some trace it back to the beginning of industrialization and the shift from a rural to an urban culture. The notion that it wasn't just jobs that drew the population city-ward, but rather a psychological evolution. Some believe the pivotal historical moment was Disney's 1942 release of *Bambi*—arguably the most powerful antihunting propaganda ever produced. Bambi was one of the first celebrity cartoon characters, a dewy-eyed fawn romping in a playland full of giggly rabbits and songs about raindrops. But he was soon joined by a gang of talking animal characters imbued with humanlike traits, only more cunning, more worldly than the doltish humans who played bit roles in their bucolic dramas. After all, who ran the farm? Didn't the spider Charlotte find a way to outfox Mr. Zuckerman, who'd been fattening Wilbur the pig for the butcher's block, thereby making him the most famous pig ever?

By the 1970s, riding the crest of a cultural revolution that demanded equality for women, blacks, and other minorities, some began to posit that animals had rights too. The idea that animals had intrinsic moral rights wasn't a twentieth-century invention. Pythagoras was an early animal rights' activist and perhaps the first celebrity vegetarian—certainly long before Pamela Anderson became a poster girl for blood-free living. However, the notion that animals had rights began to take root in the wake of Peter Singer's *Animal Liberation,* a philosophical treatise and canonical text of the animal rights movement. Singer argued that animals had rights; that they should be protected from cruelty, from laboratory testing and the destruction of their habitats. Hunting was even further up on the list; collecting heads to mount in a living room, indefensible. Taboo.

Today, what was once a consuming and defining part of North American culture is largely a blue-collar pastime, petering out—according to the official tallies—decade by decade. Hunting's tough luck may have bottomed out when Dick Cheney, apparently inspired by Elmer Fudd, shot a member of his quail-hunting party. With friends like the unloved Cheney, hunting hardly needs opponents.

Certainly it's easy to draw a line linking hunting's demise

directly to its champions. The charismatic Teddy Roosevelt hunted grizzlies and bighorn sheep in America and bagged big game in Africa, including an astonishing—if not appalling—eleven elephants, twenty rhinos, and seventeen lions.[6] Hunting trips punctuated the greatest moments in his career. He celebrated his appointment to vice-presidency with a hunting trip to Colorado. And when he received word he would become president in the wake of William McKinley's death, he was hunting in the Adirondacks. "The virility, clear-sighted common sense and resourcefulness of the American people," Roosevelt proclaimed, "[are] due to the fact that we have been a nation of hunters and frequenters of the forest, plains and waters."[7]

The whiff of wrongdoing seems to haunt Cheney's hunting adventures. He has been relentlessly chided for taking a sitting Supreme Court judge on a free duck-hunting trip and later for seeming to cover up the accidental shooting of one of his quail-hunting partners.

To shore up their faltering numbers, pro-hunting groups like the National Shooting Sports Foundation, the U.S. Sportsmen's Alliance, and the National Turkey Federation have begun to lobby states to lower the age at which children can hunt.[8] Or face the inevitable: A day when "hunter" will be added to the list of endangered species. A day when hunting will be a dead-end business.

Meanwhile, I'm feeling somewhat imperiled myself this morning as we bump along a dirt road populated with panicky rabbits. What's got me on edge—in addition to traversing a dirt path the locals refer to as the Road of No Return—is the worry I might become roadkill too. Brendan's eyes are blinking on and off like Christmas lights. I try to keep him roused with a rendition of a traditional Newfie folk song I inexplicably had been taught and remember from grade school. Brendan flinches, still only partially conscious but fully annoyed. He flips the radio dial, drowning me out with the morning's newscast. We drive along until we reach a stark patch of woods that has been clear-cut by a local logging company. A spot where new shrubbery of balsam and fir is taking root—the moose's favorite food and feeding spot.

I'm sluggish and woefully unprepared for the demands of this landscape. The ground beneath my feet is full of snarl, poking, jabbing, and scratching as we walk silently, our eyes focused on the forest. Water swishes between my toes, my heels are rubbed raw in too-small boots. Besides, there's not a moose in sight. "Sometimes you can go a long time without seeing a moose," Brendan explains. "Sometimes when you're stalking them, if you yell or somethin' you might find one." He clasps his hands together in front of his mouth and bawls. "Baaaaaaa. Wah-wah-wah. Wah-wah-wah."

No answer.

We amble back to the truck and head for yesterday's destination, praying for another hour of darkness, another opportunity at bragging rights, to see my name in the Boone and Crockett's book of records. Just off the main highway, Brendan makes a sharp right turn and jumps on the brakes. "God damn," he mutters. "We're going to be here for a while," he tells me, nodding ahead. Up the road, I recognize the telltale white hat. It's Jerry, the soft-spoken sales rep from West Virginia, and his guide Junior. They're staring into the woods, seemingly unaware of our arrival. Brendan adjusts his binoculars and rotates to the left.

"Yah. It's a big, older animal. Got a gray goatee just like Jerry. Might be a bit chewy eating. But that don't matter to him."

We watch the two men hunker down from our front-row seat in our truck. Their hats bob as they duck low, heading deeper into the forest. The buck now in reach, Jerry steadies his crossbow, and in a split second unleashes an arrow. It cuts through the air like a thunderbolt, and the moose is fatally hit.

It's a vision that's already flashed through my mind. It's déjà vu: the feeling that I've witnessed it all before. In fact, it was the night before. Only, I now realize, it was me—through my viewfinder stalking a white-tailed deer. Maybe 250 meters away. Just out of reach of a clean kill. It wasn't a dream but a game I played. Deer Hunter, the smash hit if not best-selling video game of all time—the closest I may ever get to the kill. Just like Pong was as close as I ever got to Wimbledon. But then again, if flight simulators are training for pilots, then perhaps time spent in a hunting simulator is more elaborate than a game. That it will help prep me for more time in the bush.

I'm back at the lodge, jamming hard on the joystick once again. Twenty minutes in and I've already shot two bucks and winged a bear. Now, a third deer is within shooting distance. I punch a key to call him in, but it must have been the wrong Deerlish because he's now bolting in the opposite direction. I feel the adrenaline coursing through my veins. It's like a sugar high after ingesting too many Pop Rocks or Tootsie Roll Midgets. In this moment, I suddenly feel like I can do anything—I'm Wonder Woman, I'm Buffy the Vampire Slayer—capable of forging a Middle East peace agreement, successfully defending Lord Conrad Black in court, even sticking to a strict spending limit on jewelry and accessories. An extra bonus: I can't help noticing how much easier it is on my feet, crawling here through the video screen's bulrushes. And I don't have to bother with the bloodshed, butchery, or taxidermy either.

Gradually, however, my excitement evaporates—like dew on tuckamore in the early morning. An hour has passed when I find I'm just plain bored with bagging faux heads, collecting fake racks. Could it be that I just don't have the psychological makeup of a bona fide hunter? The ego necessary to want to own the best, most complete set of moose heads? Or could it simply be explained by the fact that my sexual proclivities veer to normal? After all, according to the French postmodern philosopher Jean Baudrillard, the human desire to collect is really a form of fetishism, "a discreet form of sexual perversion."[9]

While pondering all of this, I begin to wonder why there are so few iconic women hunters. Just as a gun seemed an appropriate accessory for Teddy Roosevelt, I find it hard to imagine his wife, Edith, with a gun crooked in her arm. You might imagine that if necessary, she might have even killed a bear or two trying to get to the root cellar. But she probably preferred to leave the hunting and killing to her beloved. I scour the history books. Admittedly, I wasn't much of a history buff (my deepest apologies, Mr. Blakely, but grade-nine Canadian history was about as rousing as taking a bubble bath with a chartered accountant). I'm fascinated to learn about Martha Maxwell, "the Colorado Huntress," an accomplished naturalist, hunter, taxidermist, and early feminist. Her life's work was presented in 1876 at a Philadelphia exhibit, a diorama of mounted game that she had culled with her own hands, including elk, deer, and buffalo. Above it, a sign read WOMEN'S WORK.[10]

Not to be dismissed, of course, was the celebrated marks-woman of Buffalo Bill's Wild West Show, Annie Oakley. In the show, she wasn't so much vaunted for killing as for her gunning prowess, apparently spawning a host of trapshooting wannabes, and clubs in places like Wilmington, Philadelphia, Chicago, and Toronto. As hunting gained mass popularity in North America, increasing numbers of women began to demand their rightful place in the bush. Some historians have even gone so far as to suggest that these early female hunting enthusiasts were the precursors to the suffragettes.[11]

It's long been one of the feminist conundrums. Reconciling the right to do anything a man can do with what women want to do. In my own case, I want to believe it was more than a matter of simple cowardice. Although I must confess I would have liked to have unleashed an arrow at more than one of my male counterparts this week. I am ever thankful to those who made it possible for women like me to brandish a crossbow—Martha Maxwell, Annie Oakley, Gloria Steinem, et al.

The truth is, I'm out of my element. While I'd like to think it's a philosophical choice, I could as easily put it down to a matter of genetics. Nature trumping culture. Back in the Stone Age, it was the caveman's job to swing a big club and the woman's job to forage for wild vegetables, nuts, and berries—and, apparently, to honor the hunters with the biggest horns. In other words, the most successful hunters also got the most booty. Or so the theory goes.

Tomorrow the entire island here in Newfoundland will

become a shooting gallery. The opening of gun season. Soon fresh kills will be strung up in trees like the first ornaments of the holiday season. Pickups are already streaming up and down the roadways in the twilight, scouting for signs of moose. Their aim? A local with his hunting license isn't in it for the sport. He's not looking for a trophy any more than his missus would at the supermarket, and he goes about it with just about the same sense of purpose. He's shopping, just like her—with a fresh-bought hunting license instead of clipped coupons. Nothing more than a freezer full of meat to see the family through the winter. I try to square this with the notion that men who shoot the most impressive animals also bang the most women. What, then, explains the Newfoundland male's animal magnetism? Could it be pheromones in the moose meat? A sexual elixir culled from the velvet of the antlers?

My head is swimming, my mind still full of questions as I traipse one last time down the dirt path that leads to the meat house, one last invasion of the testosterone-drenched clubhouse. It's not feminist doctrine so much as a matter of simple human rights, the idea that no place should be shut off to an entire gender. But something else is in play in the meat house. The boys don't need to shut women out. No, it's so rank—not with meat but with men flaunting their inner delinquents—that any right-minded woman would be loath to go there. I can't imagine any of my friends lasting a minute in here. I do it only because it's my job. I cringe when I think about the crack about me in a camo bikini—if only because there's a kernel of truth in the joke. I am more comfortable in a swimsuit than holding a cross-bow in front of a moose. And that's saying a lot for a woman who hits the gym about as frequently as a supermodel dines at an all-you-can-eat buffet.

Speaking of food, inside the meat shed a black frying pan on the stove is smoking, heaped with a pile of fat and flesh. Brendan is manning the cooking station, lightly spicing a mélange of animal parts. There are rabbit legs, seal flippers, cod tongues, and, of course, the fruits of today's harvest: a couple of moose steaks. To soothe their rumbling stomachs, to fortify themselves for the twilight stalk, the boys have gathered here for an old-fashioned kind of cookout and a liquid refreshment to cleanse the palate. Soon they'll be contemplating the eternal question in hunting-lodge cuisine: What goes best with moose meat, ale or lager?

A few feet to his left, Brendan's fellow guide Dennis is carving away at a milky-white layer of fat beneath a chocolate-brown hide. Having peeled away the last slice, Dennis now flips Bullwinkle's "cape" inside out. It's clear now the intelligent designer never intended it to be reversible. It's an odd sight: beady eyes staring from beneath a flap of inner hide. In a day or two, his coat will be dry from the early autumn sun and ready for the overnight courier, on its way to a taxidermist somewhere in the Midwest.

"People swear by seal," Brendan shouts over the hiss of the stove. "They say it's as good as Viagra."

"Hell, I don't need no Viagra," Terry, the hunter from West Virginia, proclaims, wiping seal oil from his chin with a bloody sleeve, fresh from gutting and skinning the moose we're about to sample. True enough, unless she had a weakness for chainsaw killers, a woman would run at the sight of him.

Talk seamlessly turns from sex to meat, like they're all part of the same course.

"I likes grouse and seal. Not crazy about caribou, though," Brendan says.

"I'd take a rib eye any day," Bill, the snippy ad mogul, interjects.

"Now, I may be from West Virginia, but we're not like the Clampetts down there," Terry says unconvincingly. The optics couldn't be worse, for at the very moment he is perched underneath a muskrat hide that is nailed to the wall. Undeterred, he makes the best possible case for his home state being the hub of good taste. "We don't eat muskrat. We consider that a swamp chicken. The only thing worse than someone who eats muskrats is a vegetarian.

"I'd rather have squirrel on a bun any day. Every day, if I could."

The state of West Virginia probably could use a better spokesman.

There's only so much scintillating repartee I can stand, so I try to get the boys back to the meat at hand. "What about moose? Does anyone like moose?" I ask finally.

Brendan ambles over to where I'm standing, positioned between a bunch of moose haunches and the drying hide. He extends a fork with a long, twisted piece of moose meat on it. I hesitate, before pulling it from the fork with my fingers. It smells like the sweetness of the forest. The miracle of wild nutrition. I rip off a piece and place it on my tongue. The moose is just about the homeliest quadruped creature roaming the backwoods of North America. In profile or face-on, he looks nothing but forlorn. But, like they say, beauty is only skin-deep. No, it's what's on the inside that counts. I'm astonished as its wild flavors melt on my tongue. It's a bit chewier than I'd like. But utterly delectable. It's got all the robust, nutty flavor of a top sirloin. And more. It is, as the Michelin Guide undoubtedly would agree, bib-worthy. But hell, why bother? No one wears a bib around here. Given their druthers, they'd probably not even use cutlery. It's not like they're in West Virginia or anything.

7
• HAPPY MEAL •

WHILE THE PRISTINE WOODS of Newfoundland are a de facto nature preserve, here on this farm a forty-five-minute commuter ride north of New York City, it's more like a petting zoo. The hunters at Tuckamore surely would heap scorn on the very notion of the pampered and coddled meat that is raised here. But for diners from the five boroughs who make their way here for dinner, it's back to nature—as close to an idyllic, grade-school vision of farm life as you can possibly get in the suburbs.

If George Orwell had set *Animal Farm* on Park Avenue, it would surely look like this. Residents huddle in cliques on an aristocratic preserve, once the playground of the country's richest oil baron. Lolling in the shade in sleek black coats, their noses held high in the air, they snort derisively as a group of rubberneckers streams by, clamoring for a peek. As if to say, "And they think they're the pampered rich."

They are clearly a cut above: a fabled and rare breed whose lineage can be traced all the way back to the sixteenth century—

right on the first page of the Porcine Social Register. Their sweet and fatty flesh coveted by British imperials. Their rich marbling devoured by Japanese emperors. Indeed, the ancestors of those rolling in this rich, wet loam ended up on the plates and palates of some of the greatest names in history.

Here in Pocantico Hills, there's no question these swine—these Berkshire Golds—are getting the royal treatment. Do they have enough room to roam? Enough acorns and slugs? Enough tree shade and bark to scratch on? These are the things that worry Craig Haney, the man who is at once their master and their manservant. As with others in such roles, it seems no one understands the elite as well as those who attend them.

Haney and I are careening down a muddy path in a Kubota, a toy-sized RTV, headed toward a wooded hogs' lair. We pass by brightly colored carpets of radicchio and escarole, past a hill of sweating compost and a gaggle of joggers, before lurching full-tilt into a forest of trees. Haney screeches the vehicle to a stop and leaps out. As he plops one muddy Wellington after another across an electric fence, his arrival sets off a terrible ruckus. A dozen sows clamor to their feet, heading in his direction. Scuttling across the forest floor, their potbellies flapping, their newborn piglets run, screaming, behind them. Swarmed by five thousand pounds of boisterous, hairy hog, Haney suddenly looks like a feeder fish thrown into a school of piranha. These girls have chops and they, apparently, like to bite.

The slightly built thirty-nine-year-old farmer boots at a particularly rowdy sow poking her snout into his backside. "C'mon, sweetie," he coos, delivering another swift kick. This four-hundred-pound swine is having a tantrum. She's just given birth to eight piglets and her hormones are out of control. And given that this is a chemical-free zone—the antithesis of corporate farming—there is no Prozac, no growth hormones, no antibiotics here. Times like this call for an old-fashioned agricultural pragmatism even more ancient than the pigs' bloodlines. "Last night, I was up to my elbow inside of her, helping her with the piglets," Haney tells me, his pale-blue stare filled with the stoicism evoked in Grant Wood's *American Gothic*. "A few days ago, I had my thumb up another pig's butt. This job is all about body fluids," he laughs. "Sometimes you have to forget what you're doing or you'd just be a bundle of nerves."

Haney's manner betrays no jitters whatsoever. His goal is to raise livestock in peace, and that peace starts with his attitude and, yes, his conscience—raising them in good conscience, with a clean conscience. His own inner peace carries over from the belief in the approach here at the Stone Barns Center and Blue Hill Restaurant. His work here seems not so much a job as a life choice. He wants to create a utopia for his feral charges. He doesn't raise the animals; they are kept. "More and more, I find that's my overriding purpose," he explains. "Making sure that these animals have a happy life. After all," he adds, as we climb back into the vehicle and head to farm headquarters, "a happy pig is a great-tasting pig."

I feel like I've just been invited through the back door and ushered into a seat at the chef's best table. So, this is the secret ingredient! Happiness! The spice, the herb that keeps patrons lining up for months for a table here at the three-star Blue Hill Restaurant, where these Berkshires will be transformed from pig into pork.

I've traded in my writer's sweats for coveralls, for an opportunity to work here at this would-be hog heaven, an astonishingly beautiful eighty-acre farm. If I were a pig, I'd want to live here too.

I've come hundreds of miles, past Sleepy Hollow, past Tarrytown, and into one of the more affluent corners of the United States. It's here, deep in the suburbs, a veritable hotbed of civil rest, that a social and gastronomic revolution is taking hold. It's a revolution that is essentially a what's-old-is-new-again approach, built upon the notions of local ingredients, self-sufficiency, and sustainable agriculture. It's all about reducing the distance between dirt and plate. A celebration of food as much as it is a worship of grass.

I've come on this journey into the food chain—where urbanites and locals, farmers and foodies alike—gather just to breathe the same rarefied air as one of the most storied men in American commerce—John D. Rockefeller. In the 1890s, Rockefeller bought the land where today's agricultural experiment unfolds. These days, it's a $30 million showcase, functioning as part conservatory, part garden, and working farm, as well as an education center and restaurant. On any given day, you can stroll past a runaway hen digging for grubs outside the café, browse the bookstore and outdoor market, or take a class in everything from composting to sausage-making to deworming sheep. Then you can dine like a Rockefeller, supping on braised bacon and lime-infused escarole soup at the Blue Hill Restaurant.

Maybe it's just me, but it does seem a little odd: a farm owned by industrialists helping to fund the deindustrialization of farming? It's like Exxon bankrolling research into solar power. Peculiar, perhaps, that one of the richest families in America would fund a return to what is the humblest in farming—all to produce food for a restaurant that is out of reach, so lavishly priced, you might think it's tantamount to robbery by candlelight.

But there is something subversive at work. And although Haney's ethereal comportment gives him an air more of a pasture preacher than militant barnyard rebel, he has been instrumental in helping to spearhead this agricultural revolt as Stone Barns' livestock manager. He's invited me along for the ride, granting me a one-week membership in the slow-food set. During my stay, I will help tend to the heritage sheep, hens, pigs, and baby turkeys. My aim? To glean the truth about what makes a happy meal.

And while much of everything about the sprawling 1930s Norman-style Stone Barns Center for Food & Agriculture is elitist, Haney is for real. (And just for the record—he's no heir to Pat Buttram, aka Mr. Haney, the shyster farmer who sold his land to Oliver Wendell Douglas in the sitcom *Green Acres*.) Wearing dark jeans tucked into rubber boots, a beige T-shirt, and a broadbrimmed straw hat, Haney looks like a young Sam Shepard with the hard edges sawed off. He seems to have been cut out of a vintage photo and pasted into this landscape. Little wonder, then, that he also seems to be part of another time: both the past and the future. A farmer, a philosopher at heart, Haney straddles three centuries. With one eye clearly focused on his great-grandfather's farming traditions and another on the earth beneath him, he's hoping to imprint his stamp on pork belly futures.

In many ways, Haney is as rare as the Berkshires he raises. He is an endangered species in a culture utterly transformed in just two generations. It wasn't just the disappearance of an age-old legacy of family farming that came with the industrialization of farming, but millions of jobs and a way of life—destroyed by government policy, bank foreclosures, and the rise of big agribusiness.

But farming seems to be coded in Haney's DNA. "Growing up, I was probably too cerebral," he explains. "I've always been drawn to this kind of work. It just seems very immediate to me." Eight generations of his mother's family farmed the northern Catskills. They were Palatine Germans that came to New York State's Schoharie and Mohawk River valley in the 1740s. Both grandfathers were dairy farmers. After finishing a degree in social history, Haney headed back to the land he loved, establishing his own farm with a specialty in pasture-raised meats. A few years later, divorce uprooted him and he was lured to the Rockefeller farm at the behest of Blue Hill's chef, Dan Barber. He's never looked back.

He is part of a movement of crofters at the cutting edge of animal husbandry. One that would look very familiar to Laura Ingalls Wilder. "As a kid I did find inspiration in *Little House on the Prairie*," confesses Haney, whose reading tastes these days are more in line with *The Stockman Grass Farmer* and *AcresUSA*, the bibles of today's über-brainy farmer. Swept up in a mini-boom of grassroots farmers who are flagrantly defying the rules of modern-day agribusiness, Haney hopes to serve up alternatives to a world food system under corporate control since World War II. Driven by idealism, environmentalism, and animal welfare—as well as a desire to rescue taste and food safety—Haney is helping to drive growth in small livestock and poultry farms.

"Factory farms try to take as much nature as they can out of the process," he explains. "Here, we try to inject as much nature as we can back into it.

"Did you know that chickens are raised in something the size of a shoe box?" he asks, his voice incredulous now. "All you have to do is watch these guys for five minutes and you realize how much they enjoy stretching their wings and giving themselves dust baths. I can't prop up something I don't believe in. It just feels like a crime."

If you didn't know better, you might mistake Haney for an animal rights activist, or a rad vegetarian. But he's clearly no vegan wannabe. "To work here you've got to love and respect the animals—and relish eating them," he tells me matter-of-factly.

He's in strange territory, to be sure, but one with growth potential. Haney is at the forefront of a niche within a niche: he husbands not only organic meat but meat that has been raised on pasture. It looks to be the next food frontier. It's a niche that's grown from just a handful of farmers a few years ago to well over one thousand pasture-based farmers—from Kentucky to Colorado and into Alberta—in 2007. Many of Haney's breeds are heirlooms as precious as Grandma's silverware. And one day, if he gets his way, his Berkshires and Red Bourbon turkeys will rival the smash success of foods like goat cheese and heirloom tomatoes. He wants to change the world, one grass-fed ham, one pasture-raised turkey breast, one chic piece of meat at a time.

When he looks for inspiration, it's not to the Frank Perdues and Don Tysons of the world. In conversation, Haney's more likely to drop names like Rudolf Steiner, Joel Salatin, and John Petersen. They are his cultural touchstones.

"You know Steiner?" Haney asks. I offer up a blank stare. "You know, the philosopher?" he quizzes, cocking his head to one side and rubbing a blond smudge of day-old growth on his chin. Aristotle. Check. Spinoza. Check. Nietzsche, Sartre, Derrida. Check, check, check. But no Steiner. I shrug and mumble something about sleeping through too many early-morning philosophy classes way back when. Later, I find that even the staid and patrician Prince Charles is hip to the teachings of Steiner, a turn-of-the-century philosopher and muse to a new crop of farmers.

To understand the farmer-philosopher, you must go to his sources of inspiration.

Steiner was an Austrian natural historian, chemist, mathematician, and educator, who first lectured on a philosophy of agriculture in 1924 and is considered the forerunner to the modern organic movement, inspiring Haney and some of the world's finest vintners. His ideas were so old at the time that he proposed them, they were considered revolutionary.[1]

Steiner grew up on a mountainside in Austria in the 1860s—a rural peasant culture little changed since the Middle Ages. By the time he had formulated his philosophy of life—which melded the spiritual and material worlds—industrialization would sweep Europe and dramatically alter the agrarian lifestyle that had been critical to the underlying precepts of his philosophy. In one radical swoop of history, the culture of nature would be replaced by a culture that venerated the machine, and the peasants would become industrialization's new workers.[2]

Steiner lamented what was lost. "I grew up entirely out of the peasant folk, and in my spirit I have always remained there," he told a group of agricultural followers late in his life. "I myself planted potatoes....I lent a hand with the cattle. These things were absolutely near my life for a long time; I took part in them most actively. Thus I am at any rate lovingly devoted to it....I beg you to consider me as the small peasant farmer who conceived a real love for farming; one who remembers his small peasant farm and who thereby, perhaps, can understand what lives in the peasantry, in the farmers and yeoman of our agricultural life....For I have always considered what the peasants and farmers thought about these things far wiser than what the scientists were thinking."[3]

Steiner rejected the industrial model of agriculture built on the modern notions of science, efficiency, and technology. Instead, he advocated a "biodynamic" system with an eye to balance and healing. He saw each farm as a holistic, living organism that should be as self-sufficient as possible—that each should foster a rich diversity of plants and animals as a way to heal the earth. In fact, not only should crops and livestock coexist, he postulated, but he saw animal husbandry as central to restoring health and balance to the soil. His most fundamental contribution to the organic movement? The rejection of synthetic fertilizers, herbicides, and pesticides. Not just because he believed they were a chemical menace, as organic farmers now believe, but because he thought they were spiritually dead.[4]

Steiner embraced a number of unorthodox theories. He believed nature's bounty could be improved with the use of homeopathic lotions and potions derived from the ancient recipes of the peasants. He advocated the use of fifteen natural tonics to cultivate healthy soil, including—most infamously—cow dung stuffed into cows' own horns, buried in the fall, and retrieved to be spritzed on the earth in the spring. He also believed in the power of the zodiac—planting according to moon cycles and sun signs. Root days in the cycle of earth signs: Taurus, Virgo, and Capricorn; leaf days in the water signs of Cancer, Scorpio, and Pisces, and so on.[5] Stuff that anticipates New Age without the yoga mats and crystals.

Haney just laughs when I later bring this up. He's too much of this world to put his faith in constellations. "I don't know much about that," he tells me. "I spend so much of my time delving into the nitty-gritty of what we do. But he's been an important influence in that he's influenced others I've looked to as a model."

He's speaking, primarily, of Joel Salatin, the granddaddy of modern pasture-based farming, who found inspiration in the precepts of Steiner's philosophy but dramatically reworked them. Over the past twenty years, Salatin has emerged as the sort of maharishi of the sustainable-food set. He has won cult status for his innovations in animal husbandry on his five-hundred-acre Polyface Farm in Swoope, Virginia. Salatin has been an inspiration to the Stone Barns team, from conception to implementation.

While some consider him an off-the-grid crank, Salatin likes to refer to himself as a "Christian-conservative-libertarian-environmentalist-lunatic" who has learned to marshal the rhythms and symbioses of nature. But to hear him tell the story, he's more than a modern-day Thoreau with a penchant for colorful prose and provocative ideas. He's an artist. "It's not just science, it is art, and artists have to be creative. We're painting a landscape on our farms," he explains. "What I do is try to create habitats that allow the animals to express their fullness. For a pig to fully express its pigginess." At the heart of Salatin's philosophy are the notions of diversity, movement, and multiple uses for the land. That means raising several different species of animals on the same pasture—a cacophony of clucking, mooing, and bleating—switched up from week to week. Salatin says the secret is all in the "salad bar"—the forage of grass and clover that is the ruminant's caviar. Borrowing from Salatin's methodology, Haney is working to perfect his turf, the rich sward of emerald swaying beneath our feet—so key to making the ideal meat meal that many who raise animals on pasture refer to themselves as grass farmers.

The cyclical system works something like this: Sheep graze free in one pasture held in by an electrified wire. Every day or so, they are moved to a new patch of grass, and a succession of chickens—or turkeys in season—are moved into the plot that the sheep just left. The chickens dig through the sheep dung for grubs and worms and then scratch the manure into the dirt, aerating the soil and creating compost so that the cycle of growth can begin all over again. Meanwhile, the floor of the movable henhouse or "eggmobile" is opened so the droppings will fall and be left on the ground where nutrients are needed to grow more grass.

Although pasture-raised meat shares many of the virtues of organic meat—no hormones, antibiotics, or chemically modified feed—there is at least one significant difference. Organic producers feed their animals not only grass but a significant proportion of grain to fatten them up more quickly for market. Cows reared on a grain-rich diet often get sick, developing a painful disorder called "subacute acidosis," causing them to kick at their bellies and eat dirt.

Turns out, we are not just what we eat but also what our animals eat. It's welcome news in this puritanical age of culture that has dissected gastronomy into minute bits and bites of fat grams and trace minerals. At a time in which we think of the dinner table as a booby trap, jerry-rigged with potential landmines and enemies. When our first question is not "Is it good?" but "Is it good for me?"

A growing body of scientific evidence suggests that grass-fed meat is not only better for the environment and animals; it's good for us too. The more of the salad bar, the bugs and slugs, that our animals eat, the healthier our meal. Mad cow is just one among a litany of health hazards originating in factory-farmed animals. These animals have been fattened, typically obese by the time they hit the kill floor, oozing in bad fats that threaten to clog our arteries and contribute to everything from diabetes to cancer. When we eat grass-fat meat, we're consuming the same nutrient-rich greens the animal has eaten. Pasture-raised meat is higher in omega-3 fatty acids, the healthy fats found in salmon and flaxseed that are touted as a cure for everything from heart disease to depression. Grass-fed meat is also higher in vitamins A and E, two antioxidants thought to boost resistance to disease.[6]

"It's not a 'designer' food that came about through genetic manipulation," explains Jo Robinson, coauthor of *The Omega Diet* and the principal writer and researcher for eatwild.com, a website that extols the benefits of eating pasture-fed meat. "When you switch to grass-fed meat, you are restoring to your diet nutrients that factory farming took away."

Meanwhile, here on the Rockefeller farm, I'm living task to task. At the moment, I'm feeling too overwhelmed to worry much about the arc of history and the philosophical and nutritional underpinnings of farming. Feeling for all the world like *Green Acres'* inept Oliver Wendell Douglas, I spend the bulk of my first afternoon on the farm helping to build new fencing. An hour into my ludicrous attempts to connect a hammer with a nail, I've successfully secured three nails in their proper place. Haney is already halfway across the pasture. We work quietly. The cows low in a nearby pasture; a woodpecker drums on a hollow tree. The air is sweet with the smell of fresh grass. For a moment, far away from the concrete corridors of the city, away from the click, click, click of my computer keyboard, I feel like I've finally found home.

It's late afternoon when Haney hollers at me from across the meadow. "Okay, are you ready for some fun?" he asks gleefully, his teeth planing to a wide smile. He motions me into the RTV and we rumble up and down a rugged patch of pasture to where a flock of sheep are grazing. We pass by a jogger and a couple of Matisse wannabes, poised in front of their easels, taking advantage of the warm glow of a low-slung afternoon sun. "I love watching the sheep move," Haney tells me. "They get all excited when there's fresh grass. I just find it really, really pleasurable to watch them." We turn into a field where his sidekicks, farmhands Padraic MacLeish and Julie Engel, have been busy, unspooling new wire fencing in the adjacent meadow in preparation for some fifty ewes and their newborns, all Finn Dorsets. Their most famous blood cousin? Dolly, the first animal cloned in history. Cut down in her prime, the victim of premature aging.[7] And, perhaps, an argument in support of the philosophy of Steiner et al.

Engel, twenty-six, is the newest member of the crew, working on the farm for a little over a year. She's a tallish brunette with narrow-set eyes, no-name jeans, and a no-nonsense ponytail; her fierce intelligence concealed behind a slow and deliberate cadence. Her background suggests that she'll be well suited to the pace and detail of farm work. She grew up in Michigan and studied glaciers, eventually earning a degree in environmental geology, and worked as a technician before she ditched the monotony of a desk job for her dream job: working outside on a boutique farm. But she's no wide-eyed neophyte. She joined 4H as a teenager, eventually winning a string of ribbons for her prize rabbits. She's embarking on a new experiment here, raising the restaurant's first brood of pasture-raised rabbits.

And while this pretty patch of farmland is paradise to his workmates, MacLeish seems to treat it more like his personal PlayStation. Oh, he's just as committed to the cause. It's just that he seems to relish every moment of the rebellion. Standing six-feet-two, wearing a cowboy hat and aviator sunglasses, and sporting a six-pack, the twenty-three-year-old looks like he's been plucked straight from a Calvin Klein ad—freshly shorn Mohawk airbrushed out. MacLeish grew up in upstate New York, kicked around for a while doing odd jobs before landing a gig, alongside Haney, at the Farmers' Museum in Cooperstown, New York. Finding common cause, the two forged not only a working alliance but a friendship. Impressed by his commitment to getting the job done and showing the utmost respect and care for animals, Haney hired him to work on the Rockefeller farm when he could.

But this afternoon, MacLeish seems more intent on flaunting

his playful side rather than his true-blue Protestant work ethic. He leans in close and winks before letting out a great caterwaul. "G'day, g'day, g'day," he bellows until we eventually all join in the chorus. An age-old call for dinner; new grass is waiting. The sheep jostle, bunching together and bleating at the top of their lungs before proceeding, two by two, into the new field.

It's pasture perfect. We huddle together, watching quietly until MacLeish's screech shatters the silence. "Holy shit," he yells, pointing into the field where Stella, a white Maremma sheepdog is standing. It's my first lesson in the vagaries of farming. Agriculture is an attempt to work with nature, but it has its own rules, its own social Darwinism. No matter how bucolic the scene, sometimes bad things happen to good animals. Sometimes it's planned. This time it's not.

MacLeish scales the fence, followed by Haney. They bolt toward the center of the flock, where Stella is waving a small bundle of wool in her mouth, like a rag doll. It's a newborn lamb—not more than a day old. Haney coaxes gently and Stella reluctantly releases the body. He fumbles in his pocket for a knife, ripping the animal's sheepskin open like a zipper to reveal its flesh—looking for teeth marks, bruises, any hint that will reveal what prompted this calamity.

"It's going to be a long night," he mumbles, staring at the tiny corpse lying on the ground. For the next several hours, the pasture will resemble a scene out of *CSI* as Haney and his crew hunt for clues. Was it a predator? A fox that slipped through the fence? No one raises the unavoidable question: Was it Stella, the puppy, the guardian-in-training? Shortly after I leave, they will find another casualty.

We meet the next morning. Haney's eyes are ringed by dark circles. He's even quieter than usual. He doesn't say it, but I know that he feels like he let the team down. The restaurant, its patrons, his coworkers, as well as the mob of ruminants he tends to. But no one more than himself. "You just feel like every decision you make has very big consequences," he tells me later. "It's a challenge. I get very stressed out when I know there's something wrong with the animals. That maybe I should have done something different. You just never know what's going to happen next."

MacLeish taps me for help with the sheep, and we head back to the crime scene. Stella's nowhere in sight. Apparently, she's been given a temporary pink slip. All evidence suggests she's responsible for the dead lambs. Although short of catching her in the act, there is no way to know for certain.

Meanwhile, a miracle has happened overnight. At least it seems a wonder to me: a half-dozen newborns have mysteriously joined the flock. Our mission today, MacLeish informs me—catch, ear-tag, and castrate. My job is to hold the little lambs in place while MacLeish performs the "operation."

But first, it's roundup time. I feel like I've just flipped channels from *CSI* to tune in to a challenge on *Survivor: Pocantico*. It's a manic sight. MacLeish running as fast as he can, grabbing at nothing but air as these five-pound puffs of wool scamper out of his reach. Finally, twenty minutes later, his face the color of a beet, MacLeish returns with three babies in tow. "You can see why we do this right away," he mumbles sheepishly. "Three weeks from now it would be impossible to catch 'em." He keeps hold of two and hands me the third. Strapped in my arms, my little fella offers up an unruffled stare, his white eyelashes flickering ever so slightly. But I can tell he's scared witless: his heart is thumping so hard his whole body vibrates like a boom box.

We weigh them. Tag their ears. And rid them of their family jewels, not with pruning shears but by placing a small ring around their scrotums to cut off the blood supply—eventually causing their testicles to shrivel up and fall off. MacLeish finishes with my newborn, now technically a wether, who hops to his feet, seemingly unscathed, snuggling up close to me.

Researchers have only just come to realize that we do owe these sheep an apology. Turns out, they are much more intelligent than we knew. They can remember the mugs of their brethren for up to eight hundred days—and can even identify human faces a year after separation.[8] But this guy clearly doesn't recognize me for who I am: a self-respecting meat-eater that would never let the carnivore crowd down no matter how cute the lamb chop. He thinks I'm his momma! Okay, it is a little sweet. Adorable, that is, until I realize my legs are chafing. His fur feels like steel wool. I shoo him away and he scurries back to the flock, seeking a walk-by feeding, desperately trying to clamp on to every available teat.

Meanwhile, another group of greenhorns wander by. They're the first of a dozen crews of kids I'll see throughout my week here on the farm. They're on an educational tour—one of a number of tours that Stone Barns offers to schoolchildren so they can see firsthand how a farm works. Haney sees this as one of the most important tenets of Stone Barns' mission. "This is the first generation of kids who have never seen animals on the farm. I feel I have a huge responsibility to them. Like this is a very big deal," he explains. "I hope that they'll see animals like this on pasture and they'll see that they're happy. And at some point, they'll hear about the pigs and these lagoons in North Carolina, and hopefully, they'll say, 'That just seems weird to me. I remember I saw those animals at Stone Barns and it wasn't at all like that.'"

Shelby Snyder, MacLeish's fiancée, is leading this gaggle of nine-year-olds, decked out in Lacoste pastels, khaki shorts, and blissed-up attitude. The girls skip hand-in-hand while the boys shove one another, seemingly oblivious to the barnyard's sights and sounds until one little girl spots Engel's pet project. "Bunnies," she squeals, pointing toward the bottom of a hill. "I love bunnies." They run helter-skelter down the hill and to the rabbit cage, taunting some thirty black, brown, and sand-colored rabbits through the chicken wire.

It is Snyder's job as assistant instructor in the fundamentals of the barnyard to teach the children the basics of food production. To help them make the association between piglets and link sausage, chickens and wings. Connections between what happens on the farm and what's for dinner—that in just six weeks, these little cuddly bundles of cute are destined for the cleaver, and later for the restaurant, where they'll be braised and wrapped in puff pastry. "You do realize that these rabbits one day will be served in the restaurant," Shelby counsels gently. "You mean as rabbit food?" one bespectacled girl asks, her face bunching up in puzzlement. "And then they'll make rabbit boots?" a little boy chimes in. Snyder just sighs and smiles, not uttering another word as she gathers her young charges to return to their teacher. Reality, it seems, is best served in bite-size morsels.

The next morning, I arrive at seven a.m. to join the crew for egg collection. We rally in the Kubota, bouncing along the pasture in the direction of the rooster's morning crow. He's one of a handful on the farm, brought in as overlords to these hens, a cross between a White Rock and the Rhode Island Red, a heritage breed dating back to the early nineteenth century and the most prolific egg-layer in North America. At least until science learned how to trump nature.

Haney veers into the meadow where several hundred hens are busy rooting in the grass for breakfast. I trip across a rowdy crowd pecking at my feet, zigzagging toward the henhouse where a half-dozen brilliantly hued capons are perched. Above the din, I can almost hear the chiding tone of Foghorn Leghorn: "I say, I say—it's a chicken, boy. Don't you know what a chicken looks like?" Truthfully, I have never seen a chicken like this before. I have never seen a chicken in feathers, never one in anything but a Styrofoam package or cooked already in a see-through plastic tub. But that's not why I am standing here, frozen like a statue. No, what has me on edge is the idea of ransacking these nests for the eggs these hens guard like Fabergé treasures. The truth is, I'm chicken. Haney senses my dread. "Don't worry," he advises cheerily, flashing his best team captain smile. "Just stick your hand right in there." That, I think to myself, must be a joke, son. A joke. But what happens next isn't funny. It's extraordinary. A hen bustles up from her nest and preens for a moment before arching her fanny directly into my face and dispelling a quarter-pound egg, just like a Pez dispenser. I reach out to catch hold of the perfect brown orb. "Look, the hen just laid an egg!" I shout to Haney, who is bent over a wire basket, counting eggs. He just smiles and nods in recognition. "It never gets old," he tells me.

Engel and I spend the rest of the morning scrubbing eggs in the barn. Many are headed to the restaurant. The rest will be sold upstairs at the outdoor market. We stack them dozen by dozen, piled so high they threaten to topple on top of us. I'm wiping dirt from the last shell when I spot Haney climbing out of a vehicle where two pigs are on board, about to be taken to slaughter. He's just had a tape measure around their necks, trying to calculate the tonnage—how many pounds of shoulder, butt, and belly will soon be ready to be shipped off to the restaurant. He looks lost in his thoughts, like he's just lost his two best friends. "Anything wrong?" I ask. He pauses for a moment, staring at the spool of tape he's wrapping around and around again. "It's the only time I ever really think about it," he says finally. "I guess I do think about it more than I used to. Does that mean it's wrong to eat meat? No. I think we're omnivores and we've evolved to where meat-eating is part of what we do. I think in the celebration of eating meat, you honor the animal too."

Honor in sacrifice. If that's true, then I must be in line for some sort of medal, because my next chore requires not only relinquishing my dignity but my brand-new paisley-patterned rubber boots. Nothing—so far as I'm concerned—is going to be potent enough to disinfect them when I'm done cleaning the chicken coop. Engel and I have been assigned to play maid to a couple hundred hens. We've hauled the eggmobile to headquarters, where we're about to begin scouring it for the arrival of a new brood. "Not my favorite job either," Engel assures me, handing over my work tools—a scraper and shovel.

It's the first hot day of spring, and even more stifling in here. Maybe it feels that much closer because I'm being eyeballed by two roosters, the coop's only remaining residents. I've been instructed to hold them captive until the work is done and the henhouse is returned to pasture. We're only a few minutes into the job when Engel is called out to help unload the shipment of new hens. I'm left on my own to dig and scrape and, apparently, asphyxiate. I seek refuge outside for a few moments, gasping for air before I notice one of the roosters strutting the farm's long stone fence. "One of the roosters is out!" I shout at Engel, who is straining to hear me above the clucks and squawks of two hundred mouthy hens. She looks perturbed. I can almost hear her eyes roll. "Just grab him by the leg and put him back," she hollers back at me.

Sounds easy. But, truth be told, a rooster gives lie to the idea of "birdbrain." Its resourcefulness and viciousness are among the farm's best-kept secrets. The fact is, for all the jungle beasts he chased down on *Wild Kingdom*, Marlin Perkins wouldn't have had much luck snagging a rooster. Of the rooster, Voltaire once wrote, "There is no king comparable to a cock.... If the enemy approaches... he goes to battle himself, ranges his chickens behind him, and fights to the death."[9] With this in mind, I approach gingerly, strategically. I take one step. The rooster takes one step farther. I take two more. He takes three, and so on, until finally I'm chasing him as fast as I can, desperately grasping at a drumstick. Seemingly from out of nowhere, Engel swoops in, grabbing hold of the bird by both legs, swings him upside down, and ferries him back to the coop.

"Bravo!" erupts a cheer from above, where a small, well-heeled crowd has gathered outside the café, apparently both awed and amused by the spectacle. "That was so funny," another voice shrieks from on high. "You must be channeling Buster Keaton."

It's only now that it dawns on me: I am part of the agritainment. I'm a player and the Rockefeller farm is the stage—it's not only the animals but the farmers who are on show here. While Craig Haney's farming forebears were once seen as pillars of their community, these days, to visitors on the farm and in the restaurant, he's a novelty act. This epiphany brings to mind the work of British writer John Berger, who once theorized that public zoos first came into existence when man's relationship with animals was all but extinguished. "Modern zoos are an epitaph to a relationship which was as old as man," he wrote in *Why Look at Animals?*[10] Is the Rockefeller farm a future model for food production? Is it an epitaph for a way of life, a history channel theme park with its own characters and plotlines, marketed to an affluent demographic eager to devour its story? Maybe it's both.

I'm still contemplating the meaning of this social and agricultural experiment when I arrive on the farm the next morning. Carloads of teachers and children and freshly hatched chicks spill out of minivans and school buses. The children have spent the last two weeks raising the chicks as part of a classroom project. This morning, they're going to see where eggs come from. Fanning out across the meadow, they'll squeal in utter joy as they fill one wire basket after another with the morning's eggs.

They are just the first shift in a long day of collection known as the Festival of Eggs. By ten-thirty, the first group will have finished their work and will be nestled in a nearby building, seemingly mesmerized as they listen to a story about life on the farm. A half-hour later, they'll learn how to peel a hard-boiled egg. One little girl will be excused and will vomit on her way to the bathroom.

By late morning, having given all they can, the hens' nests will be empty and Haney will dispatch his crew to restock the shelves—to return many of the eggs to their nests so the next shift of children can collect them again. It's a make-work project, an inconvenience, but Haney doesn't mind. "I just love seeing how excited the kids get about what happens here," he says, folding his arms in front of him and breathing deeply as he scans the horizon, seemingly contemplating the import of his mission. It's the smallest of concessions in what for him is farming without compromise. "What we're doing here may not be the future, but I think it is part of the future. I wouldn't be here if I didn't think I was making a positive contribution." At this moment, it comes to me. If Stone Barns had a slogan, it would be: "Whole Foods Make Whole People."

I bid my good-byes. I'm off to speak to Blue Hill executive chef Dan Barber—an interview that has been granted only after I stalked him at a local event where he'd been moderating a panel on sustainable agriculture. If there's anything I've learned this week, it's that getting an interview with a New York chef— especially if you're a writer from Toronto—will take the same kind of determination that it takes to win a coveted spot at his table.

I step into the kitchen. The air is filled with a crisp bouquet of freshly chopped chives, basil, and rosemary. On the right, an army of prep cooks are already in a blur of perpetual motion.

The clatter of a dozen knives hitting the cutting board punctuates their giddy banter. The bottom half of a pig lies splayed on one counter; a tray of freshly made sausages is piled on another.

I round the corner, entering a room that is gussied up to look like a rustic yet elegant barn, washed in taupe and highlighted in dark wood. I find Barber slouched in a black leather chair, his long, lean legs stretched out in front of him. Dressed in crisp white kitchen linens and wearing a mild smile, Barber looks more smarty-pants grad student than celebrity chef. Maybe it's because he spends so much time thinking about the meaning of food.

It's clear from his first utterance that this will be less dispassionate, Socratic dialogue than fervent sermon. "My belief about pasture-based animal husbandry is pretty intense," he begins, his ink-black eyelashes fluttering like butterflies, landing on each and every syllable. "I'm writing a piece for the *Times* about why I hate vegetarians," he pronounces. "Okay, hate is a strong word." I nod knowingly, but smile inwardly. "I'm really just joking," he interjects, watching me scribble furiously in my notebook. Typically I'm the one with my foot in my mouth. I'm either too mortified or enjoying the moment too much to tell him that Gare, the man I live with and break bread with, doesn't eat meat. And he's not such a bad guy. But before I've had a chance to interrupt, Barber is expounding on the virtues of sustainable agriculture, the evils of monoculture, and the holistic interplay of nature. "To be able to insist that no one should eat meat is to kill meat in ways that we couldn't even imagine. The ecology of the world includes the wild vegetables and the wild animals. . . . You can't tell me that the carrot that

I just pulled from the ground two hours ago isn't as alive as an animal, as alive as we are. . . . I don't mean to get philosophical about it." His voice trails off.

In fact, Barber assures me in the next breath, he's downright practical about these things. Taste will always be paramount in his kitchen, even trumping concerns about how the farm animals are raised, he explains. "Animal welfare is not particularly high on my list," he confesses, "but it's extremely high on Craig [Haney]'s list and it gets higher and higher. As the years have gone by, I think Craig's become very spiritual, very close to the animals. It just seems to me that there's a connection between their happiness and his own happiness. They are totally connected and intertwined. He's making decisions in large part not on flavor but on the welfare of the animals. It just so happens that, luckily for me, the two things are a great marriage." Still, Barber concedes the precious Berkshires raised here—which roam unfettered and are fed the most ancient and natural of all pig diets—aren't the very best pork he serves here at the Blue Hill Restaurant. No, the most flavorful Berkshire pork is shipped here direct from a farmer in Pennsylvania. The Pennsylvania farmer's pigs are also raised on pasture but are fed more grain and live in somewhat more confined conditions—all of which contribute to a richer marbling of the meat. "If the ultimate goal is just animal welfare and animal happiness, then Craig is right," Barber explains. "But if it is all about the flavor and taste—if that's the only consideration—there are so many things to think about. In the spectrum of animal welfare, Craig and the Pennsylvania farmer aren't that far apart. We're talking about heavenly conditions in both cases. I have to admit," he pauses and wrings his bony hands self-consciously before lowering his voice to a whisper, "I am conflicted by these two pigs."

Few diners appear troubled by such quandaries. In fact, Barber tells me, they come here because they can eat in good conscience. "When you're sitting here looking at beautiful pastureland and what you're eating is literally helping to support the preservation of farming, of open space and the welfare of animals—it's something you can feel good about. Having that connection and knowing where your meat comes from gives you a sense of ease.

"For me to be able to cook food that people can appreciate, and then have a story line that's attached to it, is very important. From a chef's perspective, it always makes the food taste better. It's the kind of seasoning that I can't provide."

Certainly, many among the old-money set who flock here tonight look happy just to have scored an opportunity to dine at Barber's restaurant, having waited weeks—if not months—for a table. (Unless, of course, they are among the über-privileged, one of the hundreds of descendants of John D. Rockefeller, whose names the hostess keeps on a secret list at reception, who will be ushered to the front of the line while I fight for a bar stool. There's even a pecking order among the Rockefellers, an A-A list, if you will.)

What makes me different from everyone else crammed into the restaurant foyer tonight is that I've played a small role—call it a comic cameo—in this story line.

I can't get a table but I'm shown to a seat at the bar. I notice Craig Haney has squeezed into a corner on the other side of the bar to say hello to a colleague. Fresh from the pasture and still wearing dusty work clothes, he nods in my direction while he takes in the room. He's admiring his handiwork like a director looking back on the audience at the theater. It's not a job, it's his work, and it doesn't end for him when his chickens and pigs and sheep enter the kitchen.

I've decided that I'm going to break open the piggy bank tonight. I'm willing to shell out not just for a taste of the Rolls-Royce of meats—the Berkshire pork—but also to experience what both Haney and Barber have been talking about in the abstract. The notion that having an understanding of the story behind a meal seasons the meat; that a happy pig tastes better.

Indeed, if there's any justice served with my dinner, this meal will be exquisite. I'm famished by the time my bartender presents me with an elegant plate festooned in the bright hues of the garden season. The freshly picked peas, seasoned lightly in salt and pepper. Delicious. The escarole soup, served in a shot glass, even more divine. And so on down the vegetable food chain. I've saved the pièce de résistance for last: three precious slices of pork roast. A meat dish that's fit for queens and Japanese emperors and one that looks utterly unrecognizable. It's rosy-colored, like a baby's blush—quite unlike the pallid porcine protein that I typically stuff down my gullet. I carve a small piece of meat and deliver it to my tongue. Chewing gently, I eagerly anticipate a wallop of flavor, something to knock me off my stool. Sadly, it never comes. My heart sinks. I glance nervously from side to side before heaving a sigh of relief. Haney's disappeared into the night. An uncomfortable moment avoided. I doubt I could conceal my feelings, to feign enthusiasm when I don't mean it.

For me, one food critic probably summed it up best in his review of Blue Hill: "If it's a full-throttle, free-wheeling feast you're after—a vintage Brian De Palma movie of a meal—you should choose a different show. What Mr. Barber presents is like a hushed foreign film with subtitles. You have to pay attention and heed the nuances, and you can only get so carried away."[11] And while the writer was reviewing the whole show—from appetizer to dessert—his summation perfectly describes the Berkshire pork.

My tongue only knows what it knows. It is simple, uncomplicated. This pig may be rich in color, history, and legend, but its taste is as subtle as fine pearls, as the best linens. There's nothing ostentatious here. Some trumpet the lighter texture of grass-fed meat. They argue its flavors are more complex. Perhaps my palate isn't refined enough to distinguish this complexity. It only knows what it knows. And it certainly can't comprehend the ethics, the care, the farming and culinary skill that went into bringing this pig to my dinner plate. Maybe it's like the time I returned to civilization after several years spent in Canada's far north as a kid. I was so used to drinking powdered milk that I balked when first presented with the real thing. This pig is the real thing. Not man-made—fed a steady diet of hormones, antibiotics, and fattened with grain. My taste buds, in all likelihood, have been corrupted. Perhaps enjoying this genetically superior pig fattened on grass will take some taste acclimatization for the majority of us in North America who equate the taste of a good pork roast and a great steak with the flavor of meat that tastes more of grain than grass.

Ultimately, I do want to believe that the failing is mine, not

Craig Haney's, not Stone Barns', not the fault of Blue Hill Restaurant. Gazing out the window, reflecting on all that I have learned this week on the farm and the respect I have gained for farmers like Craig Haney, I take another bite of pork. I savor it for a moment. I can taste it now—the joy, the bliss. It is most certainly a Happy Meal.

8
• ODE TO THE •
• STEAKHOUSE •

It is conspicuous consumption on more than one count. Three precious commodities with price tags so high they must be burnished in gold, laid out gloriously on the heavy white china in front me: one filet, one rib eye, and a strip loin. Enough steak to feed a family of six and spectacle enough to attract the attention of my fellow patrons. Fearless or reckless, I am a five-feet-four, 115-pound unlikely trencherwoman. Having by the estimation of my partner a modest appetite, I barely make it through the first helping, never mind asking for seconds. When I was growing up, my mother always wanted me to marry a doctor. Sitting here, staring at the plates in front of me, I can't help thinking I am only thirty-five ounces away from a first date with a cardiologist.

It is eight on a Wednesday night, and I'm perched in plain view of passersby at the chef's bar at Pappas Bros. Steakhouse in Houston, Texas. I might as well be sitting on a stage under a spotlight—a new twist on the all-you-can-eat dinner the-ater. Outside, valets ferry Mercedes and BMWs back and forth under a twinkling dome of velvet sky. A private jet is on standby, and there's a helipad in back for those who commute over roof-tops. Inside, the din has already reached a fevered pitch: clink-ing silverware drowned out by the sound of middle-aged men crowded into red leather banquettes and braying at the top of their lungs.

It was once the unofficial cafeteria for Ken Lay and the dis-banded Enron boys' club. Words float through the air like so many readings on the stock ticker. This is where market bulls go to eat like bears. Where the age-old "Mine is bigger than yours" is really just a contest of expense accounts. Where the Hous-ton elite can have their steak and eat it too. It's a combination of old and new money, here to celebrate opulence and excess atop a wine cellar that houses more than $6 million in exclusive vintages. A handful of women adorn the room, decked out in big hair and big teeth and draped over men wearing pink polo shirts and Dockers, C-notes falling from their pockets. This is a male bastion—a '40s-style gentlemen's club reminiscent of the Rat Pack age. And tonight these boys are cutting deals just like they are cutting their steaks.

Knife poised in one hand, fork in another, I'm about to exer-cise my North American birthright. Or, as one freshly starched heckler jeers in passing, perform an unspeakable gluttony.

"Holy cow!" he declares in mock disbelief, inducing snorts of laughter from the pack of carnivores that promenade past my seat.

"Ma'am, please tell me you're not going to eat all that!"

Another looks at me and asks, "Are you an act?"

I suddenly feel like a nun who just walked into a Shriners' meeting. I turn crimson red, or, in point of fact, more like the color of my bloody filet. But somewhere, from a distant corner of the universe, I can hear the late Julia Child cheering me on. "To hell with all you nutritionists!" the towering, gawky maestro of *la cuisine bourgeoise* trills in my ear in her characteristic singsong voice, as she had done to so many other meat-lovers before me. "The only time to eat diet food is while you're waiting for your steak to cook."[1]

My knife glides through my first slab of rib eye like a sleigh on snow. The fat and blood gush beneath a crust lightly seasoned with salt and pepper and reeking of decadence. I hoist a piece on my fork and lift it to my mouth, when I'm disrupted by a second voice. Is it my conscience talking to me? Am I having flashbacks while going through a nostalgic exercise? Or were these steaks marinated in hallucinogenic mescal? No, the voice I'm hearing belongs to Pappas's number-two chef, Rick Aukstikalnis. Over the tumult of clanging plates, whirling waiters, and buzzing cell phones, he's trying to explain why people are lined up at the front door, eyeballing each passing steak like it's a rare ruby. "I like to think of it as controlled rotting. That's why the meat here tastes so good," he explains, donning a freshly starched white coat, looking more like a university chemist than someone who trades in animal cadavers. But then again, procuring and cooking the perfect steak is as much science as art.

I've come a long way to unearth the mysteries of this rarefied flesh. More than 1,600 miles, along a sprawling freeway, past miles of blooming buffalo clover, colonial-style mansions, gleaming glass towers, and through the back doors of Pappas Bros. company's flagship restaurant. A colossal mecca for Texas beef-eaters, rivaling the best steak in the state, if not North America. I figure that the locals must know a thing or two about a good steak and that few would disagree with Fran Lebowitz, who once declared, "My favorite animal is steak." After all, Texas is the cradle of the North American beef industry.

My steak dinner(s) are both the reward and the culmination of an apprenticeship that began here earlier in the week.

Pushing through the heavy doors, the smell of turtle gumbo floats through the empty dining room. It's barely eleven a.m. and the early shift in the Pappas kitchen is in full swing. In one corner the pastry chef is squeezing icing out of a fat tube, whipping together a chocolate confection smothered in a blanket of Godiva chocolate. In another, a butcher is slicing off thin pieces of silver fat from beef with a knife that looks like it's been pilfered from the Knights of the Round Table. His apron is smeared in blood, while the pastry guy is doused in powdered sugar.

Meanwhile, two men are huddled at the chef's bar, their heads bowed over a stack of paper. They are my culinary masters, my bosses this week. First up, there's the head chef, Michael Velardi, who is tall and round and looks like a younger, hipper version of Chef Boyardee, one for the new millennium, one with a GQ makeover, wearing a perfectly styled goatee. His sidekick, Aukstikalnis, the head of controlled rotting, looks a little like a living Modigliani, with a long face, high cheekbones, and crooked mouth. Tall and thin, with a figure any supermodel would envy, he is a veritable billboard for the Atkins lifestyle, given that his diet consists largely of beef with a side of beef and a beef garnish. At least one colossal slab of dry-aged steak—"the company product"—each and every day. Sometimes twice a day. He is like the ice cream executive whose favorite flavor is, inevitably, vanilla.

Depending on whether you think you can have too much of a sublime thing, his steak consumption is either a perk or a hazard of the job. He sees it as his deep commitment to quality control, a willingness to pay the price and accept the privilege. "I'm always getting yelled at," Aukstikalnis says, a flicker of a smirk lurking beneath a look of mock contempt directed squarely at his boss, Velardi. "He's always asking, 'What the hell are you doing?' But hey, it's just part of the job. I'm just checking the product. To see how it's aging. I don't ever get sick of it either."

If Aukstikalnis's culinary predilections skew to the functional, to the proletarian—selflessly, he eats for the common good of Pappas clients—Velardi veers into the realm of aesthetics. And ascetics. "I love the first bite. But just one bite," he says, waving a fleshy digit in the air, as if to underscore the point. "I don't ever sit down to eat a whole steak. I enjoy the first bite more than I would enjoy eating the entire steak."

No doubt the chef's prerogative. But for the few of those among us forced to take out a second mortgage to beef up on Pappas food, it may seem foolhardy. But practicality has never been the vanguard of the artiste. There's no talking logic to this meat aesthete. The chef works with each steak the way Rodin sculpted *The Thinker*. Ask him which cut is his favorite, and you're likely to be met with a steely gaze and a flummoxed silence. "Each has its own characteristics," Velardi says finally, brushing impatiently at a piece of lint on his sleeve. "It's like asking an artist, What color are you going to use? Do you like surrealism or do you like abstract expression? An artist likes art."

And art that can, apparently, only be acquired here at Pappas. "I'm pretty much jaded to other places," confesses Aukstikalnis. He admits to dining at local restaurants—"I order fish when I eat out," he harrumphs. But I can't help wondering whether he's really just doing reconnaissance on the competition while pretending to use the facilities.

The two men are like Laurel and Hardy. The yin and yang of the modern, upscale steakhouse. Some might think of steak as simply a piece of meat, but here it is a collaborative enterprise. Maybe it doesn't require men of such contrasting personalities but certainly distinct and separate expertise. Velardi is the creative maestro. Before arriving at Pappas in 1995, he earned his stripes at the kitchens of Hotel Bel Air and L'Ermitage in Los Angeles. Since taking the lead at Pappas, Velardi has earned a fistful of awards for the restaurant. These days, he spends his time dreaming up new takes on the foodstuffs you'd find in a 1950s issue of *Good Housekeeping.* More Norman Rockwell than Vincent van Gogh. He likes to tinker with the finer points of creamed spinach and scalloped potatoes—the sidekicks to the main attraction.

Aukstikalnis plays with numbers. When he's not trying to bring order to the nightly chaos of the kitchen, he's scanning spreadsheets and punching a calculator. It's his job to keep strict control of more than a million dollars in rotting corpses every year, much like a wine master overseeing a precious vintage.

"This way," Aukstikalnis instructs, clipboard in hand, motioning me into the kitchen, past a plume of steam rising from the dishwasher, cupboards overflowing with giant containers of olives and capers, and into a secret tomb. A place where the royalty of the beef world have come to rest, the USDA-stamped PRIME members of the Limousin, Angus, and Hereford crowd. It is the most exclusive of all beef clubs—maybe even more elite than Mensa—comprising a scant 2 to 3 percent of the bovine population. These bodies will stay here anywhere from thirty-five to seventy days, before being resurrected and transformed from mere flesh into art. It's called dry-aging—the slow and costly process of drying meat in a locker for weeks to enhance its tenderness while concentrating flavor. Among steak snobs, it's the *crème de la boeuf*—the only steak worth grinding between your molars.

Aukstikalnis likens dry-aging to making Kool-Aid. "The less water you have in there, the more intense a flavor you're going to have," he says, explaining that beef typically has a water content of 65 percent and that the goal of dry-aging is to squeeze out another 5 percent in the process.

Dry-aging isn't new. From as far back as the Middle Ages, people have been dry-aging beef to increase its flavor and tenderness. But it wasn't until the mid-1930s that some of the greatest scientific minds of the past century turned their attention to this grand humanitarian effort: creating the perfect steak. It was as if the New Deal needed the complement of a Perfect Meal.

It was C. L. Arnold, director of the grocery empire Kroger Food Foundation, who first approached the Mellon Institute of Pittsburgh to bring the authority of science to steak. Working over months, the Mellon chemists identified twenty-five enzymes essential in the tenderizing process. They found that in the hours directly following slaughter, these natural enzymes begin to break down protein strands in the muscle fiber—a process that not only makes it easier to chew but intensifies its flavor by changing protein into amino acids. It concentrates the flavor, some would argue, making it more "gamey."[2]

Forty years ago, most beef was dry-aged—not only at top steakhouses but at most restaurants in North America. The early '60s heralded a new era, ushering in the "cryovac" bag, and beef purveyors across North America hopped on board. The advantage of the new cryovac technique, invented in the 1930s, was that restaurants could "wet-age" beef in a bag and not lose any of its weight. Ever mindful of the bottom line, even the better steakhouses moved to wet-aged beef. The consumer forgot what the real taste of steak was.

But when the steakhouse returned in the boom-boom days of the greedy '80s, steakhouses looked to the past for inspiration. Slowly, one steakhouse after another began to offer dry-aged beef to lure consumers. Today, dry-aging is the gold standard and the only one practiced by top steakhouses—a process that usually takes anywhere from ten days to several weeks.

Meanwhile, stepping into this steel room, this repository of dismemberment, I'm assaulted by hiss and haze. The chill commands the hairs on my arms to attention. But what is most striking, even astonishing, is that despite sharing the room with five thousand pounds of rotting bodies, I can't detect any smell, any odor whatsoever. Not a thing. In an accountant's office you might be able to smell red ink. Bubble boys live in less sterile environments than this.

One tray at a time, Aukstikalnis unfurls their cotton coverings to reveal one glorious slab of beef after another, resting on large silver trays, stacked from the floor to the rafters in every direction. They are in various stages of rot, some pink, some the color of port, some tinged in robin's-egg blue along the edges, a kind of decay that is inedible and one that eventually will be sawed off. Aukstikalnis scribbles furiously on the clipboard. He is at once mortician, performing the postmortem, inspecting every strand of flesh, and actuary, determining which of the dead meat will not live again.

"How cold is it in here?" I ask after a few minutes, my teeth now clattering like cups on saucers. Aukstikalnis freezes in his tracks. "Ah, well," he says finally, his pale blue eyes flitting nervously. "Look at this," he continues with a forced smile, flouting my question. Ditto when I ask him about humidity. Although, quite frankly, I figure it must be pretty moist in here, given that my already too-big hair is working its way into a bouffant not seen since the secretarial pool closed shop. "We've worked a long time to perfect our dry-aging process," Aukstikalnis sniffs finally, looking a little chuffed. "You don't really expect me to reveal all of my secrets to a journalist, do you?" he asks, before shooing me out of the locker.

I want to tell him I've been thrown out of better places. But the truth is, one hundred years ago, I probably wouldn't have dared venture here—I wouldn't have been allowed in here—within such close proximity to the Pappas family jewels. You see, steak-eating has, throughout much of human history, been largely the preserve of men.

It's difficult to know exactly when women were admitted into this exclusive club of "beefsteak"-eaters (as it was called in the vernacular of the eighteenth to early-twentieth centuries). But one of the earliest agitators calling for her fair stake in the beef bounty was Emeline J. Clements. Emeline filed for divorce from her husband, Abraham V. Clements, a New York physician, on the grounds of cruel and inhumane treatment in 1861. "Action for Divorce," read the headline in *The New York Times*, "No Happiness Without Beefsteak." The newspaper story proceeded to enumerate a litany of marital woes: "The plaintiff now alleges that since her marriage with her husband she has been the victim of much abuse from the one who should be her protector. That the ordinary comforts of life have been denied her; that she has suffered from the want of food; the defendant limiting the amount of beefsteak for the breakfast table, from which four persons were accustomed to eat one pound, and upon one occasion, when she overstepped this limit by purchasing from the butcher one pound and a half of beefsteak, he grossly abused and ill treated her."[3]

Likewise, women were similarly rebuffed in the public arena. Beefsteak wasn't just food. It was an event. A place where men gathered, unfettered by the niceties of polite society like knives and forks and genteel manners. Beer in one hand, steak in the other, they'd gather around barrels, belching and jabbering into the wee hours of the morning while waiters slipped up and down sawdust floors ferrying trays of beef.

It was a cultural event that borrowed heavily from the earlier "beefsteak societies" in Britain. While it was the preserve of the British elite in England, it was a decidedly middle-class diversion of the North American male—and one confined largely to New York City. Not only did refrigerated railway cars make mass consumption of beef possible, but New Yorkers also had the money to fund their appetite for beefsteak.

New Yorker writer Joseph Mitchell usually focused on the Fulton Fish Market and seafood but occasionally turned his eye and palate to the particular culture of beefsteak. "The New York steak dinner, or beefsteak, is a form of gluttony as stylized and regional as the riverbank fish fry, the hot-rock clambake, or the Texas barbecue,"[4] Mitchell wrote.

Meanwhile, beefsteak also was quickly becoming the staple of the burgeoning restaurant scene in New York. Early restaurants like the Old Homestead (1868), Keens Steakhouse (1885), Brooklyn's Gage & Tollner (1879), and Peter Luger (1887)[5] promoted the beefsteak as their main attraction. (That most of these establishments endure is a testament to the staying power of steak, especially in contrast to long-gone seafood establishments that Joseph Mitchell wrote about.)

But it would take Prohibition to ultimately democratize and neuter the beefsteak. Not only did speakeasies like the Palm (1926) and Gallagher's (1927—although the restaurant brazenly claims it is America's first steakhouse[6]) infamously served up beer and bathtub gin to flappers and mobsters, it served beefsteak too. Not that beefsteak was illegal, only that it tasted so good it seemed illegal.

Mitchell, a Carolina-born, old-fashioned gentleman who never knew a tradition he could not embrace, mourned what was lost in his much-celebrated lament for the beefsteak: "It didn't take women long to corrupt the beefsteak," Mitchell charged. "They forced the addition of such things as Manhattan cocktails, fruit cups, and fancy salads to the traditional menu of slices of ripened steaks, double lamb chops, kidneys, and beer by the pitcher. They insisted on dance orchestras instead of brassy German bands. The life of the party at a beefsteak used to be the man who let out the most ecstatic grunts, drank the most beer, ate the most steak, and got the most grease on his ears, but women do not esteem a glutton, and at a contemporary beef-steak it is unusual for a man to do away with more than three pounds of meat and twenty-five glasses of beer.... When beef-steaks became bisexual, the etiquette changed. For generations men had worn their second-best suits because of the inevita-bility of grease spots; tuxedos and women appeared simulta-neously. Most beefsteaks degenerated into polite banquets at which open-face sandwiches of grilled steak happened to be the principal dish."[7]

Polite banquets? I can't imagine what Mitchell might con-sider impolite—he was so civilized he seems to have worn a tie to bed—but I've yet to witness a bare-chested man ripping through a rib eye like a crazed jackal. And I can't help but notice that despite the luxe banquettes, velvet curtains, and a wine list that includes a $30,000 bottle of Château d'Yquem, there is a whiff of the primitive in the modern steakhouse. Perhaps it was a top Morton's executive who said it best: "When the caveman beat something over the head and dragged it back for dinner, it sure wasn't sushi."[8]

I put the question of its enduring appeal to some of the fin-est minds who make their living pondering the meaning of the steakhouse (among other things). "I think the steakhouse satis-fies a social hunger more than a real hunger," explains Harvard anthropologist James L. Watson. "It's about power and control. It's a political arena where young and middle-aged men come together to celebrate machismo. It's a declaration that I can eat whatever I want and I'm not going to get sick."

If he's right, Frank Pastore may well qualify to be the most powerful man on the planet. The one-time pitcher for the Cincinnati Reds turned radio preacher maintains his twenty-year-old record for gluttony. It was 1987, and on his way to spring training in Florida, Pastore stopped at the legendary Big Texan Steak House in Amarillo. Nine and a half minutes later he had hit the jackpot: a free dinner as prize for consuming six pounds of beef in record time. How did he do it? "It's all in the wrist," he quips. "Now, when I see those twelve-ounce steaks, I think they should be eaten on crackers."

While no one has yet beaten his record time, 42,000 have tried; some 8,000 have succeeded in finishing the seventy-two-ounce steak, including a sixty-nine-year-old granny and an eleven-year-old boy.[9]

Meanwhile, it's still too early in the evening to gauge what sort of social contest, what forms of gluttony and machismo will unfold here in the temple of tenderloin tonight. It's late afternoon, the calm before the storm, and I find a seat at the kitchen bar as I await my next tutorial. Glancing over my shoulder, I catch a glimpse of Velardi pacing distractedly back and forth across the dining room, cell phone in hand. "I *said* I want him to have *diet* shakes," he screeches into the phone before spying me out of the corner of his eye. He glowers in my direction, and lowers his voice.

As I shift nervously on my stool, I'm reminded of my mission. With my science lectures now behind me, I am here this evening for a lesson in the art and theater of the steakhouse. And what better way to kick-start my tutorial than with a soupçon of melodrama.

Like any great artist, Velardi will spend his evening creating. He has handed me off to his minions for my lessons in the art of the grill. But not before first telling me to study up on the menu. Tonight's special is filet Oscar, a surf-and-turf number with a ten-ounce filet topped with a medallion of broiled lobster tail meat and béarnaise sauce. That's in addition to the everyday fare: peppercorn steak, veal chops, and sides and starters like bacon-wrapped scallops, onion rings, and baked potatoes. Maybe it's Tony Bennett crooning in my ear, but I can't help thinking that had I been sitting here a half-century ago, I would be perusing the same menu. And maybe that's what the modern steakhouse is selling. If you believe in it, tradition. If you are skeptical, nostalgia. If you are hostile, schmaltz.

At precisely five p.m., a half-dozen line cooks parade past my seat, peacocking and preening on the way to their workstations. I'm suddenly overwhelmed by a flood of my own memories. A chill runs down my back. Could it be a haunting from Freddie, the petulant rogue chef-genius who drank himself to an early grave while terrorizing the waitstaff at the Toronto restaurant that helped fund my education? Or a gust from his phantom kitchen knife whooshing past my head?

No, I finally surmise, the chill I'm feeling is coming from these grillhouse veterans. There's Sal, George, and Ricardo, all decked out in the uniform of the line: baggy checkered pants, stiff white jackets, black baseball caps, and derisive sneers. These guys have earned their stripes with some forty years' grilling between them—and they demand their props, even from a hapless grilling rookie like me.

"Hi, I'm Susan," I say, extending my hand toward Sal, the

head grill guy. He reciprocates with a grouchy look, twirling a set of tongs in his right hand that reveals the telltale signs of his trade: welts on top of scar tissue. Fading blisters.

"You ever done this before?" he asks finally, with a sideways glance.

"Oh, sure," I trill, trying to muster some of Emeril's BAM-bastic confidence to disguise my panic. "I barbecue ALL the time."

Sal's lips curl ever so slightly. A smirk that spreads like a contagion down the line. "Okay," he barks, motioning me into a corner of his workstation. "I'll let you watch. I'll try to show you some of what you need to know," he says before leaning in close with a half-crazed stare and whispering, "Just don't get in the way."

The first ticket, the first dinner order of the evening, soon spits out of a machine to the right: one rare filet, one medium-rare rib eye. José, the butcher, reaches into the reserve he has prepared for the evening, fetching two plump and hefty steaks. I brace myself against the blast of the grill, as Sal plops the rib eye at the back of the grill first. Two minutes later, he throws the filet on.

Meanwhile, a gaggle of slinky hostesses dressed in all black and high heels totter back and forth across the restaurant. A party of six in tow. Party of four. A deuce. Soon the restaurant is squeezed nearly to capacity, sounding like the clattering of a thousand sterling-silver steak knives. Waiters in white butcher aprons and black bow ties are magically balancing colossal-sized trays heaped in beef overhead. Busboys ferrying baskets of dinner rolls are running in every direction. A small crowd is gathered in front of a meat display, chewing over which steak has just the right amount of marbling, the perfect distribution of fat for their dinner tonight.

Sal is in full flight. His tongs poking here and there, he moves each steak in and around his grill as though he's playing an elaborate game of checkers. One that he alone understands.

Meanwhile, Aukstikalnis is working the other side of the grill line to smooth the bumps of production. He shouts a litany of nonsensical commands. "Sell it!"

Someone else yells, "Move it!" and I jump to the right, catching my heel in the plastic mat on the floor. I tumble to the ground, threatening to take Sal with me.

"Would someone please get her out of the way?!" Sal shouts.

Aukstikalnis appears out of nowhere and grabs my elbow. "I hope you haven't eaten much," he tells me, leading me to a bar in front of the grill, where I have a bird's-eye view of the kitchen drama. Where I will soon be part of the floor show.

My waitress is lovely and knowledgeable. Even Joe Mitchell might approve. She dispatches the sommelier, who suggests a $150 number, extolling the cherry and red berry flavors that will make it the ideal accompaniment to my meal.

Rick smiles proudly as he watches me tuck into a transcendent twosome of crabcakes. I'm still scooping up crumbs with my forefinger—so much for the "polite banquet"—when my waitress arrives with three beautifully charred meat masterpieces. Sitting in front of this heap of meat, I feel like a she-wolf, although admittedly there's enough food here for a pack of wolves.

I pick up my knife in one hand, a fork in the other. The couple seated next to me at the bar go slack-jawed, their whispers drowned out by the melee at the grill. I glare in their direction, narrowing my eyes into slits before baring my fangs. Sphincters clenching, they suddenly turn away, sucking in their heads like a couple of sea turtles. Completely spooked. But not me: I feel emboldened. Ready to tap into my inner glutton. I decide to go primitive, summoning the leftover reptilian part of my brain that anthropologists say rules the desire for excess.

I can feel my nostrils flare, my adrenaline pulsing. I exhale through pursed lips, pondering the vexing decision of my week: Will it be the strip loin first? The filet? The rib eye? I fawn over these exotic beasts, hemming and hawing until I finally settle on the ladies' choice: a filet, which is as high as a featherbed. I saw into it and hoist a slice to my mouth. It's nutty and smooth. No aftertaste. Next up? The rib eye—the steak of the wrangler, the rustler, and the cowboy. Its deep beef flavor is even more intense and far chewier. Even more delicious than the filet. And finally, the strip loin—the choice of steak snobs everywhere. What can I say? Pappas knows best. I am much plated, fully sated.

In the spirit of my assignment, I figure I'd better taste again. And again. And again. A full forty-five minutes later, my steaks are no more. They say you are what you eat. More pointed, in the spirit of our material culture, you are what you consume. It's not just a matter of gastronutrition. I may look like a beached whale, but I am rich, wealthy beyond my means. Certainly more so than those sad-sack fellows in the banquette at the back of the room, who have polished off their twelve-ounce rib eyes, who chided me on the way to their dinner. That's not me in the day-to-day, just a one-time turn. I've had more steak bling than anybody else in the room, but socioeconomically I might have more in common with the people who manicure their lawns and wash their cars. Do I feel guilty? Do I feel like a trespasser? Not for a second. Do I have a steak-driven case of class envy? Perhaps.

Tumbling off my stool, carrying nearly three pounds of steak with me, I leave a beefed-up but wiser version of myself. As William Blake aptly once noted: "The road of excess leads to the palace of wisdom." So here it is, here's what I've learned: What Blake said of men is no less true of steaks, that they are *alike (tho' infinitely various)*. If Blake had finished his artistic rendering of Dante's *Inferno*, I doubt that it would look anything like Pappas's. (One can only imagine Ken Lay flagging a waiter at the *Inferno*'s Sizzler.) But something like this steakhouse might have come to Blake in one of his visions—as close to heaven as he'd ever get on earth.

9
· PRIMAL SCREAM ·

"The Sexy Chicken is my favorite," declares a paunchy man with pale blue eyes that gleam like marbles under the warm glow of the kitchen lights where a group of forty has gathered this evening for dinner. "Do you know why I call it that?" Aajonus Vonderplanitz asks rhetorically while scanning the room before locking his gaze upon a busty Cameron Diaz look-alike. "I call it Sexy Chicken," he continues, "because it makes you really, really horny."

An older couple holding hands on my right exchange a come-hither look. Clearly, at $4 a pound, it's a low-cost alternative to Viagra, although it's unlikely that Sexy Chicken would ever get the Food and Drug Administration's safety stamp of approval.

"Is the recipe in your new cookbook?" queries a dishy young man with glossy dark locks, perfect teeth, and a chin that looks to have been chiseled straight out of the Colorado Rockies beneath our feet. The crowd erupts with laughter. Apparently, I'm in good company. Pretty boy's a rookie too. "It's not a cookbook," Vonderplanitz grunts derisively. "On the Primal Diet, we don't cook anything."

It's more than simply a matter of semantics. Those who follow the Primal Diet don't order in, pick it up from the caterers, or have others prep the meal for them. The cuts of meat here are not prepared in any traditional sense. They've never seen the inside of an oven, or touched a grill. Their temperature is determined by nothing more than the setting on the thermostat—room temperature, that is.

This is a raw meat potluck. The ultimate in fast food. And those gathered here in one of North America's most exclusive playgrounds have come to dine on dishes like Sexy Chicken, orange-glazed duck, meat au gratin, and steak tartare. But this is more than a meeting of raw meat gourmets, a sharing of epicurean secrets. Those milling around the buffet table tonight are deadly serious about their diet. A diet that's similar to the one that *Homo erectus* consumed when he first roamed the savannah more than 10,000 years ago. A typical day's feast? Several raw eggs, a pound of raw meat, and a couple of green salad shakes. In fact, many gnawing on raw animal flesh behind the cover of silk drapes in this swank Aspen mansion are former vegetarians. They've come from as far away as Connecticut and Arizona to find a cure for everything from cellulite, acne, and depression to multiple sclerosis and cancer. But first, they're going to learn how eating like a cave dweller will have them swinging from the trees.

"When I was a fruitarian, ejaculatory orgasm was pleasurable but exhausting," Vonderplanitz explains with the same matter-of-fact tone he will employ in a detailed discussion of bowel movements following dinner. "I got depressed and irritable if I had regular ejaculations." I suddenly have an urge to invoke the "table talk" rule, but I can't get my jaw off the ground fast enough to hijack the conversation and head Vonderplanitz off his unusual prescription for the boudoir blues. "Now that I consume so much raw protein and fat," he continues, "I enjoy sex from one to six hours daily and have up to three ejaculations. I finally feel like I have achieved heaven on earth."

To the some 20,000 North Americans reportedly following his Primal Diet, Vonderplanitz is a messiah for the new millennium. A charismatic leader with an evangelical jag. His prodigious claims are a strange brew of New Age meets Stone Age. Think caveman with the chimes and crystals and you get the picture.

He says he played a construction worker on the soap opera *General Hospital* before finding his calling as a nutritional palm reader, iridologist, and "scientist." This evening, the sixty-year-old Vonderplanitz (who's also been known as John Richard Swigart, John Planitz, Richard Garritt, and Brock Bison) is dressed as Everyman. Light-colored khakis, a long-sleeved gray T-shirt, and hiking boots. His hair is the color of gingerbread and the texture of a chia plant in full bloom. It frames a face scorched by one too many noonday sessions at the pool. The fact is, with his looks, he's perfect to play a desert-island castaway. But look deep into his crystalline eyes, he explains, and you'll see evidence of a heart, lungs, and organs operating like those of a man twenty years younger. The healing miracle of a rejuvenating diet composed of more than 90 percent raw meat and fat. Food laced with microbes like *E. coli* and salmonella—the "janitors," the "cleanup crew" he claims has helped cure him of a litany of health woes, including diabetes, autism, and bone and blood cancer. A diet fit for the gods and goddesses who walk among us—among them a string of Hollywood celebrities, one reportedly being Mel Gibson, who has, on more than one occasion, extolled the virtues of eating like a tiger.

Tonight's potluck is hosted by Kim, a slinky, early-forties woman dressed in all black with a cascade of dark hair sweeping midway down her back. She slopes her way around the room, from guest to guest, making introductions while her pet rabbit, Vanilla, hops underfoot. The local fixer, she's a former pharmaceutical saleswoman and a self-taught nutritionist who hopes to spread the word about the pure primal pleasure of dining on uncooked meat. It's an eclectic crowd. There's Mary, Pat, Robert, Lisa, Fabio, and a Cher among us—seemingly drawn from all age groups and social strata. From high-tech moguls to sweat-lodge owners to hippy-dippy snowboarders.

The introductions out of the way, the group forms a line in front of the buffet table. "Chicken ceviche!" someone squeals. I can't tell if it's a shriek of delight or horror, because for staunch meat-eaters like me, the only thing crazier than no meat is a serving of raw meat on the dinner plate. As the odd woman out, I suddenly feel prudish, fanatical, kooky. This, I think to myself, is how it must feel to my tofu-lovin' boyfriend. The spoilsport of the banquet who secretly irks every carnivorous host who feels compelled to add a veggie dish to their carefully planned meat menus. One more look at the buffet table piled with caveman nibbles and meat slushies and I feel weak at the knees. I reach for my cell phone, desperately searching the speed dial for Boston Pizza's delivery number, only to find it's accidentally been deleted. Desperate for a way out, I consider pleading that I am a breathetarian who lives a wholly aerobic existence. No claim, I figure, would be too outrageous, given the company I'm keeping here.

It seems an ideal backdrop for a celebratory meatfest. Located in the clouds—some 8,000 feet up in the Rocky Mountains—Aspen was once the summer hunting grounds of the Ute tribe. And although these days you're more likely to be shooting elk through your camera lens than with a gun, demand is booming in the town's chichi restaurants for factory-free, low-fat meats like elk, bison, and venison. And consider this fashion fact: Aspen may well be the only place in North America where a full-length fur coat is still a vogue manly thing.

But it's more than that. Maybe it started with the prospectors who flocked to the town in the full swing of the silver rush in the 1870s. Or in the 1940s with Walter Paepcke, a wealthy industrialist who wanted to create the "Aspen Idea." He hoped to transform Aspen from a mining town into a cultural utopia, a place where great thinkers would travel to renew their spirits and exchange ideas.[1] Whatever Paepcke had in mind, it probably wasn't what Hunter S. Thompson envisioned when he ran for local sheriff on the "freak power" ticket. By the time the granddaddy of gonzo journalism narrowly lost his bid for power in the mid-'70s, Aspen was already a well-established haven for misfits and oddballs. A countercultural sanctuary, where a renegade like Thompson drank away his

days and nights, living on a liquid diet of Nyquil and Wild Turkey.[2] In other words, a place that would be welcoming to any
group such as this—one whose collective mantra is "Eat shit
and live."

It is with this in mind that I find myself at the end of the
buffet line with an empty plate in hand. Some guests, like
Aaron, have gone primitive and opted out of cutlery and china
altogether. He's cutting a New York steak with scissors and
eating directly from the supermarket styrofoam. "It's like
sushi," the effervescent acupuncturist and the town's longest
Primal Diet devotee explains. "You've got to cut against the
grain. It's the same trick," he says, plopping a cube of meat
in his mouth. "When you start to eat all raw you go, 'Wow.
Wow!' It's from the higher vibration of the food. You get feeling better and clearer in your mind and eventually you have
no fear about bacteria. You finally realize you don't have to rely
on outside entities for your health care. You can take care of
yourself."

It's a recurring theme this evening. Just as the hippies of the
early '60s sought to wrest corporate control of the food supply,
those who've come here tonight view the Primal Diet as a kind
of personal vindication. Triumph over a conspiracy perpetrated
by the establishment: big government, Big Pharma, HMOs, and
Fortune 500 companies. These raw-meat rebels are driven by
the most American of impulses: the rejection of authority from
on high. They are living the American dream—albeit one on
the cultural fringes—in a world where much of what we eat is
handed to us through a window by a kid dressed in a polyester
costume, who asks, "Do you want fries with that?" oblivious of

the nutritional and environmental devastation caused by his company's nuggets and burgers.

Robert was once one of those kids. These days, he'd never eat at McDonald's, never eat meat from a factory farm. But he admits he's made some strange bedfellows of late. The gun-toting, red-plaid crowd, for example, who are going to teach him how to stalk, kill, and dress his own animals. "I never thought I'd take up hunting," explains the hip thirtysomething, similar in mien to Elvis Costello, wearing thick black glasses and a velvet dinner jacket—which is to say, a long way from the hunting lodge. "I like the idea of being completely self-sufficient. And eating food that's free of poisons."

Scanning tonight's spread, I want to tell him that the poison thing is debatable. But I bite my tongue, hoping he'll offer a recommendation on dinner. "I couldn't do the raw chicken," he explains. "I'll never go there. So I opted for the raw elk liver instead." "And?" I ask. "Was it good?" Judging from the flicker of disgust that flashes across his face, I rightly figure it's not a rave. "It crunched like a carrot," he explains, "had the feel of an oyster and tasted like liver. It was truly frightening."

I feel an eating disorder coming on. It's not just the thought of eating mystery meats. I'm panicked by the idea of eating foodstuffs I've been taught to avoid for dear life. Raw meat laced with potential pathogens like *E. coli* 0157:H7, salmonella, campylobacter, and listeria. It seems every day there's another recall of meat tainted with *E. coli*. One day it is 40,000 pounds of beef shipped to Wal-Mart stores in twelve states; the next day it is a recall of 5.7 million pounds shipped across the west from another beef purveyor in California. In the United States, an estimated 73,000 Americans are sickened and another 61 die each year after eating food contaminated with *E. coli*, according to the Centers for Disease Control and Prevention. The bacteria is most commonly found in raw and undercooked meat as well as bean sprouts, spinach, and unpasteurized ciders and juices. Meanwhile, salmonella packs an even more lethal punch, killing about 700 people in the United States every year. In late 2006, *Consumer Reports* tested more than five hundred assorted chickens and found that 15 percent of all chickens were infected with salmonella and more than half were infected with the bacteria campylobacter.[3] However, salmonella is found not only on raw and undercooked meats and poultry but also on shrimp, eggs and dairy, fresh produce, chocolate, and unpasteurized orange juice. While the CDC reports about 40,000 poisonings from salmonella each year, it estimates the actual number is likely thirty times higher.

So it's little wonder that health authorities go apoplectic when they hear stories of consumers willingly chowing down on raw meat. "It's absolutely crazy," explains Toronto nutritionist Fran Berkoff. "You can get really, really sick. Or worse. There might have been a time in our history when we didn't have to cook meat like we do now, but these days, it's a real safety issue. People will say, 'Show me a chicken that's got salmonella.' But all you need is one to make you really ill. Besides, it's incredibly gross."

Recently, there's been a dramatic rise in consumer demand for raw dairy products teeming with the same kind of bacteria found in raw meat in both Canada and the United States. Black markets are booming. Police are cracking down on illegal producers in states and provinces where it's illegal to sell raw dairy products. In late 2006, one of Canada's most feted chefs rallied to the cause of a local farmer shut down for selling raw dairy products to hundreds of Toronto families. Chef Jamie Kennedy lined up alongside dozens of customers who waved placards like hardened protestors to oppose the police confiscation of bottled raw milk and blocks of unpasteurized cheese. Kennedy argued alongside like-minded consumers that raw dairy contains natural enzymes, antibodies, and vitamins that are destroyed in the heating process of pasteurization.[4] Despite the consumer surge, federal health authorities aren't swayed. They warn of lurking pathogens, pointing to the outbreak of illnesses in recent years.

Meanwhile, Aaron, the glowing acupuncturist, assures me there's nothing to worry about. The meat being served here at the raw meat potluck tonight is organic—the good stuff—and it's not going to make me sick, he says. Armed with the CDC stats, I figure I have less chance of dying from *E. coli* than from salmonella. So I set my sights on a scrap of carpaccio, gussied up with bocconcini, tomato, and basil—the equivalent of Primal Diet pabulum, specially made for novices like me. I try to mobilize my inner warhorse, contemplating the words of my favorite bad-boy food scribe, Anthony Bourdain, who explained in his blockbuster book *Kitchen Confidential,* "Good eating is all about risk. Whether we're talking about unpasteurized Stilton, raw oysters or working for organized crime 'associates,' food for me has always been an adventure." I cross myself, raise my meat square to my mouth, when I'm suddenly saved by divine intervention. Vonderplanitz calls an end to dinner and the beginning of the evening's discussion.

We gather in the living room, squeezed side by side on leather couches and oversized ottomans. Vonderplanitz claims a seat at the front of the room, perched like a lion overlooking a den of cubs.

"Dr. Aajonus," a whippet-thin woman with a pinched face begins, "do I really need to put on ten pounds to heal?" Here in the land of the scrawny haunches, it seems that asking Kate Moss wannabes to eat shit is one thing. But ask them to swap their size zero for a size six? It's tantamount to lunacy: like asking them to break the final taboo in a taboo-devouring culture. As with any diet, success requires self-denial. Here, it seems, you can keep your BMW but not your runway-model looks.

Vonderplanitz calls it like he sees it. "Women like you wouldn't have been given much of a second look in earlier times," he explains. I scour the room, observing this super-class of cadavers shift nervously in their seats while the woman who posed the question visibly deflates, like a balloon releasing its last gasp. In a vernacular that runs from the pseudo-technical to the sophomoric, Vonderplanitz continues, explaining that the cycle of weight gain and loss helps rid the body of toxins typically stored in fat. In the past, he explains, we had an intuitive understanding of the link between health and fat. "A heavyset, Rubenesque woman was probably considered the best asset that a man could have when they were considering women as assets. A man would look at a skinny woman and say, 'Oh, poor thing.' She couldn't get married off. No one would take her."

He confesses a penchant for beefy women. No skin-and-bones types for him. In fact, it was modeling icon Twiggy herself who turned him off skinny women forever. "In 1972," he explains, trumping up his minor, long-ago celebrity, "at the request of my publicity agent, I took Twiggy to the *Butterflies Are Free* premiere at the Westwood. Everybody was so intimidated by this young girl. But she was a hyperactive basket case. I mean she was an emotional roller coaster. I couldn't handle it. I never called her again."

The moral of the story? "Fat, mellow, and happy. That's a better way to live," he says.

A shy, middle-aged woman, neatly dressed in a twin set and freshly pressed khakis, falters in a childlike voice as she begins to recount her own story—of what brought her to the Primal Diet in the first place. A few years ago, both she and her husband were diagnosed with Lyme disease. For two years, the couple meticulously followed doctor's orders, gobbling down one dose of high antibiotics after another. But when traditional medicine didn't work, they started looking for alternative ways of healing, eventually stumbling upon the Primal Diet. They've been following it for months. The only problem? "Well, I don't know how to say this," she utters, sotto voce. "It's the parasites. I have parasites and I'm having trouble getting rid of them."

You'd think it might be a conversation killer. In days past, guests would head for the drawing room after dinner for a discussion of world politics and literature. But here, at a raw meat potluck, nothing seems to get an after-dinner conversation rocking like a discussion of parasites. Everyone's got war stories. Naturally, no one can top the guru's. "I was in Vietnam when I shat out a forty-five-foot tapeworm," Vonderplanitz explains, waving his hands excitedly, his students nodding knowingly. "I know how long it was because I chased it across the room and measured it. Then, for some reason, I had a craving for onions. I ate two of them and immediately felt better."

Orange alert. My head is spinning. Maybe I'm suffering from low blood sugar from my no-cal dinner. Truthfully, I couldn't feel worse right now if it were me passing a forty-five-foot tapeworm. I'm grateful when I realize that talk has shifted from the practical aspects of housing intestinal freeloaders to the theoretical—although some might say heretical: to the "science" behind the doctor's Primal Diet. (Although he doesn't discourage his "patients" from addressing him as doctor, he tells me he prefers to be referred to as a scientist and that he has a Ph.D. in nutrition.) "Modern medicine's fear of pathogens is based on speculation, fear, and junk science," Vonderplanitz explains. "The idea that microbes are always harmful and must be eradicated is based on ignorance. Health department officials are living in the cerebral dark ages.

"I say, crack some eggs. Let them get rotten. Eat your raw meat with your salmonella, eat your *E. coli*," he shouts now, pumping his fists in the air for emphasis. "They are your body's janitors. They go in there and eat up the damaged tissues. They eat your cancers." Although extreme cases sometimes call for more extreme measures, he explains. Sometimes terminal cancer patients may find a speedier recovery dining on "high meat"—animal flesh that has been aged for a few months in the fridge—completely decomposed and swimming in worms and bacteria. Or by dining directly on the feces of a healthy herbivore—a gopher, a sheep, or a goat, for example.

Who am I—a liberal arts major—to argue with science?

To question such astonishing success? Or at least his claims of success. More than 90 percent of cancer victims following the Primal Diet, Vonderplanitz tells us, are now in remission. Unfortunately, he has no scientific backup; no researchers have followed his lead. When pushed on it, he has all the answers, counters all doubt. Keeping records, he explains, might be construed as a medical act and land him in deep trouble with the authorities.

I feel compelled to speak up—to rally on behalf of humanity. "Shouldn't we let the world know you have the cure for cancer?" I implore him. "Shouldn't we be trying to get scientists on our side—studies underway that will give the world the evidence that they need?"

I suddenly feel eighty eyeballs upon me, as penetrating as diamond drill bits. A counterculture cresting behind me.

"What you don't understand," an older woman barks at me from the couch, "is that nothing in our system of capitalism and democracy is going to allow that. The pharmaceutical industry doesn't want people to find out about something as simple as this."

"The only way someone is going to find out about this is if they are lucky and have enough gumption to follow through with it…"

"Most people want to be told what to do—they want to be in a health crisis all the time…"

"The pharmaceutical industry would find some way to discredit the Primal Diet…"

"You're part of the problem. You're part of the media. The media's in cahoots with the pharmaceutical companies…"

I dodge invectives like bullets, until Vonderplanitz raises his hand in a bid to speak.

"There's no money to finance a study. Since 20 percent of our GDP is generated by the pharmaceutical industry, our economy would collapse. We'd be in a depression. That's everything you need to know," he tells me.

It's the same argument with which Vonderplanitz found an audience first in his 1997 book *We Want to Live: The Primal Diet* and later in *The Recipe for Living Without Disease,* published in 2002. I leaf through a well-thumbed copy of *We Want to Live.* Admittedly, it's the first book I've ever read that comes with a warning absolving the author and publisher of any liability due to injury or damage caused by its contents.

Reading on, I find the only thing harder to swallow than a pound of raw flesh is Vonderplanitz's explanation as to how he stumbled upon the Primal Diet. A story told with such utter simplicity, you might expect to find it in a kid's library, sandwiched somewhere between *The Three Little Pigs* and *Lord of the Flies.* A story that began more than thirty years ago. A story that begins like this: Weak and sick, and poisoned by the "cures" of modern medicine, Vonderplanitz went to an old Indian burial site to fast himself to death. One night, he was awakened by a coyote, motioning him to follow his lead, and Vonderplanitz trailed the animal to a clearing. There he met a pack of coyotes who offered him a freshly killed jackrabbit. "All eleven of them stood, staring at me. I kept getting this thought: 'It's what you need, take and eat it.' They seemed to be sending me that thought. . . . I looked at the coyotes and said, 'I don't know, guys, I haven't eaten meat in six years.'" But Vonderplanitz did eat it, reluctantly at first, and then voraciously once he came to the realization that the pathogens in the raw meat might kill him quicker than his fast. The next morning, to his astonishment, he woke up completely revitalized. He quickly expanded his diet, feeding on rattlesnakes and birds and raw goat milk. His health improving daily from eating raw meats and fats, Vonderplanitz eventually returned to Los Angeles to spread the word.[5]

About the same time, a group of scientists halfway across the country were about to set the diet industry on its head, advocating another version of caveman cuisine. Writing in the stodgy *American Journal of Medicine* in 1988, three Atlanta academics from Emory University looked back—way back, to the way we were before the advent of agriculture—for clues to human health. S. Boyd Eaton, Melvin Konner, and Marjorie Shostak also looked to the caveman for ideas on how to remedy the plagues of modernity, such as obesity, heart disease, and diabetes. The journal article, "Stone Agers in the Fast Lane: Chronic Degenerative Diseases in Evolutionary Perspective," would soon expand to the blockbuster bestseller *The Paleolithic Prescription: A Program of Diet & Exercise and a Design for Living* and spawn a string of dietary tomes espousing a similar thesis. Works that included *Neanderthin, The Evolution Diet, The Origin Diet,* and *Metabolic Man.*

The main thrust behind the Paleo diet is the notion that although we are people of the twenty-first century, genetically we remain citizens of the Paleolithic era. Up until five hundred generations ago, humankind hunted and foraged. People lived on lean protein, wild plants, and fruits. But with the agricultural revolution that began some 10,000 years ago, man was launched on an unnatural dietary path—one comprising root vegetables, grains, and meat from domesticated animals—one for which millions of years of evolution hadn't prepared him. The mismatch between his modern diet and his Paleolithic genes, these scientists argued, sowed the seeds for modern illnesses and chronic disease. Their prescription for health? A return to the cave and the realignment of diet with our ancient genome.[6]

That's where Vonderplanitz and the Paleo diet types part ways. According to Vonderplanitz, not only did we take the wrong turn with invention of the till and the hoe, but also with the taming of fire. "Heating food destroys many health-giving properties and produces disease-causing toxins that accelerate bodily deterioration associated with aging processes," he writes in *The Recipe for Living Without Disease.* "Cooking protein-foods, including all meat, above 104 degrees F produces toxins. Higher cooking temperatures create more dangerous toxins…that have proved to be carcinogenic in laboratory animals."[7]

Cooking meat not only produces toxins, it kills nutrients and pathogens like salmonella and *E. coli* that clean up our systems and break down our cancers, Vonderplantiz argues. Inconceivable? Maybe that's why Vonderplanitz has had difficulty finding a mainstream platform to pontificate his views, save a scant few appearances on shows like *Ripley's Believe It or Not!* And why media juggernauts like *Oprah* have backed away or canceled scheduled interviews at the last minute.

However, it's doubtful that researchers were following the former soap actor's lead when they stumbled on a strikingly similar finding. In 1998, researchers at a Yale study center stunned the scientific community when they announced that they had had some success in treating cancer in mice with a modified form of salmonella. Since then, hundreds of dying men and women across North America and Europe—at research centers such as Harvard, Stanford, and the University of Toronto—have jumped on the bandwagon. Cancer patients have been injected with everything from the common cold virus to measles, herpes, and even the chicken flu in a bid to cure their illness. The results have been nothing short of astonishing, pushing many cancer patients into remission.[8] "Duke University is using a weakened polio virus, Mayo Clinic is using a measles virus," Vonderplanitz notes in his book. "The projected retail price of injection to the patient will be $8,000. I suggest that we get colds or flu, eat high meat regularly, and pay nothing."[9]

Pay nothing? If only it were that good a deal. As the evening here at the raw meat potluck winds down, Vonderplanitz's patients are gathering at the door, bundling into their ski jackets and boots. A light dusting of snow is falling on the Victorian mansions and log cabins that look like pebbles resting beneath the sweep of the Rocky mountains. Some guests are headed to the exclusive, members-only Caribou Club. Some are going to the Belly Up to listen to a local band, and others are headed home to bed. After all, there are only so many days of powder in a season. A small group lolls behind, squeezed around Vonderplanitz. Hoping to glean one last kernel of wisdom, to finally press the flesh of their raw meat guru. Some will be back tomorrow, meeting with him privately. For $300, he'll gaze deeply into their eyes, scanning the patterns, flecks, and color of their irises before giving them a prognosis and a prescription. How to adjust their raw meat and fat diet to heal what ails them.

There's no time to book me in. His schedule is full, Kim, our host and event organizer, tells me. A good thing too, since I've already cracked open the vault for this dinner. If I include the price of my airline ticket and hotel, I figure this dinner has set me back $1,200. It would have bought me three meals at my most coveted dinner spot, Susur, in Toronto. It is undoubtedly a lot to shell out for a piece of carpaccio the size of a postage stamp. The one now stuck to a napkin that I've just retrieved from the sleek marble countertop. Maybe it's a case of finally seeing the light. Or being too cheap, too bone-headed, too conscientious in my mission. But I won't leave Aspen without eating this piece of raw meat. My hand shakes as I make a couple of foiled attempts before finally getting it into my mouth. I completely blank out. I have no recollection of chewing, or tasting the most expensive piece of beef I'll ever eat. I reasonably conclude that this is no way to have dinner. Without taste, without enjoyment.

Meanwhile, I finally find my own audience with Vonderplanitz. We chat briefly about the weather, his trip into Aspen tonight, and his small but growing following in Canada, some three hundred raw-meat eaters, mostly in Toronto. Frankly, I'm a little surprised that, at least for the moment, he seems like a regular guy. Like the plumber down the street, or the construction guy you'd hire to fix your roof—just like the guy he played so long ago on *General Hospital*. The male leads on the soap were dashing doctors, the love interests. Having watched him work the dining room in Aspen tonight, I sense that he's stumbled upon the role of a lifetime, and his ideal audience. It's a little more like dinner theater here—these partygoers suspend disbelief while Vonderplanitz plays Dr. Feelgood, a raw-meat therapist. Of course in this role, the dining room isn't all that different from the set of *General Hospital.* Just like the soap opera doctors, Vonderplanitz isn't bound by the Hippocratic oath.

10
· CARNIVORE CHIC ·

GIL YOUNG is suited up in green rubber coveralls splattered in slime and meat scraps. Standing ankle-deep in a pool of mud and blood, he thrusts his lean frame behind a hacksaw, working furiously to behead a hog. The freshly shaved swine, sent to hog heaven by way of a bullet between the eyes less than thirty minutes earlier, lies splayed on a table in the midday sun, his skin the color of a boiled potato.

A half-dozen men are crowded around. One has his hands clamped on the snout. Another grips a hind leg. Others hover nearby holding large silver bowls, waiting for their pound of flesh to throw on the barbecue. I'm standing alongside a small group of rubberneckers, well behind the massacre, doing my best to avoid the blood spray.

His brown eyes as small and blank as the buttons on a stuffed toy, he moves methodically, without pause. It's little wonder. This pig is being prepped by a guy who helped ship many of the townsfolk into the afterlife. He's not only a master butcher, and a onetime mayor, but a retired undertaker. To an outsider, it may seem a strange cycle of life. But if they've trusted him with the repair of the town's sidewalks and the interment of their loved ones—why not dinner?

Young's blade razes the pig's esophagus, before stuttering as it hits the neck bone. The sound of steel on bone rises above a melancholy tune accompanied by fiddle and accordion from somewhere in the distance. *"Les haricots ne sont pas salés,"* a voice intones, a song about leaner times when there was no salt meat to flavor the bean dinner. It is early November, at a *boucherie* in the heart of Louisiana's Cajun country, a fall ritual as old as the singer's refrain and the two-hundred-year-old oak tree I'm standing under. A communal butchering tradition once rooted in necessity in the days before refrigeration and later transformed into a celebration with the joie de vivre of a once dispossessed and now proud people.

"I don't think the patient is going to survive the surgery," Young's son Wendel avers, wincing from beneath an orange baseball cap and standing just out of the reach of the hacksaw. A spirited peal of laughter erupts from the crowd, comprising both locals and those who have come from Connecticut and California and from as far away as France to witness the making of pig into pork.

Young begins the dirty work of hollowing out the animal's interior. He slices through several layers of fat, into the hog's pale belly. A twisted spiral of gray intestines suddenly bubbles out, like a soup pot boiling over with noodles. Young then slices off a cloven hoof and absentmindedly tosses it aside. It falls, brushing my foot on its way to its final resting stop, directly between two reedy kids—a boy and a girl—and a local trucker-cum-biker sporting a graying ponytail and denim overalls.

The girl squeals as it rolls to her feet, before burying her head in the puff of kitten fur she holds in her arms.

"Oh," the little boy yells excitedly, turning to the girl. "I remember this part from last year. But last year we used a different pig."

The rumblings of a naïf. But for a moment, I'm reminded of just how different this pig really is. Raised on acorns and bugs, he grazed in a nearby pasture before he met his maker. Not like the pigs we buy at the supermarket, bred from the same gene pool, they look like stretch limousines. Pigs confined to cages under the roof of the mega-barn, pumped full of growth hormones and antibiotics to ward off the diseases that fester in such crowded conditions.

Meanwhile, Young begins plopping hunks of animal guts and gore into the men's bowls. "Okay, all vegetarians should leave the premises," he jokes. "The rest of you, get your plates ready!"

I'm a little taken aback. The first time I saw a half-butchered hog on display in front of me on the factory floor in Brandon, Manitoba, I was more inclined to run for the toilet bowl than a dinner plate. Admittedly, I'd never tasted boudin. (Apparently, I didn't know how to pronounce it either—it's boo-DAN, I learned after several misfires.) Nor did I understand this spicy rice and pork sausage's vaunted place in this culture. Yet boudin isn't reserved for special occasions. No formalities are needed. It's not just an everyday foodstuff but an everywhere snack. One served up sizzling hot at practically every corner store, every gas station. Best eaten on your way to the car, or while waiting on a margarita at the drive-thru Daiquiri Shack.

Given its ubiquity here in southwestern Louisiana, you'd think some enterprising folk might have figured out a way to crank out enough boudin to feed the rest of a sausage-loving nation. Sadly, boudin rarely makes it out of the parking lot on Laurel Avenue, out of the St. Landry Parish (county), let alone outside of the state. Dozens on death row next door in Texas reportedly have requested boudin as their final mortal meal—the ultimate takeout order—only to be told that it's unavailable. To their minds, unusual, cruel, and inhumane treatment, which says a lot about the power of boudin's appeal.

I don't know about boudin, but I've yet to meet a sausage I didn't like. My love of the humble "variety meat" is a secret I've worked hard to hide from my significant other. I'm assuming that hot dogs are what he misses most since he gave up meat decades ago, given that he's willing to endure the most frigid Toronto winter weather to barbecue a ghastly faux version made from tofu and fashioned into a tube. It must be the simple portability and architecture of the tube steak or maybe even the condiments that he still has a longing for—it can't possibly be the taste. Soybean curd in a bun: a combination off-putting enough to make any diehard carnivore reach for the Maalox.

Truthfully, Gare has never given me much grief about my carnivorous habits. Until that night I came home from a sausage-making course—a sell-out and favorite among the bridesmaid set—at the Healthy Butcher, situated along one of the trendiest retail and club strips in Toronto. Gare was working at the computer when I arrived home. "What's that smell?" he yelled from the office as I stuffed my freshly made links into the bottom of the fridge, excited about giving them as a gift to his best friend, a guy arguably even more enamored of everyday charcuterie than I. "It's pork sausages!" I exclaimed. "I'm going to give them to Joe."

I awoke a few hours later, at three a.m., alone in the bedroom. "Why don't you come to bed?" I asked, stumbling in the darkness of the living room, trying to rouse Gare from the couch. "I'm sorry," he replied, still half asleep. "But I can smell you in the bedroom all the way from here."

"But I showered!"

"I can still smell it," he gasped, before turning away and burrowing his head in the cushion. "I'm sorry, but you stink."

It is, admittedly, one reason I've come this far, to Louisiana. Not only to search out the world's best sausage, but to keep my relationship intact.

I scour the Internet. I make dozens of phone calls. Eventually, I'm referred to Curtis Joubert, a tenth-generation Acadian and onetime state legislator. A suave southern gentleman with a common man's touch, known to have quipped on more than one occasion, "If it grows or moves, we have a festival for it."

Joubert is credited with establishing the World Championship Crawfish Étouffée Cook-off in Eunice, the town he served as mayor for nearly fifteen years. He passes for a common man to the townspeople, but he always plays to his audience. He is, in fact, a closeted intellectual—one who has read the classics and can talk offhand with authority about Raskolnikov in *Crime and Punishment*. Surely if anyone can help me with my research, it's Joubert. "Miss Susan," the seventy-six-year-old croons into the phone with a drawl that belies any hint that French was the language of his boyhood, spent just outside Eunice, in the heart of the Cajun prairies. "Why, the best boudin comes from right here where I live," he tells me.

What makes this boudin so special, I demand to know. What's in the recipe?

Joubert stammers. "Well," he begins, "I'm not sure anybody's ever going to share that with you. You've got to understand, Miss Susan, these recipes are handed down from generation to generation. They are closely guarded secrets."

My heart sank at the word "secrets." I contemplated all the recipes never disclosed: Kentucky Fried Chicken, Coca-Cola, Cadbury's Caramilk chocolate bar, Crème de la Mer's $200 miracle in a jar. The list goes on and on. Corporate secrets kept deep in the vault. The KGB and the CIA may have been able to breach KFC's competitor's trove of highly sensitive intelligence. But they'd never have been able to get a foot in the kitchen door when Harland Sanders was mixing up—as they used to advertise—his "secret blend of herbs and spices." Just like the kill floor at the Brandon disassembly plant was Maple Leaf's dirty secret—one left off the company tour.

I worried that members of an insular culture like this may be even more protective of their secrets. That this might be a dead end. The secrets of the whale hunt in Barrow, Alaska, remain so by dint of geography rather than culture. But for the Acadians—who fled British persecution in Nova Scotia during Le Grand Dérangement, which began in 1755, before settling here—it may be something more. Perhaps that for a people who define themselves by their distinctive cuisine as much as their idiosyncratic music, to give up the secrets of boudin would be to give up a significant part of themselves.

I plead. I beg. Joubert resists, but eventually relents. I can't help thinking that despite his ample generosity, he can't resist a little showboating, maybe even gloating. That by giving the world a tiny window into his culture, he's letting us in on what we've been missing.

Joubert agrees to be my fixer. He will find someone to teach me about boudin. But first I must pledge that no patents will be violated, no copyrights broken. That I won't steal any family recipes—like the one stashed in the vault over at Bourque's in nearby Port Barre. I suddenly feel like I've just been admitted to the Freemasons or Skull and Bones—a secret society without the arcane handshakes, whispered passwords, and naked wrestling.

That's the back story. The story of how I find myself here this afternoon at a *boucherie*, playing footsie with a pig's hoof. Gil Young, the man now cleaning his bloody knife with an apron, is not only the master butcher here, but the resident boudin crafts-man. A *boudinière*, if you will, who has promised to show me the ropes. He's going to teach me how to make boudin.

I ARRIVE IN LAFAYETTE several days earlier. Hailing a taxi, I head northwest to meet Joubert in Eunice, about fifty miles away. It's late afternoon and the sun glints on the rice fields and crawfish ponds that line the highway. Heading deeper in Acadiana, we pass a small house dwarfed by a large blue flag accented in one corner by three silver fleurs-de-lis—the flag of French Louisiana.

Though the wetlands and bayous of Louisiana define Cajun

country in popular consciousness, its cultural heartland is actually the Cajun Prairies. A vast expanse beginning in Lafayette that extends toward Texas. Eunice, a town of 12,000 located northeast of Lafayette, bills itself as the capital of the Cajun Prairies. It's home to twenty-seven churches—one for every 450 residents—and one of the state's largest Mardis Gras festivals, as well as a satellite campus of Louisiana State University. But its most lauded landmark is the Liberty Theater, a restored vaudeville house that serves as the community's cultural hub, and my host's crowning achievement as mayor. A place where townsfolk meet every Saturday night for the Rendez-vous des Cajuns—to listen to breathless a cappella ballads and one rousing, foot-stomping fiddle medley after another. A place where the sexiest thing a young man can wear is a well-loved pair of Levi's and an accordion.

"Want some cracklins?" my cabbie queries, thrusting a greasy bag across the backseat, one full of a snack food he's been popping back like peanuts. Somehow I doubt that deep-fried skin and pork fat is going to help me squeeze into the already too-tight dress I'm hoping to wear to a splashy event as soon as I return to Toronto.

"I'm saving my appetite for boudin," I decline as politely as I can.

"Boudin!" he cackles, wiping the grease from his moustache onto a shirt sleeve. "You heard the joke?" he asks, barreling ahead before I'd had a chance to answer. "What's a seven-course dinner for a Cajun? A six-pack of beer and a link of boudin!"

Sigh. A joke so old it has a beard. I can only hope this represents the low point in local color. Either that or I have arrived on the set of *Hee-Haw*.

However, I'm happy to stock up on this spicy pork and rice sausage, given the other choices on the Cajun menu: alligator, muskrat, and squirrel. Maybe a little too audacious for a white-bread woman from the milquetoast heartland of Canada. But the truth is, even Cajuns have their limits.

More than a decade ago, the state of Louisiana recruited its top culinary talent to help find a solution to public enemy number one: nutria, a large South American rodent reportedly imported by fur traders decades earlier, now wreaking environmental havoc throughout the state. Paul Prudhomme, the New Orleans chef who put Cajun food on the map in the 1980s, was among the star-studded cast of cooks that stepped forward, vowing to stew, fry, and fricassee the *Myocastor coypus* into extinction. Or at least out of the state.

Sadly, not a single animal rights activist rallied to the poor vermin's cause. It was a beast that even PETA couldn't love.

The state sponsored a cookbook that included recipes for fettuccine with poached nutria and nutria à l'orange, trumpeting it as "the most exciting delicacy to come along in years." Prudhomme contributed recipes for nutria sausage, étouffée, and gumbo. "It's wonderful fixed with popcorn shrimp," he gushed at the time. "You just have to get over the idea of it."[1]

Joubert tried to get over it the day Prudhomme came to town to promote his nutria-inspired creations, he recalls on this temperate November afternoon. We're sitting on the front porch of his verandah, the entrance to an opulent brick house where Joubert likes to entertain friends with a batch of his homemade gumbo. Mostly local city council types.

Until a few years ago Joubert's gatherings featured one of the most infamous and colorful men in Louisiana political history, bad boy Edwin Edwards, spiritual heir to Huey and Earl Long. Back in the day, Governor Edwards would have been feasting on Joubert's boudin at the legislature's dining room up in Baton Rouge, but these days he's supping on rice and beans while serving time in the federal penitentiary in Oakdale for racketeering. Edwards, now eighty, is slated for release in 2011—while most younger men look forward to female company on release, Mr. Edwards probably will only be longing for boudin.

Back in the '90s, you could make the case that Prudhomme's star power rivaled even that of Edwards's. People lined around the block in Eunice to see what all the hubbub was about, even if they weren't keen on tasting Prudhomme's newest creation. But as town mayor, Joubert took his oath to heart. It was his civic duty to move to the front of the line, to be the guinea pig—so to speak. "How was it?" I prod, anxious to get to the meat of the matter. Joubert pauses, stretching his lips into a characteristic wobbly smile. "I'll tell you what I told CNN back then," he begins, leaning his six-foot-two frame deeper into the wicker chair he's sitting in. "A good Cajun cook can make even old shoe leather taste good.

"Here people will tell you with pride, we don't eat to live. We live to eat." Joubert's not the first, of course, to assert that there is an elemental relationship between food and a place, a place and its people. In *The Raw and the Cooked,* French anthropologist Claude Lévi-Strauss argued that food is one of the most important ways in which people express themselves. This was certainly true of Arnold Brower and his Inupiat clan in Barrow. Never before had I witnessed the reverence with which food is consumed and talked about in any other region or culture—

except, perhaps, here in Louisiana. As writer C. Paige Gutierrez notes in her book *Cajun Foodways*, "Cajuns are uniquely distinctive in their ability to enjoy food."[2]

Boudin, one might argue, is an emblem of triumph—although you won't find many citations or references to it in the local history books. Its very existence is testament to the resiliency of the Cajun people. A people who battled adversity for centuries—first as exiles from Nova Scotia, and later in their new homeland of Louisiana, colliding with a class of French-speaking white Creoles intent on transplanting feudalism from France to the shores of Mississippi. For decades the Cajuns clung to their traditional way of life and Catholic religion, retreating into the bayous, marshes, and prairies. Far from the seat of influence in Louisiana politics and the corridors of finance.[3]

Although some white Creoles, Anglos, and later European immigrants married into the community, by the turn of the century Cajuns increasingly found themselves the targets of intolerance. The state instituted compulsory education in 1921, and later coopted leaders within the Acadian educational elite in its campaign to wipe the French language out of the state. The effect was not only to marginalize the language of their culture, but all things Cajun. Worse, many Cajuns internalized this negative view of themselves. "Many outsiders—and insiders as well—associated Cajun culture with ignorance and poverty. Following in the footsteps of their nineteenth-century predecessors, twentieth-century observers continued to stereotype Cajuns as either virtuous peasants living in an idyllic, romanticized setting, or as mysterious, violent, hedonistic swamp dwellers."[4]

By the '60s, the cultural tides began to shift. Pockets of regional ethnic pride were cropping up in other parts of North America. They provided a blueprint for Louisiana's Cajuns, where a powerful grassroots backlash was taking hold. By 1968, the movement had gained enough momentum that the state vowed to rebuild the Cajuns' core institutions. It thereby designated a twenty-two-parish French-speaking region of southern Louisiana as Acadiana in honor of the area's pioneers.

Ruby's is a Cajun institution, even if not a state-sanctioned one. Locals have been coming to Walnut Street in Eunice since the 1950s for the restaurant's legendary biscuits, the down-home Cajun cooking, and, more recently, to bone up on their French on Thursday mornings. It's just past ten-thirty when I arrive on this particular Thursday. Locals are already jostling to get a lunch table. Today's special? Pork steaks smothered in gravy, served with Wonder Bread and a side order of local politics—a diversion that seems second only to food in the catalogue of local amusements.

"What ya'll doin' today?" hollers Dot in a voice as loud as her dress. The grandmother and café owner lumbers around, turning sideways to make her way between tables, to greet the couple directly to my left. "Can you believe last night's election?" she says, her mouth sagging in an exaggerated gesture of mock disbelief as they discuss last night's bitterly contested battle for the local sheriff's seat. "Well, I always say the best man will win," she continues, "and he did just that."

Nods all around the table.

Dot's eyes suddenly fix on a plate piled high with meat in front of a slim and pretty forty-something woman. "You having that without rice?" she wheezes, her penciled-in eyebrows flexing in astonishment. "You'll starve," she admonishes the woman, before turning in my direction and shouting over her shoulder, "Y'all enjoy your food!"

She settles into a chair next to mine. "How's your biscuit, hon?"

"It's unbelievably delicious," I tell her truthfully. She beams proudly before asking where I'm from and what I'm doing here. I tell her about my mission. Not only to find and eat the world's best boudin, but to learn its secret recipe.

"Can y'all believe it?" Dot suddenly erupts, flinging her arms in the air and crying to everyone and no one in particular. "The girl's never had boudin!"

Gasps of disbelief all around. Meanwhile, Dot's already out of her chair and on her way out of the restaurant. She won't have me leave her café, she tells me, reaching for the doorknob, without having had some boudin—even if it means bringing it in from another food purveyor. I want to tell her that I can't possibly eat this boudin; that I have sworn boudin celibacy until I attend the invitation-only *boucherie* on Sunday. But before I've had a chance to speak up, she's already waving good-bye from the front seat of her pickup.

"You know," a man at a nearby table intones from deep under a cowboy hat. "Boudin is French—you must have it up there in Canada. Up there in Quebec."

"It's not French," a woman on the other side of the café interrupts, her voice filled with certitude. "It's Spanish. I know it's Spanish."

Another voice pipes in, "No, I think it's German."

And soon a full-scale melee over boudin is under way. Again.

Turns out, they are all correct. Just like Louisiana's Gallic melting pot, boudin is a cultural collision. Adapting and borrowing from several food cultures: Native American, African American, German, British, Italian, and—of course—from France, the country that gave boudin its name.[5]

Still, I can't help wondering who came up with the idea to take a pig's intestine and stuff it with food. While his name is undoubtedly lost in history, the sausage has existed for centuries. The Chinese are believed to have made sausage as early as 4000 B.C. They were first noted in Western literature in Homer's *Odyssey*.[6] Even back then they were a controversial food— but apparently more because of their utility during orgies than for their heart-clogging attributes. During the Roman Empire's conversion to Christianity, sausages were banned reportedly because of their use during festivals like Lupercalia—and not merely just as food.[7]

The word *sausage* is derived from *saussiche* in Old French, and rooted in the Latin word *salsus,* meaning "salted." Salting helped preserve meat in the days before refrigeration, and sausage is the granddaddy of all prepared foods. It evolved as a result of efficient butchery—the use of bits and pieces, organ meats, fat and blood that otherwise would have been relegated to the scrap heap of the butcher's table or the dog's bowl. But it wasn't just about satisfying hunger. During the first millennium A.D., in France, charcuterie quickly evolved as a respected trade, its craftsmen legendary. Recipe books from seventeenth- and eighteenth-century Europe provide detailed recipes for blood sausages, and "puddings"—a reference to any food stuffed in animal intestines.[8] Meanwhile, as sausage-making began to evolve as a true craft in Europe, its popularity expanded across the globe. Explorers traveled with them throughout the 1400s to the 1700s, introducing sausage to locals who experimented with their own spices and ingredients.[9]

Not only did France have its boudin, Spain had its chorizo. Britain its bangers and snorkers. China, yap cheung. Poland, kielbasa. Meanwhile, countries like Italy produced regional variations of salami alongside coppa and mortadella. While the Germans produced bratwurst, weisswurst, knockwurst, and, of course, the frankfurter.

When the first European settlers arrived on the shores of North America, they brought their age-old sausage recipes with them, packed in their suitcases alongside other precious family heirlooms. For the early settlers, sausage-making was a fall ritual. A time when neighbors from nearby farms came together, pooling resources to make use of every bit and scrap of the pig. To provide enough protein to last the long North American winters.

Street vendors were likely peddling sausages as early as the 1860s, and they eventually were called "dachshund sausage" for their resemblance to the low-slung dog. A German named Charles Feltman, who sold pies from a cart on Coney Island, added a burner to his wagon and is generally credited with being the first visionary to fork a warm sausage into a split roll. By 1900 he parlayed this invention into a sprawling empire, in which he employed 1,200 workers capable of serving 8,000 consumers at a time. Soon, hot dogs came to be seen as the ultimate patriotic fare, Americanized through their association with public events like the baseball game.[10]

Maybe it was due to urbanization and rising prosperity, a desire to buy into middle-class aspirations and fulfill the American dream by consuming beef, but somewhere early in the twentieth century sausage lost its cachet. It didn't mean that North Americans weren't consuming a healthy (depending upon how you measure it) per capita share of pork-filled casings in the privacy of their kitchens, but consumers no longer displayed the same kind of gusto that they had at festivals like Lupercalia. Certainly, sausage still had its champions: Marlene Dietrich, for example, who once confessed that her favorite dinner consisted of frankfurters and champagne. But when the Depression hit in the '30s, the humble tubesteak was seen as a cheap meal. Fluky's hot dog stand in Chicago, for example, offered a "Depression sandwich"—a hot dog and fries for a nickel.[11] From there on, it seemed the poor sausage had been relegated to the breakfast table and the truck stop—a poor man's dinner served with eggs, beans, and toast. Or a snack food consumed at the carnival sideshow, gobbled down before taking in the bearded lady and the human pincushion.

One could argue that the nadir came in 1936, the year that hot dogs were thrust into an international controversy, involving President Franklin D. Roosevelt, the First Lady, and the British monarchy. Even Eleanor Roosevelt's mother reportedly was mortified when she found out that her daughter planned to serve hot dogs at an official state dinner held in honor of George VI and the Queen Mother. The First Lady eventually calmed the storm by issuing a statement from the White House, advising that there would be more dignified food items on the menu. It has been suggested that this also may have been the beginning of the royal tradition to always have a handbag at the ready.[12]

And then, just as the sausage's exalted reputation fizzled like a wet firecracker in elite circles in the earlier part of the last century, it came back with a bang at the dawn of the new millennium. Charcuterie books suddenly were flying off bookstore shelves. Restaurants like Salt in Vancouver and the Butcher Shop in Boston began to spring up to feed a *salumi*-loving public. Riding the artisanal wave—and the desire to turn a sow's ear into a silk purse—top chefs began to go whole hog, devoting their attention to perfecting their own charcuterie. Even royalty embraced the commoners' most humble dish, with Prince Charles pumping out his gold-wrapped "super premium" sausages. A category killer, made from free-range, organic duchy swine, which, naturally, had been given the royal treatment. Mudbaths in summer, footballs to kick around the sties to relieve their stress—undoubtedly a blissful scene calculated to appeal to discerning consumers.

In Canada, the bar was set by Toronto's Michael Stadtländer, who built a smokehouse to turn his own hand-raised pigs into delectable cold cuts. In the United States, even star chefs like Paul Bertolli were getting in on the action, following their passion. Bertolli, the onetime celebrity chef from Olivetti in California—and before that the storied Chez Panisse—stunned the culinary world when he hung up his chef's hat to devote his life to a sausage-making business. Yes, the Michelin Guide was passed over for wieners. A food craze clearly tied to the trend in "whole animal eating." One that corresponds to the celebration of offal at white-tablecloth dinners across North America. Indeed, foie gras, truffles, and other staples of gastronomic excess now find themselves sharing space on menus at five-star restaurants with cheeks, jowls, sweetbreads, and cold lamb's brain on toast. Nothing is wasted. It's not merely a competition among chefs to make bad things taste good; it's an ethical movement. The ultimate in feel-good carnivorousness, designed to respect the entire animal and thereby soothe the guilty conscience of the meat-eater.

Meanwhile, here in Louisiana, it's a movement that's never had a moment. It never needed one. Artisanal food? Snout-to-tail eating? It's what has always been in fashion. While Bertolli seems intent on resurrecting his great-great-grandfather's ancient recipes, in Acadiana food is part of the culture's living history. Recipes are always being revamped and reworked, just as the culture is constantly evolving.

It's clear that the spicy pork and rice boudin found here today in Acadiana has little in common with sausage of its origin in France—a link made with pork, chicken, veal, and cognac (and arguably even less with its other French cousin, the blood-filled boudin rouge). Just as it's difficult to draw a culinary line between North America's first batch of boudin and the one now feted here in Cajun country. Testament, perhaps, to how Acadians always have been able to adapt their traditions and culture to their surroundings. The first recorded recipe for boudin is over two hundred years old, prepared by Toussaint Charbonneau, a fur trader cum cook, hired to work alongside Captain Meriwether Lewis and William Clark on their famed expedition. Charbonneau apparently had little talent for hard work on the trail and no interest in cartography and exploration, but he did exhibit an early flair for the culinary trade. The explorers recorded their first taste of American boudin in this journal entry, on Thursday, May 9, 1805: "Killed one buffaloe.... We saved the necessary materials for making what our wrighthand cook Charbono calls the boudin blanc, and immediately set him about preparing them for supper; this white pudding we all esteem one of the greatest delicacies of the forrest." He then followed with an elaborate explanation of how he squeezed out a buffalo intestine, stuffed it with meat and kidney suet, "baptized" it in the Missouri River with "two dips and a flirt," and boiled it before frying it in bear grease.[13] By this account you might have presumed that Lewis and Clark were on a gastronomic tour.

Although the rites and rituals of boudin may be somewhat less elaborate these days, Charbonneau's fervor for variety meat is still very much in evidence. It's Saturday morning, a high holiday in these parts, when friends gather to celebrate the holy trinity—community, music, and boudin. My guide Curtis Joubert and I are rumbling through town in his fancy pickup, headed to an old farmhouse for a jamboree held here every weekend for more than twenty years. The tunes are blaring on the radio, and we drive by a sign that reads FRENCH DANCE HERE TONIGHT, $4. No mention of who's playing. To locals, it's clear that whoever is playing is whoever shows up.

Joubert is now wearing his weekend attire: a yellow golf shirt and a baseball cap that sits high on his head. He tours me through the historic part of Eunice, crossing himself as we drive past a local church. We turn on to the main artery, passing a parking lot jammed with trucks and minivans and a local sheriff's car. A line of men, women, and children stream out the door, waiting for local specialties like smoked ponce—a hog belly stuffed with sausage—and black-eyed peas and andouille sausage. But mostly they're here for boudin. "It's like that every Saturday morning," Joubert tells me. "There's an old joke around here," he continues. "You'd better not have your surgery scheduled for Saturday morning because your doctor's going to have to leave halfway through to get his boudin."

"Some people eat it every day. I love it but I can't have it every day. Just on Saturday. It's a little tough on your cholesterol, you know, Miss Susan."

Cholesterol. Right up until this point I presumed that nobody in the parish noticed or cared. I would have asked Joubert if he was speaking in his capacity as Eunice's surgeon general, but I let it slide.

Two miles out of town, we pull up on the shoulder of the road, outside the Savoy Music Center. "There will be boudin from all different stores in here," Joubert says as we push open the door. "The guy who brings boudin is always the most popular guy in the room. At least for two or three minutes."

It's barely ten-thirty a.m. and the room is already in full two-stepping swing. A teenage boy is squeezing on the button accordion, his ninety-year-old great-uncle playing the fiddle. A dozen or more musicians are gathered round, waiting their turn. It's a typical Saturday session where young musicians come to learn from old hands. Where locals come to slide around what passes for a dance floor here, and tourists come from far out of state to witness this ragtag orchestra—young and old, playing together, eating, joking, singing.

Joubert tips his chapeau by way of greeting, and we make our way to a bench on the side of the room.

I soon find myself swept up in the revelry. My toes tapping, my head snapping to the beat of an old ditty, the Eunice two-step. It's even more crowded here than usual. A few dozen friends are in from out of state for tomorrow's *boucherie*—an annual event staged by the shop's owner, Marc Savoy, who is also a master accordion-maker and musician. It's hard to miss him as he strides through the sea of merrymakers, at six-feet-six towering over them all. When he speaks, you'd think it's the PA system, a voice coming from a high-hanging speaker. "Curtis, you fixin' to have some boudin?" he booms. "Have some cracklins," Savoy implores me. "You'd better get up there now if you're going to get any."

I sidestep the makeshift dance floor to a counter where a dozen hands are grabbing at cracklins and boudin links that have been sliced into bite-sized pieces. I'm saving my boudin-tasting for tomorrow, but I'm curious for a glimpse of boudin imported from exotic-sounding places like Mamou and Opelousas and even farther-flung locales.

"This one's from Poche's in Breaux Bridge . . ."

"This is Best Stop's [a store in nearby Scott] and it's the best . . ."

"Not any better than the one right here from Eunice Poultry . . ."

Boudin one-upmanship is just typical party banter in these parts. Luckily, it's relatively civil. Not like the dustups that Robert Carriker has been in. Ones in which he's been shouted down. Cussed out and nearly punched out—all for asking boudin zealots to justify why their coveted supplier's recipe is the best.

"I've had people get really angry. I've been challenged," Carriker explains, confessing he was completely befuddled by the impassioned squabbles inspired by the simple foodstuff when he first moved to Lafayette from Washington State nearly ten years ago. "I've had people scream at me: 'What does a Yankee like you know about this?'"

A man of science, a man of letters, Carriker has worked hard to bring a measure of reason to the debate. The head of the University of Louisiana's history department has made boudin his hobby, eating his way across the Acadian boudin trail. He and his friend, a teacher who prefers the anonymity of "Coach T" (for reasons that will become abundantly clear), hit the road early every Saturday morning on an epicurean pilgrimage. Stopping at every gas station, every corner store and restaurant to taste as many variations of boudin as possible. They post their ratings on the website www.boudinlink.com, which also features a detailed description of each link's characteristics—i.e., rice-to-pork ratio, wet/dry consistency, and so on. Just think of their work as the Better Boudin Bureau.

Not surprisingly, the ratings have sparked no end of controversy. One irate boudin-maker—miffed at his rating, the worst in the history of the website—reportedly lost it the day he stood in front of the principal at the school where Coach T was teaching. He and his boudin had been unfairly maligned, he spat with fury before issuing this warning: unless the rating was removed from the teacher's website, the boudin-maker vowed to transfer his kids out of the school. Coach T complied at the principal's request, but reposted the same rating a year later when he moved out of the district to take a position at another school. No one would have blamed him if he had docked the boudin-maker a grade for customer service.

Hearing all of this has set me on edge for my boudin lessons. How can I, a boudin maiden, be expected to compete? After all, these Cajuns have a head start of several generations. And, truth be told, I'm not a born natural in the kitchen. With memories and wounds of that chicken beating the shit out of me in Pizzuco's New York butcher shop, I can feel the job performance anxiety welling up. I try to keep it together as we pull into Savoy's farm this afternoon for the *boucherie*. Sidling up beside my master boudin-maker, Gil Young, fresh from the slaughter, I suddenly picture myself on the production line at the chocolate factory next to Lucy Ricardo, unable to keep pace, stuffing the overrun in my mouth and down my blouse. I grit my teeth and steel myself for the challenge—I'll have to be at the very top of my game to avoid total humiliation. I can't help wondering: Does Young ever get nervous? Might be one explanation for why he's nursing a tumbler of straight vodka. Perhaps I need a couple of shots of courage, too.

"It is a competitive sport, and you'll need to get your hands dirty," Young says, pouring me a shot of vodka before handing me a well-worn apron. "Don't worry," my seventy-nine-year-old *boudinière* continues with a wave of a bony hand. "I'm not expecting any customer complaints. And if we do get some, hell, they just won't be on the guest list next year!"

Meanwhile, the sun is trying to poke through the cloud cover. A group of children have gathered at the edge of the farm where an elaborate dance is taking place. A tom turkey fans his feathers and stomps his spurred feet before thrusting his chest out and circling a hen, who looks perturbed by the spectacle. The rituals of mating under way here. A funeral turned dinner party a few feet away.

While the women are busy setting out trays of rice dressing, yam and marshmallow bakes, and biscuits, the men have set up their fire stations. Terry, a biker and former military guy, is stirring his special backbone stew. Claude, a transplanted Quebecker, is barbecuing back ribs. Brother Johnson is in charge of the cracklins.

"You ready?" Young asks, and before I've had a chance to answer, he's clutching a knife in one hand and a bag of onions in the other. "It's one-thirty. We've got two hours to get boudin on the table. Let's go!"

Young begins to chop frantically, his arm pumping like a woodcutter's as he hacks into pieces of loin, heart, liver, and kidney. I try to keep pace, slicing onions. We heap the meat and onions into a massive black cauldron filled with water and stir it every few minutes with a big stick. At Maple Leaf, I had been rattled by the fact that the disembodied heads tumbling toward me had been chopped off exactly forty-two minutes earlier. But that was just a matter of the speedy turnaround in processing. Maple Leaf, though, has nothing on boudin. Locals might speculate about the ethnic origins of the recipes, but their efficiency probably traces back to the Germans. The pig parts floating in the pot are from an animal that was grazing peacefully in a pasture a little over an hour ago. And in a few more dances and another tumbler of vodka, this boudin will be down some Acadian gullet. (If the raw-meat cultists were here, I guess they could feast on the uncooked pork while it was still warm.)

Truthfully, I can't help feeling a certain gallows empathy as

I stare into the pot. After all, I made eye contact with this pig as he was being walked down the plank to his death. I take a big gulp of vodka and vow right here and now that this pig won't have died in vain. Our boudin is going to be the stuff of myth. Of legend. Or at least grist for my book, the nearest thing to a porcine obituary. Of course the rest of the folks at this gathering aren't thinking about posterity. They're not thinking about haute cuisine either, just good, tasty, honest food. The same kind of food that's been served up here on these *boucherie* grounds for the better part of a century.

"Back in the old days, we'd start first thing in the morning," Young explains, now chopping a bushel of parsley. "It was a lot of hard work, but it taught us how to work, you know? These days it's about Cajun pride, but back then it was about necessity. We had to stretch the meat as far as we could. The whole community came out. The men would do the butchering and most of the cooking. The boudin was always the woman's job. That and the cracklin cornbread. They'd first have to clean the original casings [the intestines] and that wasn't a pleasant smell. They'd be boiling on the stove and you couldn't walk in there without passing out. Back then, they didn't have all the seasonings either for boudin. Not tasty like it is now."

Young's tone isn't mocking. Not like the cooks who sneered at me from under their baseball caps at Pappas steakhouse in Houston. They demanded respect, while Young asks for nothing. He's generous, willing to share his secrets for the betterment of humanity. By his thinking, if the rest of the world were more like Eunice, it might not necessarily be a better place, but everything would at least taste better.

It's hard enough for me to follow a recipe, let alone recount one, and surely I've forgotten an item or two. Memory plays tricks with the hard details. Or maybe—just maybe—Young has slipped a couple of things past me. Sprinkled a couple of secret seasonings in the pot when I wasn't looking. So with this blow-by-blow, slice-by-slice account, one word of warning: Don't try this at home. Because if you do, no guarantees.

Take one heart, one kidney, one liver, several pounds of fresh pig loin and shoulder.

Boil it furiously in a fifty-gallon drum filled with water.

Add a few handfuls of onion, a cupful of black pepper, paprika, cayenne.

Stir in a few Cajun bon mots.

When the onion has wilted just enough—about forty-five minutes into stewing—remove it, along with chunks of meat, and stuff it in the grinder.

Add parsley.

Grind. Mix it with rice. About a fifty-fifty ratio. Put it into the sausage stuffer and imagine yourself making balloon animals. When you've got a link about two feet in length, begin to carve it into eight-inch pieces.

"Okay, Marc, taste test," Young shouts at our host Marc Savoy, who happens to be passing by. Savoy stops, scoops a sticky glop of cooked boudin mix out of Young's hand, and stuffs it in his mouth. He closes his eyes and leans his head back, staring into the sky. "Gil, you never let us down," he sighs after a moment. "You're the master. I've been lovin' boudin ever since I've been knowing my name."

Young beams. He turns to the revelers and bellows, "Boudin! Boudin!" A crowd stampedes our workstation. Children, locals, and boudin virgins all anxiously grabbing at links and a napkin.

I seek out Joubert to bring him a piece of boudin. He's seated nearby in a lawn chair, next to his wife, Kristine, and a couple of folks from out of town, including former governor Edwin Edwards's brother, Marion, and his wife, Penny.

"I hear you ate some mukluks!" Penny squeals as I approach the group. "It just sounds so disgusting. My, you are a brave girl..."

I don't feel the need to correct her. That it wasn't footwear but muktuk, or whale blubber, I had dined on in Alaska. I don't feel the need to tell her that eating muktuk required no more bravery than did eating the alligator I'd had here two days earlier. No, I didn't want to insult her. Just like I didn't want to insult my Inupiat hosts, who had so generously shared their most precious, most coveted food with me. I'd grown to realize that had I grown up in these parts, I'd love alligator just as I would have loved muktuk had I been raised north of the 58th parallel.

However, it's our elder statesman, Joubert, who makes the connections that elude both Penny and me. "You know, Ms. Susan," Joubert begins, "when the Eskimos get together on the ice and chop up the whale—why, that's a *boucherie*. That's no different from what we're doing right here this afternoon."

I imagine Joubert and Arnold Brower Sr., one of the Arctic's greatest whalers and my host in Barrow, would have much to talk about. In many ways, they're both preserving the most important aspects of their culture. Their food cultures. And while no one up in Barrow or here in the Cajun Prairies talks much about the slow-food movement—trumpeting the virtues of the culinary wing of the antiglobalization movement—it's what they do naturally. It's organic in a purely cultural sense.

While I can look at the bottles of spices, the pile of ingredients at our cooking station, I'll never really be able to reproduce boudin, despite my culinary immersion. The secret is safe; it can't be violated. And then it suddenly comes to me: The secret of boudin is the secret of all good food. You can watch, you can learn at the hands of the master, but the fact is that all good food is rooted in time, place, and culture. It is idiosyncratic, unique, and expressive of the place where it's made and the people making it. The closer the food is to the place, the more it defines its makers and eaters, the more intense its flavors. Not like the meat that is mass-marketed from factory farms, cleansed of all flavor by modern breeding and feeding.

Cajun food had its Warholian fifteen minutes of fame in the 1980s, but now it's strictly out there with acid-washed jeans and, well, Andy Warhol himself. Not just passé but, in the wider culture, dead. At one point, it'd become so popular that Cajun spices, once daring, were then considered no more exotic than ketchup. But never mind food fashion as defined by the likes of *Food & Wine* and *Gourmet*. Forget the food critics. The Acadians, with no intention other than eating well, are leaders in a culinary trend. Respecting the pastoral, agrarian order while turning their backs on the hegemony of our supersized, super-processed, superbland diet. Somehow they've managed to reconcile what eludes most of us eaters here in North America: the marrying of virtue with pleasure. It probably would amuse the folks of Eunice if I told them they were leaders in anything other than boudin. The rest of us are finally coming around to where they've been and what they've been doing all along.

It's with this in mind that I finally bite into my boudin. *Eh bien!* "All animals are equal, but some animals are more equal than others." The words of George Orwell. He was getting at something else entirely (and God knows a chronically unhappy ascetic would have been a bad fit with the party-happy folks of Eunice). Still, there's no doubt that people seriously underrate the pig's place in the food chain. This boudin melts on my tongue. Delicious, warm, and slightly spicy. A mélange of perfect ingredients and perfect artistry. This is pig perfect. Meat perfect. That pig did not die in vain.

• EPILOGUE •

THE SCENE in the dining room is one part June Cleaver, one part Henry VIII, at once prim and oblivious of etiquette. We have the pearls on and the best silver out, but those at the table tonight have their forks and knives at the ready, poised to be wielded like a tradesman's pickaxes and saws. Thankfully, the scene is bathed in candlelight. More brightly lit, the centerpiece, a prime rib roast wrapped in fat and wafting with nostalgia, would look like only so much meat thrown to wolves. In a harsher light, our convivial smiles would look more like barred teeth.

This same bit of dinner theater is playing out in homes up and down the streets around as families gather for one of the year's most important repasts: Easter dinner.

It's a coming together and a meeting in the center. And that's something put to the test here in Ottawa, Canada's political hub, where everyone is on one side or another. Where it seems no one stands in the middle. And given their political leanings, it's a wonder that our hosts can see each other from where they stand on issues. My sister Lisa is a public school teacher, while her partner, Don, a speechwriter, puts words in the mouths of the capital's better-known right-wingers.

Among the guests, Don probably could count on the support of Randy, the straight-laced neighbor. No slave to fashion, he could have walked right out of a Norman Rockwell illustration on the cover of a vintage *Saturday Evening Post*. But Ottawa doesn't just play to type, and neither do our guests—some are wolfish conservatives gussied up in liberal clothing. Jenny, an artist, is wearing an all-black ensemble and a chic bob. She's here with her husband, Bill, fresh from a three-month stay in Africa, where he was working on a new book. They could easily pass for fixtures on the alt-culture scene, but they're card-carrying Tories. Seated to the left of them are my nephew Nicholas, who found his calling at chef's school after reading Anthony Bourdain's *Kitchen Confidential,* and my two young nieces Madeline and Georgina. My friend Vicky, an environmental economist and my best friend growing up, is the only other Liberal here outside my blood relatives. She doesn't consider the dining room a fit place for political discourse. Thankfully, our guests leave the political talk for the next fund-raiser.

On this day of spiritual renewal, the issues that typically divide us are supposed to be set aside. The political news cycle has given way to more religious matters this weekend. Meanwhile, I've been preoccupied by much more material concerns. Prepping for this dinner over these past few days, I've been wondering: How much prime rib do I need to feed ten people? What sort of rub should I apply to my meat? How do you make gravy from scratch? Resolving these seemingly trivial concerns would be the answers to my immediate prayers. The truth is, getting this prime rib onto the dinner table tonight requires something approaching divine intervention.

The timing is fitting. It's the end of Lent—a period when historically Christians the world over have abstained from meat-eating. And this is the main course, the grand finale to my adventures in meat. Before my guests have even taken a bite, I'm trying to digest the lessons I've learned over the past year.

One thing I've discovered is that each successive generation seems to have staked out its identity by rejecting the foods its parents hold so dear. A quirk of North American food culture. My meat-and-potatoes childhood evolved into a sampling of international cuisine. I traveled the world plate by plate, my credit card statements stamped with the names of exotic restaurants, like a diplomat's passport. This carried over into my own kitchen—instead of Fodor's guides to far-flung lands, I collected cookbooks featuring foreign cuisines. Over the years, I've prepared my share of pad thai, kimchi, curry, burritos, and risotto. If there was a common thread that ran through most of the cookbooks and the dishes, it was that they tracked to places where meat is hard to come by. All of which is to say that when I did venture into the kitchen, I always cooked meat as a garnish rather than the main event.

And yet I longed to serve a prime rib just as my mother had done all those Sundays. She made it look so easy, almost intuitive, although she worked hard doing triple duty in the kitchen as prep cook, pastry maker, and executive chef. With the prime rib ready and resting before being carved for the table, my mother would be busily whisking her gravy, one eye on her vegetables, the other on the cheese sauce, while I watched the Yorkshire puddings rise through the oven door window. There was always a sense of self-satisfaction when she brought her roast out to a tableful of guests, many of them looking like our fresh-scrubbed neighbor. There was something about this Sunday ritual that left an indelible mark in my mind about the way in which food nourishes and sustains us.

That's the back story to this dinner party. For me, serving this roast is a rite of passage. It's my coming-out party. The only haute couture here tonight is, of course, our blue-blood prime rib, selected for its impeccable breeding and character.

My sister and I had set out for the butcher shop in Ottawa South the day before our soiree. The start of the search for the repast from our past. Fittingly, it's a neighborhood where the new and old converge, where heartland traditions endure. Passing the gable-roofed homes hunched under century-old oak and maple trees, I couldn't help thinking that the prime rib I was now shopping for wasn't all that different than the prime rib that would have been served here at the turn of the century. What was good meat back then is here in the new millennium. It's just packaged differently—stamped with "Organic," "Hormone-free," and "Free-range" labels. Just like the glorious-looking five-rib roast our butcher is wrapping in brown paper.

Our $85 roast safely in lockdown in the refrigerator back at my sister's house, we spent the afternoon scouring cookbooks. We finally settled on a rub for the roast that included red and green peppercorns and a recipe for gravy that called for mustard, horseradish, cranberries, and Merlot.

By the crack of dawn the next morning, Lisa and I were in the kitchen, furiously chopping vegetables and grating the chocolate for our torte. By lunchtime, the cake was in the oven and it was time to turn my attention to our prime rib. I ground the peppercorns, chopped garlic, added olive oil and rosemary before fetching the roast from the refrigerator and placing it in a roasting pan. Like a surgeon performing delicate surgery, I carved a series of X's up and down the roast—all too aware that unlike the physician, I didn't have any malpractice insurance. I scooped the rub onto my fingertips and began pressing into the meat. It wasn't long ago when I would have been uneasy even touching this roast—its utter foreignness would have seemed threatening, like I was violating some sort of natural order. But rather than fear, I was filled with anticipation. I knew I was going to savor this meat in a way I never had before.

I rubbed and patted while I reflected on the writings of Wendell Berry, the Kentucky farmer and man of letters who admonished North Americans for having too little appreciation of the connections between the farm and the dinner plate. Eating, he once wrote, is both an agricultural and political act. "Eating ends the annual drama of the food economy that begins with planting and birth. . . . The industrial eater is, in fact, one who does not know that eating is an agricultural act, who no longer knows or imagines the connections between eating and the land, and who is therefore necessarily passive and uncritical— in short, a victim."[1]

I no longer felt like a victim. True, I couldn't countenance what I'd seen at the slaughterhouse, what I'd learned about factory farming. I had come to the conclusion that if I were to eat an animal, to take another creature's life in order to nourish mine, I had a responsibility to do it in good conscience. And that required a radical overhaul of both my shopping and consumption habits.

The most pressing reason for change is environmental. To ignore the facts is to do so at our peril. According to a United Nations report released late in 2006, our collective meat consumption contributes more to global warming than trains, planes, and automobiles put together. The combined effects of cattle belching and methane gas from the manure left behind by the billions of animals we raise for food contributes 18 percent to all greenhouse gases. And the future looks even bleaker if we consider that global meat consumption is expected to double by 2050. In North America, we're now consuming the equivalent of a medium-sized steak each day—twice the daily protein consumption recommended by the U.S. Department of Agriculture.

"Oh, I wish I was an Oscar Mayer wiener," a little voice chirped merrily from the TV screen of my youth, "for that is what I'd truly like to be." Clearly, this jingle writer never visited a factory farm, because the reality of how a cow becomes a dog is much crueler. Animals pumped full of growth hormones and antibiotics just to keep them alive in filthy, overcrowded conditions. Hens crowded into cages so small they can't stretch their wings. They are routinely debeaked so they don't pluck their own feathers or cannibalize their neighbors'. Pigs similarly crowded into confinement pens, so stressed they chew one another's tails. The list of indignities goes on and on. As journalist and author Michael Pollan has written: "More than any other institution, the American industrial farm offers a nightmarish glimpse of what capitalism can look like in the absence of moral or regulatory constraint."[2] The meat industry depends on our ignorance to conduct its everyday business.

As we climb the evolutionary ladder, it seems appropriate that our relationship with animals should evolve too. Leading us back to the question of whether we should all give up meat cold-turkey. Will there be a day when the majority of humanity sees meat-eating as an act of depravity—much as we have historical customs like public stonings and slavery? It seems unlikely. Man's first memoirs were the cave paintings in which he etched portraits of the things that filled his imagination. Not his longings for God, or community, but the bison and aurochs he planned to club and cook for dinner. Anthropologists tell us our brains grew in complexity as a response to the hunt, and that our culture flourished around the campfire. Meat-eating, then, is what made us human. The animal rights movement was once the epitome of a fringe group. PETA as cranks, and dangerous ones at that. No longer. Ironically, as Pollan points out, the upsurge in concern for animal welfare comes at a point in human history when we are inflicting more pain and suffering on animals than ever. Major food corporations— like Burger King and McDonald's—know which way the wind is blowing. It's not their moral compass but their reading of public opinion that has inspired some important changes in the way they source animal products over the past few years. For that we owe a big debt to the avatars of the animal welfare movement: Paul McCartney, Chrissie Hynde, Pamela Anderson, and others.

In historical terms, the causes vegetarians espouse and the ecological disasters they alert us to are relatively modern, the by-products of factory farming. In effect, the vegetarian orthodoxy has never been more emphatic and its influence on carnivores more profound. Yes, vegetarianism influences many more people than actually subscribe to the practice. Its lessons certainly have influenced me. Instructing me in how I might eat meat with a clearer conscience. How can we do this? The solution is really quite simple: Eat less meat. Eat better meat. That means eating meat twice a week instead of every day; eating organic and pasture-raised meats. And choosing lesser cuts—brisket instead of sirloin, pork hocks instead of roast pork loin. It's about respecting the entire animal by utilizing all of its edible bits, but also a vote for the small farmer and one against factory farming. This may sound like a jejune indulgence to the single mother with four mouths to feed. Admittedly, it's a luxury to even contemplate such food choices, and maybe not always practical. But it's not an all-or-nothing scenario. We don't have to buy organic meat every time we line up at the checkout counter. But each time we do, we are making a positive contribution to animal welfare, our own health, and the well-being of the planet. This should contribute to our pleasure.

Speaking of pleasure: It's eight p.m. and my sister Lisa is busy serving up soup to our guests. Meanwhile, I've got my head in the oven. If friends had witnessed my distress the last few days and just entered the kitchen, they might fear the worst. In fact, I'm just checking the meat thermometer, which is now pointing at 130 degrees Fahrenheit—perfect for a medium-rare prime rib—and coincidentally my own body temperature. The result of the feverish pace I've kept all afternoon to get this dinner on the table. I remove the roast—exquisitely browned on the outside, perfectly pink at the center—from the oven to rest while I begin my gravy. I scrape the bits and scraps of meat from the bottom of the roaster while whisking in a cup of Merlot, a few tablespoons of horseradish, Dijon mustard, salt and pepper, and dried cranberries. It's not long before my gravy is bubbling and I poke a finger in for a taste test. I'm astonished: the gravy is utterly delicious.

Don is summoned to carve the roast. He's against the welfare state, but as an enthusiastic host, he is concerned with the welfare of his guests. He slices two thick slices for each diner—anything more might be a test of a national health care system his party would like to see stripped to the bone. The artist and her husband—why, the amount of meat on their plates is twice what the families in the African villages they visited would have eaten in a week. Don even slices two pieces for each of the kids. I can't help looking at my nephew and nieces and wonder what it is that they'll rebel against. They've tasted traditions from past generations and also had their sampling of world cuisine and fast food. What's left?

Well, in fact, by the end of the meal there's not much of anything left. There are no reviews of my cooking, just this judgment: a lonely shard of meat stuck to the bone. One by one, the men take their turns parading into the kitchen, their smiles fading when they realize the roast has been stripped bare save for this piece that my sister Lisa stealth-rescues. For her, this meat means lunch sandwiches for tomorrow. It's quite a dramatic departure—her claiming this animal flesh as her own—given that she was ahead of the curve and she typically pushed meat away as a child despite my mother's protestations. I wonder what Lisa's growing swell of vegetarian charges will be thinking as she lights into her roast beef sandwich in the lunchroom at school tomorrow.

Meanwhile, as we sit back and enjoy a little wine-aided digestion, I can't help but notice how pleased Don looks. I know he enjoyed this prime rib—not just the taste but the look and the aroma—but his satisfaction goes beyond senses to sensibility.

There hasn't been any political debate at the table, no attempt to coax anyone over to his side. Still, our meal is a political act. The prime rib is homage to his hometown of Calgary, the center of Canadian cattle country, the epicenter of the conservative movement in Canada. And Don, who sees political context where others might not think to look, is also keenly aware that our meal is also an endorsement of the meat industry, a powerful lobby squarely in the Conservative (right-wing) corner.

But for him—as for all good hosts—the meaning of this dinner goes much deeper. It transcends politics, transcends borders and cultures. The raw-meat people might have appropriated the word *primal*, but really it's the best description of the act of gathering around meat. Tonight we were as civilized as we could be at the dinner table, but were we really so far removed from cavemen tussling over the last scrap of bison? The same might be asked of the Cajuns wrestling for that last boudin link in Eunice—that scene wouldn't be so different from the Pilgrims stripping the turkey carcass clean. What we are really celebrating when we gather for a meat meal is our reconnection to the earth, to our communities and our collective history.

ACKNOWLEDGMENTS

Without Gare Joyce, my partner in life and words, this book never would have happened. Not only did he encourage me to pursue this project when it was nothing more than a glimmer of an idea, but he has been a source of constant inspiration and support—not to mention a sufferer in silence—when I would come home smelling like a butcher's apron. I must also extend a big thank-you to my agent, Rick Broadhead. Every writer should be so lucky to have such a committed, enthusiastic agent cheering them on from the sidelines; someone who will even respond to their e-mails at eleven on a Saturday night. And thank you to my two editors on either side of the border. First, to Rachel Kahan at Putnam, who was the perfect editor for this book. Other editors might share my passion for food, but I can't imagine any as adventurous as Rachel. In our conversations about our dining history she'd casually mention the pleasures of deep-fried Thanksgiving turkey (worth risking a third-degree burn with every mouthful) or the presentation of South American guinea pig (rendered in a real-life pose by a cook who must have moonlighted as a taxidermist). Rachel's gentle prodding, incisive questions, and enthusiasm contributed enormously to this manuscript. Also at Putnam, I'm much indebted to Rachel Holtzman who was always there in support of the book and who kept her sense of humor and glass-half-full positivism even under deadline pressures. Diane Turbide, at Penguin Canada, improved not just the smallest details in the manuscript, but the bigger narrative arc as well. She has shown unflagging support for this project from its inception.

I thank my family for understanding why I missed so many family events during the year I was researching and writing this manuscript. In addition, I owe a debt of gratitude to a number of friends, chief among them Carol Davies, who was willing to read my manuscript at various stages. Also Kaly Vittala, Dawn Walton, Shelley White, and Margaret Webb, for their passionate discussions about food along the way; Andrew Mitrovica and Carolyn Leitch, for all their coaching; and to Dave Pyette, who gave me my first big break in journalism.

And finally, I owe much to the many warm and generous people I met while researching this book. Thank you to everyone listed here: Curtis and Kristine Joubert in Eunice, Louisiana, for their hospitality; Gil Young, for taking me under his wing; Arnold Brower Sr. in Barrow, Alaska, for keeping me out of harm's way and introducing me to his magical world; the government of Newfoundland and all the folks at Tuckamore Lodge, especially Barb Genge, Randy Strangemore, and Brendan Fitzpatrick, for keeping me laughing. Thanks to Dan Barber, Craig Haney, and their wonderful team at the Rockefeller farm, and the folks at Pappas Bros. in Texas. Warm regards to the Brown family in Beeville, Texas, as well as Mario Fiorucci and Tara Longo at the Healthy Butcher in Toronto. Thanks also to Benny Pizzuco for, well, being Benny Pizzuco. And thank you to all of his wonderful staff at the Florence Meat Market. Also, I must express my gratitude to my editors at *Report on Business* magazine, Maryam Sanati and Laas Turnbull, for encouraging me to pursue the story of the Maple Leaf meat-packing plant in Brandon, which would eventually inspire me to write this book. In that way, the blood is on their hands as much as it was on mine.

• NOTES •

1. BUTCHERED

1. Christopher Phelps, "Welcome to the Jungle: Meatpacking Then and Now," *Canadian Dimension*, 39.6, November–December 2005, p. 45.

2. Todd Scarth, "Labour Pains in Brandon," *Fast Facts*, Canadian Center for Policy Alternatives, 2003, pp. 1–2.

3. Roger Horowitz, "The Decline of Unionism in America's Meatpacking Industry," *Social Policy*, March 2002, pp. 32–36.

4. Karen Olsson, "The Shame of Meatpacking," *The Nation*, September 16, 2002, pp. 11–16.

5. Scarth, pp. 1–2.

6. Ibid.

7. Olsson, p. 16.

8. Gail A. Eisnitz, *Slaughterhouse: The Shocking Story of Greed, Neglect, and Inhumane Treatment Inside the U.S. Meat Industry* (Amherst, NY: Prometheus, 1997), p. 158.

9. "What 'Risk Based Inspection' Means for Consumers," Food and Water Watch Insitute, January 2007.

10. Ibid., p. 171.

11. Ibid., p. 167.

12. Ibid., p. 155.

13. Susan Bourette, "Butchered," *The Globe and Mail's Report on Business*, December 2003, pp. 46–54.

14. *Brandon Sun*, November 29, 2003, p. A1.

2. MEAT, MYSELF, AND I

1. Mark Kurlansky, *Choice Cuts: A Savory Selection of Food Writing from Around the World and Throughout History* (London: Jonathan Cape, 2002), p. 225.

2. Steven G. Kellman, "Fish, Flesh, Fowl: The Anti-Vegetarian Animus," *American Scholar*, 69 (October 2000), pp. 65–96.

3. Tristram Stuart, *The Bloodless Revolution: A Cultural History of Vegetarianism from 1600 to Modern Times* (New York: W. W. Norton, 2007), p. 133.

4. Ibid., p. xix.

5. Researchers discovered that the life expectancy of a thirty-year-old vegetarian Adventist woman was 85.7 years, and 83.3 years for a vegetarian Adventist man. This exceeds the life expectancies of other Californians by 6.1 years for women and 9.5 years for men. http://news.adventist.org/data/2001/06/0995375716/index.html.en.

6. Kellman, pp. 65–96.

7. J. M. Coetzee, "Meat Country," *Granta* 52: *Food: The Vital Stuff* (Winter 1999), pp. 44–52.

8. Ibid., p. 47.

9. Ibid.

10. Kellman, pp. 65–96.

11. Margaret Visser, "The Sins of the Flesh," *Granta* 52: *Food: The Vital Stuff* (Winter 1999), pp. 112–19.

12. Ibid.

3. THE NEW CELEBRITY CHEF

1. Jackie Wullschlager, "Humanity in All Its Agony and Emptiness," *Financial Times*, June 20, 2006, p. 12.

2. Derrick Rixson, *The History of Meat Trading* (Nottingham, England: Nottingham University Press, 2000), p. 54.

3. Madeleine Ferrières, *Sacred Cow, Mad Cow: A History of Food Fears* (New York: Columbia University Press), pp. 66–67.

4. Ibid., pp. 263–64.

5. "A complicated balance of trust and tension characterized the point-of-sale relationship between retail butcher and shoppers. Studies conducted in the 1920s and 1930s agreed that customers bought meat from stores that were very near them, generally within 1,000 feet or two blocks, and patronized the same store for years at a time." Roger Horowitz, *Putting Meat on the American Table: Taste, Technology, Transformation* (Baltimore: Johns Hopkins University Press, 2005), pp. 32–33.

6. "Packers Picture New Meat Stores," *The New York Times*, October 22, 1930, p. 48.

7. Nick Taylor, "Slice of Life," *The New Yorker*, January 29, 1996, p. 31.

8. Joseph Dale, "Dale's Collection of Twelve Favourite English Songs, Adopted for the Voice & Piano Forte...," Book 15 (London: J. Dale, 1809), p. 240.

9. Colin Spencer, "The Beef That Built an Empire," *The New York Times*, March 30, 1996, p. 23.

10. Will Yandik, "The Meat Market: Developers Eye New York City's Meatpacking District with Lean and Hungry Looks," *Online Preservation*, August 8, 2001.

11. Jack Ubaldi, *Meat Book: A Butcher's Guide to Buying, Cutting, and Cooking Meat* (New York: Macmillan, 1987), p. 194.

4. OFF THE EATEN TRACK

1. Marian Botsford Fraser, "First Rule: No Killing Your Dinner Companions," *The Globe and Mail*, June 15, 1991, p. C18.

2. John Balzar, "To Catch a Whale with Handmade Sealskin Boats and Snowmobiles," *Los Angeles Times*, July 24, 1994, p. 14.

3. New Bedford Whaling National Historical Park. http://www.nps.gov/archive/nebe/inupit.htm.

4. Charles D. Brower, *Fifty Years Below Zero: A Lifetime of Adventure in the Far North* (Edinburgh: Riverdale, 1948), p. 254.

5. Scott LaFee, "Eye-Opening Research Suggests Bowhead Whales May Live for Centuries," *The San Diego Union-Tribune*, January 24, 2001, p. A10.

6. Charles Wohlforth, *The Whale and the Supercomputer: On the*

Northern Front of Climate Change (New York: Farrar, Straus & Giroux 2004), p. 251.

7. Kurt Kleiner, "Meats, No Shoots, No Leaves," *New Scientist*, May 29, 2004, pp. 50–51.

8. Ibid.

9. Barbara Bodenhorn, "I'm Not the Great Hunter, My Wife Is: Inupiat and Anthropological Models of Gender," *Inuit Studies* 12:1, 2 (1990), pp. 55–74.

5. THE NEW PONDEROSA

1. LeeAnn Blankenship, "The Cowboy's Home on Wheels," *Highlights for Children*, 58, no. 3 (March 2003), p. 40.

2. John Mack Faragher, "Gunslingers and Bureaucrats," *The New Republic*, 207, no. 25 (December 14, 1992), p. 29.

3. Barbara E. Willard, "The American Story of Meat: Discursive Influences on Cultural Eating Practice," *Journal of Popular Culture*, 36, p. 108.

4. Jeremy Rifkin, *Beyond Beef: The Rise and Fall of the Cattle Culture* (New York: Dutton, 1992), p. 77.

5. Ibid., pp. 62–63.

6. Ibid., pp. 88–89.

7. Ibid., p. 90.

8. Camp Ezell, *The Historical Story of Bee County, Texas* (Beeville, TX: Camp Ezell and Beeville Publishing, 1973), p. 101.

9. Michael Pollan, "Unhappy Meals," *The New York Times Magazine,* January 28, 2007, p. 38.

10. Dan Mathews, "Bold Beginnings," *The Advocate*, November 12, 2002, p. 52.

11. Richard Huff, "At Last, Oprah Can Shoot the Bull," New York *Daily News*, March 2, 1998, p. 72.

12. Jane E. Brody, "Feeding Children off the Spock Menu," *The New York Times,* June 30, 1998, p. F7.

13. Jessica Reaves, "Where's the Beef (in the Teenage Diet)?" *Time*, January 30, 2003 (online edition).

14. Katharine Mieszkowski, "Luring Preteens with Red Meat: A

Website Produced for Girls by the National Cattlemen's Beef Association Solves Self-Esteem Problems with Heaps of Ground Round," *Salon.com,* February 11, 2003.

15. Karen Kaplan and Betty Hallock, "Cloned Beef: It's What's for Dinner," *Los Angeles Times,* March 4, 2007, p. A1.

16. Ben Macintyre, "Will the Petri Dish Put Daisy Out to Grass?" *The Times* (London), January 13, 2007, p. 26.

17. Alice Waters, "The Farm-Restaurant Connection," in Molly O'Neill, ed., *American Food Writing: An Anthology with Classic Recipes* (New York: Penguin, 2007), p. 561.

6. ANTLER ENVY

1. Jim Casada, "It Was Always Our Game," *Outdoor Life,* 201, no. 5 (June 1998), p. 52.

2. Brian Luke, "Violent Love: Hunting, Heterosexuality, and the Erotics of Men's Predation," *Feminist Studies,* 2, no. 3., pp. 627–53.

3. Daniel Justin Herman, *Hunting and the American Imagination* (Washington, DC: Smithsonian Institution Press, 2001), p. 1.

4. Ibid., pp. 1–2.

5. Ibid., p. xii.

6. Lance Morrow, "Bears and Rhinos: Never Underestimate the Role of Sentimentality in the Making of American Myths and Heroes," *Smithsonian,* October 2001, p. 125.

7. Herman, p. 219.

8. Mary Anne Magiera, "Encouraging Young Hunters Is a Challenge," *Worcester Telegram & Gazette,* November 11, 2005, p. D4.

9. "Books—Maverick Tastes," *Financial Times,* April 16, 1994, p. 21.

10. Herman, p. 229.

11. Ibid., p. 227.

7. HAPPY MEAL

1. Hilmar Moore, "Rudolf Steiner: A Biographical Introduction for Farmers," *Biodynamics,* 214 (November/December 1997).

2. Ibid.

3. Ibid.

4. Ibid.

5. Ibid.

6. Margot Roosevelt, "The Grass-Fed Revolution," *Time,* June 11, 2006, p. 76.

7. Robin McKie, "Where Dolly Went Astray," *The Observer,* February 18, 2007, p. 20.

8. T. J. Kelleher, "Remembering Ewe—In Sum—Sheep Intelligence," *Natural History,* February 2002, p. 16.

9. H. I. Woolf, *Voltaire's Philosophical Dictionary* (New York: Alfred A. Knopf, 1937), p. 184.

10. John Berger, "Why Look at Animals?" *About Looking* (New York: Pantheon, 1980), p. 19.

11. Frank Bruni, "Food You'd Almost Rather Hug Than Eat," *The New York Times,* August 2, 2006, p. 98.

8. ODE TO THE STEAKHOUSE

1. Linda Kulman, "Steakhouse Craze Defies Healthful Eating Edict," *U.S. News & World Report,* March 4, 2001.

2. Waldemar Kaempffert, "Science in the News: Air Conditioned Beef," *The New York Times,* March 26, 1939, p. 56.

3. "Action for Divorce, No Happiness Without Beefsteak," *The New York Times,* February 12, 1861, p. 3.

4. Joseph Mitchell, "All You Can Hold for Five Bucks," *The New Yorker,* April 15, 1939, pp. 35–42.

5. John Mariani, "Ready for Prime Time: A Good Steak Is Hard to Find," *Cigar Aficionado,* Winter 1993–1994.

6. Ibid.

7. Mitchell.

8. Kulman.

9. www.bigtexan.com.

9. PRIMAL SCREAM

1. Peters Brooks, "The Aspen Idea," *Opera News,* 66, no. 12 (June 2002), p. 36.

2. Kirk Johnson, "With an Icon's Death, Aspen Checks Its Inner Gonzo," *The New York Times,* February 23, 2005, p. A12.

3. Jeff O'Connell, "De-bug Your Dinner," *Men's Health*, March 2007, p. 96.

4. Margaret Philp, "The Milkman Cometh," *The Globe and Mail*, December 2, 2006, p. M1.

5. Aajonus Vonderplanitz, *We Want to Live: The Primal Diet* (Los Angeles: Carnelian Bay Castle, 1997), p. 123.

6. James H. O'Keefe and Loren Cordain, "Cardiovascular Disease Resulting from a Diet and Lifestyle at Odds with Our Paleolithic Genome: How to Become a 21st-Century Hunter-Gatherer," *Mayo Clinic Proceedings*, 79, no. 1 (January 2004), pp. 101–108.

7. Vonderplanitz, p. 118.

8. Carolyn Abraham, "The Promise of Viral Therapies," *The Globe and Mail*, November 30, 2006, p. A1

9. Vonderplanitz, p. 172.

10. CARNIVORE CHIC

1. Sheila Stroup, "First You Make a Roux," New Orleans *Times-Picayune*, July 29, 1993, p. B1.

2. C. Paige Gutierrez, *Cajun Foodways* (Jackson: University Press of Mississippi, 1992), pp. 4–6.

3. Ibid., pp. 6–10.

4. Ibid.

5. Robert Carriker, "Boudin by the Bite," *Louisiana Life Magazine*, Winter 2006–2007, pp. 34–39.

6. Lynn Petrak, "Sausage Masters," *The National Provisioner*, 219, no. 10 (October 2005), pp. 44–45.

7. Martin Wright, "I Have Seen the Future, and It's Pork," *The Guardian* (UK), September 30, 2005, p. 12.

8. Derrick Rixson, *The History of Meat Trading* (Nottingham, England: University of Nottingham Press, 2000), 178–79.

9. Petrak.

10. Donald Dale Jackson, "Hot Dogs Are Us," *Smithsonian*, June 1999, p. 104.

11. Ibid.

12. Wright.

13. Carriker.

EPILOGUE

1. Wendell Berry, "The Pleasures of Eating," in O'Neill, *American Food Writing*, pp. 551–58.

2. Michael Pollan, "An Animal's Place," *The New York Times Magazine*, November 10, 2002, p. 58.

ABOUT THE AUTHOR

Susan Bourette is an award-winning investigative journalist based in Toronto. She is a former reporter for *The Globe and Mail*, and her writing has appeared in *The Christian Science Monitor*, *Maclean's*, and *Elle*. She lives in Toronto with her boyfriend, Gare, a lifelong vegetarian.